THE L S OF A COCKNEY KID FROM HOXTON

ROY WILD

ISBN, hardback: 978-1-80227-340-3
ISBN, paperback: 978-1-80227-341-0
ISBN, ebook: 978-1-80227-342-7

This book is typeset in Cochin

For my children and their unwavering enthusiasm and encouragement as well as the occasional metaphorical kick up the deaf and dumb to get me to flex my literary muscles and record my life story.

ACKNOWLEDGEMENTS

To all my old pals from my teen years who lived in the Hoxton area, all thirteen of them. Many of us, with the inexorable march of time, broke away from the old gang, gave in to wedding bells and settled down to family life. Sadly, many of them have now passed away: Lennie Myring, Frankie Hudson, Teddy Reece, Michael Isaacs, Kenny Fields, Freddy Groves and Frankie Shea. May they all rest in peace, and I'll see them at the crossroads. I thank them all for the laughs and capers we got up to, all the parties and the good times in the fifties and sixties. Every one of them has left me with indelible memories that I will always cherish. I am forever thankful and offer a fervent prayer of gratitude to the Almighty that I'm still standing.

To all the latter friends that I have amassed throughout my life who brought colour to a black and white world, my heartfelt thanks to you all for allowing me to be part of your lives and making my life so much richer.

A special mention of my good pal Mark Aaron whom I sadly lost in 2016. I still mourn him tremendously, a guy who was generosity personified and was much revered and respected by everyone he came into contact with. His memory will be woven forever into the fabric of my future life. Hold a place for me Mark, and as I said in the eulogy that I wrote for you, "I won't say goodbye. This is just a passage in time. We will meet again when it is my turn to depart this mortal plane and take my place in antiquity."

In telling my life story, I have used false names or just first names for people who were involved in my life and used full names in cases where I have first run it past them and have their full permission to do so. I have used the full name of my old pal, author Lenny Hamilton, as he has now passed away and is far beyond the reach of any authority.

There is so much more to my life than has been written between the covers of this book that I have chosen to omit to protect the innocent and not cause embarrassment to my children.

Despite the wrong paths I chose in my younger life, I can still face my reflection in the mirror and not suffer too much shame, except on one count, the pain I caused my family. I can say in mitigation, not once did I harm anybody physically in my criminal endeavours. I am a different man now to the guy I was when I was young and involved in villainy. I was sensible enough to know that it was never going to be long term for me; I knew I had to straighten up and fly right, and I did! I now enjoy great *joie de vivre* – zest for life.

I have written my life story from my rich reserve of notes and memories, and I hope I have written with compassion, warmth and, of course, humour.

CONTENTS

Andy was the eldest son of another large family consisting of four boys and two girls. He grew up on the streets where he became, like most kids his age, very savvy and wise beyond his years. In 1914, when he was seven years of age, the First World War started. By the time it ended in 1918, he was growing into a young man well-versed in the ways of the world. He drifted in and out of various jobs, never settling into any of them. He decided to join the Army, but at sixteen he was too young; anyone wishing to enrol in the Military had to be seventeen or above. At age seventeen Andy applied at the Army Offices in Whitehall, Westminster, and was enlisted into the Military. Shortly after, he was dispatched to Maidstone in Kent, the home of the prestigious Queen's Own Royal West Kent Regiment, for a term of seven years.

After his training, his battalion was shipped out to Madras in India where he excelled in sports. He became a marksman with a rifle and won awards for proficiency in firing machine guns; his crowning glory was the Silver Medal he won for bayonet fighting, presented to him by the Viceroy of India. Andy went on to become part of a Guard of Honour for His Excellency the Viceroy.

Andy also excelled at boxing and became a regimental champion, fighting in the All India finals. This love of boxing stayed with him all his life, and he passed it on to his young son Roy.

After serving his seven years, Andy was ensconced back into civilian life in 1933, with four more years to serve in the Army Reserve. At the end of the four years, Andy left the Army completely, with an exemplary record as a serving soldier. In his pay book and record book, his Commanding Officer described him as ***"a hard working clean and sober man of smart appearance; he can be trusted to carry out his duties without supervision; intelligent and reliable, a good type of man."***

Andy worked on the underground, laying train lines, but left that job and started work for a company in Putney, London, called The French Dyers & Cleaners as a Hoffman presser.

Shortly after his homecoming, his brother Freddy introduced him to Rosie. In no time at all, they were stepping out together and fell in love. In 1936, they knew they were meant for each other and the bans were put up at St Luke's Church, which was nearby; they were married on August 2nd of that year.

Their first son was born in the famous Barts Hospital amid the celebrations of the signing of the Armistice at the end of the First World War. A ward nurse asked Rosie whether she could pick a name for her son and Rosie asked her what she had in mind. She replied, "Basil." Rosie recoiled in horror. Nobody in Rosie and Andy's circle was named Basil, so their son was registered as Royston and was christened in the same church where his parents had been married. An interesting fact emerged at this time that the Armistice had been signed at 11 am on the 11th day of the 11th month, and it was decided that all children born at 11 am on the 11th day of the 11th month would have their names recorded for posterity in the local paper. Roy was born on the eleventh day of the eleventh month, also at eleven o'clock, but his birth was at 11 pm so he missed out on having his name in the paper. But whichever way you view it, it is still 11-11-11, which is pretty unique.

CHAPTER 2

ENTER ROY

To be born within the sound of Bow Bells, as the old adage goes, is to be a true cockney. The Bow Bells are situated in Cheapside within the City of London, a few minutes' walk from Barts Hospital, which makes me a true cockney and also the son of cockney parents, who were both born within the sound of Bow Bells on the East Side of the River Thames.

Shortly after I was born, we moved into Arlington Avenue, just off of the New North Road, Islington, where Mum and Dad rented two rooms, which were hardly adequate for a young family. When I was a year old, we moved into the upstairs part of a house in Northport Street, Hoxton N1, where we had more room and the bonus of a garden. In less than a year, the Second World War broke out. When the British Government declared war on Germany on September 1st 1939, I was heading towards my second birthday. Hoxton became alive with workers supplied by the Shoreditch Borough Council who were engaged in building brick shelters in the roads and delivering to all houses six corrugated sheets measuring 6ft by 4ft 6in, with steel plates at each end and the whole lot bolted together. These had to be assembled by the householder and then covered with earth to form a blast shield. They were known as Anderson Shelters, named after Sir John Anderson, who, at the time, was the Lord Privy Seal and responsible for preparing air-raid precautions immediately prior to the outbreak of World War 11 to protect the British public against the German air attacks that started on September 7th 1940. Other British cities, such as Birmingham, Liverpool and Coventry, also suffered bombing raids. As the night raids intensified, many people tired of repeatedly interrupting their sleep to go back and forth to the brick shelters in the road and virtually took up residence in the Anderson in the garden, but families had to put up with the damp and dank conditions that existed in these makeshift shelters. There was no electricity, gas or any other service in the shelter, just lots and lots of creepy crawlies. Mum would make us cups of tea on an old brass primus stove, and lighting was provided by a couple of paraffin lamps.

Mum used to make us a picnic, as she called it, which was some cubed cheese and pickles, and we would take it up to bed, which was in the front of our house. Most houses in the street had sticky paper stuck across the window panes to stop flying glass caused by the blast of a nearby bomb. We were lucky in as much as our large bedroom window had stout shutters that could be pulled right across, and then a bar secured them shut, giving some protection from shattered glass. When we were woken from a sound sleep by the nearby air raid siren (it was located up on the corner of Southgate Road and Bridport Place, we had to head for the Anderson shelter with our bed clothes, eiderdowns and gas masks. Looking back now, I realize that we were no safer there than we were in the house, as a falling bomb has no conscience! At least in the house we had a floor above us and a house made of bricks, which gave more protection than a couple of feet of loose earth piled onto no more than a damp, uncomfortable doll's house, so Mum decided that in future we would stay put in our nice warm beds. She probably thought, if this is the night when our number comes up, so be it. Brick shelters in the road were receiving direct hits, Anderson shelters in people's gardens were being blown up, so where was safe? They were about as useful as air conditioning on a rowing boat.

Dad's role at The French Dyers and Cleaners was similar to an Air Raid Precautions Warden (ARP); at night, he would be up on the roof of the company watching for approaching enemy aircraft. When they were detected, air raid sirens would be sounded, and after a bombing raid, the "All Clear" would be sounded again. People would emerge from their shelters to see the damage done to the local area; where once stood a pub, there was a heap of rubble, or a block of houses had been flattened. I think the women took it harder than the men folk. I can remember some women running around screaming, holding their heads in their hands, and people trying to pacify them. I remember playing out in the streets some way from home when the air raid siren sounded and in no time a bomb exploded nearby, with dust and rubble everywhere. I could hear Mum shouting my name hysterically. Opposite us in Northport St lived the Stripe family, and young Freddie Stripe's dad, also Fred, had grabbed me by the hand and was shouting out to my mum through the dust, "It's OK, Rose, I've got Roy. He's safe!" Mum took hold of me, filled with relief that I was alive, while I probably thought, "What is all the fuss about?" Mum, like many mothers, would sew the names of their children into their coats for two reasons: it would help pupils to find their coats in the cloak room at school and also identify a child who had been killed in the bombings.

Mum and I were evacuated to Wellingborough in Northamptonshire and stayed in the house of one of the women who were paid by the government to give safe haven from the bombings in London. She was a terrible woman, always complaining and saying, "Don't touch this, don't touch that!" Mum found herself at loggerheads all the time with this querulous woman, and after a week we caught a train back to our own home. By this time, Hitler's forces had come up with the devastating V1 and V2 rockets that could reach London across the English Channel. When we heard the engine cut out, that was when the rocket dropped. We used to look up and see and hear them, and when the engine stopped, we ran for the shelter or our house; at least there was some degree of safety, as opposed to being killed in the street by the blast.

After a period of intensive and consistent bombing, Mum and Dad realised we would be safer down the underground, and many people were thinking the same. Our nearest stop was Old Street tube station on the Northern line. Mum and I would walk or catch a bus in New North Road, carrying our bedding along with sandwiches and flasks of tea, and secure our place on the crowded platform for the night. People would while away the nights sleeping, playing cards and engaging in a sing-along. This was one of their favourite ditties:

"Let's all go down the tube,
Let's all go down the tube,
People standing on your toes,
Sticking their fingers up your nose,
Let's all go down the tube!"

These kinds of songs kept morale up. But we would also listen to the muffled sound of the bombs being dropped above us, and people would comment, "Another poor soul has copped it..." When emerging in the morning into the daylight, we would see whole streets and houses demolished and ARP wardens and volunteers digging out the bodies of people who had been killed and the injured who were still alive. All of the hospitals must have been terribly overloaded; I have no idea how they coped. Maybe it was because in those days, hospitals were everywhere in abundance, unlike the present time when most of them have been closed due to cutbacks, which seems to be the popular terminology used by Government departments.

This was the time of the "blackout", which meant that any light that could be seen from outside a building had to be dimmed or blacked out completely so that enemy bombers could not see the factories, docks and residential areas. Even the smallest chink of light would bring the sound of loud knocking on the door from an ARP Warden, telling you to cover up the offending light. All motor vehicles had their headlamps masked by black tape, and the gas street lights were extinguished before darkness settled in. One evening, Dad's half-brother Teddy popped over to see Dad about something and in the pitch black walked into the lamp post outside our house, giving his forehead a very nasty gash. Dad had to walk Teddy over to St. Leonard's Hospital by the light of a small torch to have the wound attended to and stitched. Most people had a small torch for emergency use, but as long as it was fairly subdued and aimed at the ground, an ARP Warden would let you carry on. If Dad had not been allowed to have the small torch to light the way to the hospital, we might have had two casualties with their heads split open!

On the corner of our street was a pub, The Rushton Arms, run by Tommy Gorman and his wife Franie. We emerged into our street one morning after a heavy night of bombing to see most of the pub demolished, as well as some of the houses adjacent to it. My Nan, my dad's mother, was luckily spared any damage although her house was in the block of houses that was hit.

Mum and Dad were quite friendly with Tommy Gorman, and his wife Franie would mind me sometimes when Mum went out to work. On Sunday mornings, in nice weather, parents would have a drink inside the pub and their children would wait outside for a lemonade and a packet of crisps or an arrowroot biscuit. A favourite trick, naughty as it was, was for kids to take glasses that had been left outside by previous drinkers, turn the glass at an angle and rub it continuously on the granite kerb, which resulted in a hole at the bottom. The pot man, who was employed to collect glasses that had been left outside, would then take them back into the pub to be washed and reused. When they were filled with beer, the glasses would leak, spilling beer all over the place. On this occasion, Tommy Gorman came rushing out in a terrible mood and grabbed hold of me, giving me a shake. One of the kids rushed into the pub and told my dad what was happening. Dad rushed out, stuck Tommy up against the wall and was about to sling a couple of shots into him but was pulled off by friends and other customers. When it was explained to Tommy that I had nothing to do with the leaky glass business, he relented and apologized to Dad and me. He should have known you don't mess with a regimental champion boxer.

Dad was still working for the company in Putney and had been promoted to foreman. He was then called up by the War Office to be conscripted into the Army. Dad's governor contacted the war office authorities, and because of the job he had been assigned to do, looking out for approaching enemy bombers, as well as being an ARP Warden, he was exempted from serving in the Second World War. After a while, the company brought another guy into the company and asked Dad to take him under his wing, so to speak. This new man had been given a higher position and a higher salary than Dad, with no knowledge of the cleaning business, which was cleaning expensive, high-end carpets, as well as dry cleaning and pressing clothes for the public. (Dad was a no-nonsense guy, and much I have inherited from him.) Dad's reply to their request was, "You expect me to teach him all I know, and when that is complete, he will be ordering me about?" There was a dispute that could not be settled, no impartial adjudicator was assigned to give a decision, and the management would not change their mind or see how unfair this was, so Dad said, "Keep your job!", gave a week's notice and left. Prior to this unhappy incident, Dad had been happy there, had received promotion and was well thought of by all the staff. The company would put on a lovely Christmas Party at the nearby Star & Garter hotel, and Mum, Dad and I would go every year. All the children of the staff would receive a present, and on the face of it, it was a good company to work for. This one thoughtless and unfair decision had spoilt a good working relationship, and sadly, it was somewhere where Dad was happy.

Within a short time, Dad found himself a job in the same trade as a Hoffman presser of suits, ladies' dresses, costumes and other articles of clothing for a high-class dry cleaners in Victoria Street SW1 patronised by many of the stars of the day due to their high-quality work. The guy who owned the shop was a certain Mr Jones, a nice Jewish guy whom Dad hit it off with immediately, and there was much mutual respect. I remember once Dad, on a day off, took me to the shop where he worked and introduced me to Mr Jones, who, in cockney parlance, was only "six penn'orth of coppers high" but a friendly man. He lived above the business in an upstairs flat, and Dad said to me, after having a word with his governor, "I want to show you something." We went up a side staircase that led to the upstairs flat, and on the left going up the stairs were numerous aquariums, all lit up and flush with the wall. I was amazed and very impressed, as I feel Dad had been when he had first seen them.

My dad was a very experienced and good Hoffman presser and told me that before pressing suits or anything with pockets, you had to check in case there were any matches in the pockets, especially Red Top matches, that could easily ignite, aided by the cleaning fluid that would act as an accelerant. Searching through the pockets of a religious-type garment one day, Dad found a large, important-looking gold ring, which he handed in to his governor. It was concluded it belonged to the Bishop of Westminster, and Dad was thanked by the Bishop and received some kind of commendation.

We lived at number eight Northport Street and shared the house with another family, Ted and Flo Jones and their two children, Olly (Olivia) and her brother Eddie. I was one year old, heading towards my second birthday, when World War Two broke out and all hell was let loose. We stayed in the downstairs area of the house with access to the back garden. Cooking and washing took place in a scullery as we never had a kitchen. Mum had an old-fashioned stand-alone gas cooker, and over in the opposite corner was a copper for washing the clothes; washing machines had yet to be invented, at least in this country. The copper had a small aperture towards the bottom where Dad would light a fire with paper and kindling, then it would be fuelled by a couple of shovels of coal. The top of the copper had a large metal bowl where the soiled clothes were put; it was filled up with water which was heated by the fire. Mum used a large pair of tongs at intervals to lift up the washing and turn it over so everything was washed evenly. Then the washing was taken outside to an old mangle or wringer, as Mum called it. It had two big rollers that were turned by a handle on the side; the water wrung out of the washing was caught by a bowl that rested on a small shelf just below the rollers. The clean washing was then hung out on the clothesline, which was supported by a long pole called a prop. There were no problems with this procedure in summertime, but come winter, the clothes hung out to dry would freeze on the line and would be brought in stiff as a board, leant up against a clothes horse until thawed and then hung over the "horse" until dry. That was the easy bit; the hard part was the ironing of Dad's shirts, my school clothes and anything of Mum's.

Mum had a couple of cast iron smoothing irons, also known as flat irons, that she would heat up on the gas rings of our old cooker. When one was almost red hot, and with a piece of thick cloth wrapped around the handle, she would iron the clothes, which were always ironed damp so they weren't burnt. By the time the first iron started to lose its heat, the other iron would have been heated sufficiently to use, and that's how they were used, alternatively. How Mum and other housewives coped in those hard times is beyond me. Mum's refrigerator was a bowl of cold water put on the outside scullery windowsill; a couple of bottles of milk were put in the bowl to stop them curdling. Her vacuum cleaner was a broom, a brush and a dustpan. Women cleaned the front steps of their houses with a block of what was known as whitening; some steps were done in red ochre, which spruced up the facade of the house.

Long before the days of central heating, Dad would get a fire going in the front room, or best room as some people called it. It looked out to the front of the house where two doors opened onto an outside area known as the airey where there were two cellars. The local coal man, who worked for a company called Range, would drop your order of coal through a cast iron round plate that sat flush on the pavement. I can still see his poor old horse pulling that coal cart for miles around the streets of the East End, as well as the milkman's horse and the horse that would pull the dustcart. There was another small room in between the front room and the scullery with an old-fashioned dresser and a cast iron range fire with an oven attached to the side of it; today they would be of antique value and cost a fortune.

In those war years, part of our staple diet was Spam with just about everything, powdered eggs, and powdered milk tablets at school. Mum and I pushed an old pram round to the coal shop and joined the line of other women with their prams waiting to be served with a quarter cwt (25 lbs) of coal; that was used very sparingly in the front room. If you had a cat or dog, you could go to the cat's meat stall in Hoxton Market and buy scraps of meat from the abattoir, wrapped up in newspaper. Round the streets peddling their wares were the knife grinder, who would sharpen all your knives and scissors, the hot chestnut seller in the evening, the hurdy-gurdy man playing his tunes, the ice cream seller on his three-wheeled bike selling frozen choc ices and tubs of ice cream, and late at night a man on his bike shouting out, "Dog Winners!" These were the greyhound results from the Greyhound Stadiums at Haringey and Clapton. All these characters added to the rich tapestry of my life.

In those post-war years, life was hard; much was endured and little was asked. Many people depended on Dawson and Provident cheques, which were loans that you could pay back over a certain period. Those companies had the best of both worlds: not only did the amount borrowed have interest added but you had to spend the cheque in their own stores. Despite the ration books and all the privation, Mum always made sure we had food on the table. Hoxton was like a village where everyone knew everyone and neighbours still believed in helping out if you had a problem.

We had a cupboard under the stairs where Dad would store coal that he would bring in from the outside cellar to keep the fire going for a couple of days. Also under the stairs, Dad had put up a small shelf where he kept an old OXO box. He had started a small Christmas Club, and he and Mum, his brother Freddy and his half-sister Maggie would pay in on a weekly basis. The amounts were recorded in Dad's little book and shared out at Christmas. When I returned home one day from school, Mum said with a rather sombre look on her face that Dad wanted to see me in the front room. Dad said, "Sit down, son," and asked me whether I had seen the OXO box that was in the cupboard under the stairs. I of course replied, "No Dad, why?" He told me it was missing with all the Christmas savings in it. Dad had fixed the shelf high up so it was just under one of the stairs, well beyond my reach, and the only other person who knew the Oxo box's location was

Dad's sister Maggie, who lived upstairs. Maggie had a brother who was a well-known tea leaf (thief) and maybe she had mentioned it to him. It was never discovered what happened to the missing money, and maybe that was for the best. If Dad had found out who had taken it, his retribution would have been terrible to behold.

Many people kept chickens in the backyard, mostly for egg production. When the chickens stopped laying, possibly through old age, "young pullets" (as they were called) would be bought down Club Row, which nestled in Bethnal Green Road and ran down to Brick Lane. Here one could buy puppies and kittens, as well as birds in cages. Dad once purchased a kitten for 10/- shillings, 50p in today's money. Our old birds that were beyond egg laying would sadly provide a meal for the family; they would be killed by Dad, which now fills me with great sadness. I have a great love and respect for all sentient creatures and have been a vegetarian for more than thirty years.

The toilet and ablution facilities during the war years and after were pretty meagre and antiquated. Mum had an old tin bath hanging up on a hook on the outside wall in the back yard which would mainly be used for my convenience. Water would be heated in the copper or by kettles on the gas rings on the old cooker in the scullery. I was lucky that I had the bath to myself, unlike in some larger families where two children would share the same water, and, as the bath was vacated, another two would step in and have to use the same soiled water.

Dad and Mum would use the communal public wash houses, which opened in 1897 and served the people of Hoxton. They stood at the far end of Pitfield Street and are still there to this day but in another format, namely, a library. We had an outside toilet, with a large gap above and below the door, and a cistern high up on the wall with a rusty old chain that you pulled. This was years before toilet rolls were available, so newspapers would be cut up into squares and hung up, diamond-shaped, on an old nail, followed by a piece of string looped over the nail. That was all we had as far as personal hygiene was concerned.

The war ended on December 2nd1945, and Mum gave birth to my brother Tony on May 16th the following year. Tony was born at home in Mum's bedroom, and in attendance was Mum's sister Millie. My job was running up and down to the scullery, bringing up bowls of hot water. I had no idea what was going on. I was just nine years old and was suddenly told by Aunt Millie that I had a baby brother. I must have wondered where he came from as there were no gooseberry bushes in our garden!

An outing I always looked forward to was when Dad and I would catch the bus to Kingsland Road Waste. This was a roadside market full of stalls that sold almost everything, and in the middle of the market was a stall that sold sarsaparilla drinks and apple fritters. On a cold day, you would always see a crowd of people surrounding the stall, sipping their hot drinks and eating their hot fritters. Then we would pause at the toy shop that sold Hornby Train Sets and slug guns, me with my face pressed up against the window longingly hoping that one day I would own a slug gun. As I reached fourteen and fifteen, I became interested in Speedway Riding and with half a dozen pals would catch a bus to the old Harringey Arena to support the local team. It was always very thrilling watching the bikes tearing around the cinder track, amid the noise and exhaust fumes. I can still remember the names of a couple of celebrities of the time – Split Waterman, Jack Parker, Vic Duggan and his brother, Ray – such special memories. I have just learnt via Google that Split Waterman died in 2019 aged ninety-six. Vic Duggan died in 2007 aged ninety-one and Vic's brother Ray sadly died on the track in an accident in 1950 aged thirty-seven. My heroes! Thank you for all the thrills and spills you provided in my youth.

Children had to make their own amusement and would play street games like Knock Down Ginger, which meant knocking on a person's front door and then running away, or tying a long piece of string to somebody's door knocker and the other end to the opposite knocker on the door of the house on the other side of the street. One door would be banged on, and when the door was opened, it would tauten the string and knock on the other door. Great fun or so we kids thought at the time. Another game was Run Outs, in which one of the kids faced a wall with his eyes shut and would have to count to twenty, giving the rest of the gang time to run away and hide; when they were found, the game was over for them. The favourite game for us boys was football, played in the middle of the street or road. Two boys who had been picked as captains would toss a coin, heads or tails. Whoever called correctly would pick his player, and then the other captain would pick his player and so on, until there were two teams. A couple of coats or jumpers would act as goal posts at each end and the match would begin, now and again having to be stopped as vehicles passed by. We all enjoyed the Saturday morning picture show at the Hoxton Cinema, also known as the Bug Hole, where we would watch films like *Tarzan and the Apes* and the exploits of Buster Crabbe in *Flash Gordon*, but we loved the cowboy films the best, with Hopalong Cassidy, Roy Rogers and his horse Trigger, Gene Autry and Johnny Mack Brown. It was sixpence entrance fee, and my pocket money at the time was one shilling and sixpence, which my Dad would give me every Friday night. That was quite generous, and I would have plenty left over for the next morning picture show to buy ice cream in a little tub with a minute wooden spatula or an ice lolly. When I went with Mum and Dad as a family, we always sat up in the circle because sitting down in the stalls you took the chance of things like empty ice cream tubs, lolly sticks and half-eaten toffee apples and sandwiches raining down on you. Another reason for taking a seat in the circle was that at ground level, in the stalls, you never sat in any seats that were close to one of the aisles because an elderly gentleman in an usher's uniform would walk down the aisles spraying some kind of disinfectant from a hand-held spray and you would receive an earful of said spray. I can't remember ever seeing this gentleman, who was affectionately referred to as "the bug hunter", in the circle; maybe his duties didn't extend to that more hallowed area.

The main entrance to the Hoxton Cinema was in Pitfield Street, but the side entrance joined a large block of old dwellings in Haberdasher Street where we would take the staircase to the roof, which looked down into the men's toilet for the cinema. Running all the way down into the toilet was an old cast iron drain pipe, which, despite the enormous height, we would fearlessly shin down. Sometimes there would be a man standing there taking care of business, and imagine his surprise when he looked up and saw a couple of kids descending from above. We would cautiously open the toilet door that led into the cinema and crawl up the side aisle and into an empty seat. It was quite amusing to see a line of kids on their hands and knees looking for empty seats before being seen by one of the usherettes and thrown out. I realise now how dangerous this stunt was; we could have been killed by a fall. The old Hoxton Cinema stood derelict for many years and is currently being converted into luxury flats with the original facade intact.

Whenever I pass by, I find myself gazing wistfully and with great reverence and affection (and not without a drop of silver creeping into the corner of my eyes), remembering those far-off days with Mum and Dad and later with that old gang of mine.

Living in Hoxton was a magical time for us kids. There were lots of things to do and places to explore. At Christmas time, all the stalls in the market would be open until late at night, and on Christmas Eve, at about ten o'clock, Dad would make a trip to the market and buy all our Christmas fruit. There was always a lovely atmosphere. All the stalls would be lit up by paraffin lamps, the stallholders dressed in their festive red and white Santa hats, calling out their wares, trying hard to seduce you to buy from them.

There were many well-known characters that operated stalls in Hoxton Market. One, in particular, was a certain Henry Brown, whom my mum had known for many years, even before we moved to Hoxton. He later became the governor of a well-known and much-frequented pub called The Bacchus, in the middle of the market. Mum related this story to me: Opposite The Bacchus were the undertakers Hayes & English, who would go on to bury most of the people of Hoxton. Henry Brown and a couple of his pals went into the undertakers and nicked a ready-made coffin. Henry climbed into the coffin and lay in a dignified pose with his hands folded solemnly across his chest. He was carried the length of the market, and people probably thought he had passed away until he sat up and waved to the crowd of shoppers. Everyone then started cheering and laughing. These were the kind of people I grew up with in Hoxton. Mum would occasionally take me shopping at Dalston in Hackney, which was where the famous Ridley Road Market operated. When we had done all the shopping, Mum would take me to Lyons Corner House, one of a chain of tea rooms which used to be all over London and always on a corner, hence the name! We would have a pot of tea and a cream cake – wonderful! These are some of the magical memories of when I was a young boy.

CHAPTER 3

OFF TO SCHOOL

In 1942, at age five, I started school at Whitmore Street School which was situated between Grange Street and Gopsall Street, a couple of minutes' walk from our house. The school bell would ring out every morning at nine o'clock, telling the local mums to bring their children to school as lessons were about to start. My very first teacher was Mrs Kelly, an elderly, rather rotund, kind and "mumsy" lady. We would start the day with Assembly. Every class in the school would line up in the school hall, and taking centre stage would be the Headmaster, Mr Watts. He would give us talks on various aspects of our school, then all of us would, as one voice, sing hymns and finish up with The Lord's Prayer. After we had filed back to the classroom, Mrs Kelly would show us how to make things and teach us to read and tell the time and other essential life skills.

At 11 am, a teacher would ring a large hand-held bell signalling Play Time, and all classes would make their way to the playground. Some boys would play a game of football or marbles, and others would play throwing cigarette cards up against the wall. The cigarette cards had initially been inserted into packets of cigarettes to protect the cigarettes from being damaged in transit, but it was not long before tobacco companies came up with the idea of printing advertisements on these cards. In 1876, these companies began producing a series of cards that the smoker could collect. They believed that this would encourage the smoker to continue using that particular brand. The first British company to issue cigarette cards was W.D. & H.O. Wills. These cards were in every packet of "fags" and fathers would give them to their sons. Nearly everybody smoked in those days, and boys would accumulate hundreds of cigarette cards, which would be swapped. They consisted of photos of footballers, cricketers, boxers, trains, flowers, jockeys, golfers and various other things of interest.

I enjoyed my time at Whitmore School. As I grew older, I moved up into Miss Conway's class. One day the Headmaster told us that Miss Conway had got married and we had to refer to her in future as Mrs Yewkins. After a year or so, I graduated into the class of Mr Bragg. It was during this time with a male teacher that my interest in football took hold of me. My dad had always been an Arsenal supporter and in 1947 took me to my first Arsenal game at Highbury. I was just ten years old and so excited by the sheer size of the stadium. It couldn't compare with the new Emirates Stadium that is home to the Arsenal team now, and which my son and daughter and I visit regularly, but my heart will always belong to Highbury Stadium. At this point, I must mention that very first game I attended with my dad we won; we beat Leeds United 2-1, so that was the icing on the cake for me. At Whitmore School, there was a roof and a lower playground. I was consigned to the lower playground, which was at street level, and I seemed to have a natural ability in football. I would always play in goal, at which I became quite adept; so much so, that I enjoyed the sobriquet of "George Swindon", the resident goalkeeper for Arsenal. He lived to the age of ninety and died in 2005. Thank you, George, for being my hero whom I always tried to emulate and live up to.

On most days at Whitmore, I would come home at dinner time, but on a few occasions, I would stay at school and have my dinner with another couple of hundred kids in the dining hall. We would all sit at long tables covered by crisp white table cloths. The dining hall was policed by numerous teachers to make sure you ate your dinner. The afters could be jelly and custard or something equally enticing, but the main meal might not look very tempting, and some things on the plate you might refuse to eat. Teachers in those days would more or less force you to eat; they were far stricter than today. The caretaker, who lived on the school premises, had a large white Alsatian dog which roamed about the dining hall quite freely, so anything on your plate that looked inedible would be given to the dog that would gladly devour it. He was always lurking about under the tables, a practice that would not be allowed with all the health and hygiene laws there are today.

I stayed at Whitmore until I was eleven and then had to start secondary school, which was about the same distance from our house as my primary school. Little did I know what was to follow!

CHAPTER 4

FUN AND GAMES

The war years for us kids were not as traumatic as they might have been as they represented one big adventure playground and many things and places to be explored. In New North Road, there was a bombed-out church, and one of our pastimes was climbing up onto the roof that was still intact and stripping off the lead, which we would sell to the local scrap yard. Where houses had been razed to the ground, we would dig out the lead inserts from the railings and sell those, too.

When Guy Fawkes Night came around on November 5th, there was plenty of wood available for a bonfire – doors, floor joists and floor boards in abundance – and what was left over would be chopped up and sold to people to warm their houses. One bonfire night in around 1950, we had a huge heap of wood and any old armchairs people did not want stacked up in a wigwam shape ready to be lit in the evening. In the morning, when the fire had expired, there was a large crater in the road filled with ash. The concrete surface had erupted with the tremendous heat generated, and the local authority had to send round workmen to resurface the road. That was the end of bonfires in Northport Street.

A week or so before November 5th, we would make a "Guy" out of an old sack stuffed with any old clothes the kids could cadge from their mums, an old pair of strides (trousers) and a piece of cardboard with a face drawn on it. We would position ourselves outside a pub or Old Street Underground Station or even Shoreditch Town Hall, which was opposite the Old Street Police Station, and ask for "a penny for the guy". Not once were we approached by anybody from the Police Station and told to move on, as they would today. I suppose that the practice was so widespread, certainly throughout the London area, and completely innocent, although really the pennies were for us to buy fireworks with. There were no restrictions on the purchase of fireworks; they could be purchased in almost any newsagents shop and were made mainly by a company known as Brocks Fireworks. I now realise just how dangerous these explosives were. Some of the more powerful bangers were called Thunder Flashes, and you would have to stand well clear when you lit the blue touch paper. Some boys would put an elastic band around two or more Thunder Flashes and – of all things! – put them inside an empty milk bottle. One of these bangers could blow off a finger quite easily. Imagine the explosion from two! You certainly had to take cover when the milk bottle disintegrated. One of my old pals, Elby Silk, had a small bag slung over his shoulder holding a substantial number of fireworks (Bangers, Catherine Wheels, Sparklers, Roman Candles and Rockets) and a spark somehow found its way into the bag. The whole lot were ignited, and we had to tear the bag off him, but not before he suffered some not-too-serious burns. He was rushed to A & E at the nearby St Leonard's Hospital. I never really liked fireworks as a child and even less now as an adult because of the noise they make and the way they terrify animals. I do not agree with how they can be bought over the counter by anyone over sixteen. I think firework displays should be put on by local authorities where there is strict supervision and safety rules are in place. A display is put on by the Local Authority in the town where my daughter lives. I understand it costs many tens of thousands of pounds to produce, and the authority has received many letters from irate people complaining that housing rates and various other taxes could be better spent on housing the homeless who have been huddled up in shop doorways on cold nights. I have stood in awe at a firework display in the Disney Complex in Florida – magical to behold!

We also enjoyed fishing down the cut (canal) and would make what was known as a drag from an old bike wheel. We would remove the spokes, place it on a flat hessian sack and thread string all the way around the wheel, holding the sacking in place; finally, with four pieces of string meeting in the middle and another length of string tied to the four pieces, it could be lowered into the water and dragged along while we walked on the tow path. Every so often, the drag would be pulled up and was invariably filled with fish such as sticklebacks, red throats and sometimes the larger gudgeon. These were put in large water tanks that had been constructed in most London boroughs, so there was much wildlife swimming around other than in the canals.

After the First World War, there were problems with the supply of water right across London because water supply mains had been damaged during the bombing. Water could not reliably be pumped from the Thames because it is tidal and at low tide it was almost impossible to pump water. In July 1938, in anticipation of war breaking out again, the Government decreed that new water pipes were to be constructed across London. The London Fire Brigade built large brick water tanks, lined with asphalt, as emergency water supplies for their fire engines. They were usually situated on street corners so they were accessible from both sides. These tanks held approximately fifty-five thousand gallons of water and had brick stanchions leading down to the water's edge. We kids would string together a couple of room doors taken from a bombed house and go sailing across this large expanse of water – "Pirates of the Spanish Main"! My parents would have thrown a fit if they had seen me! Even more so if they had seen me swimming in the cut. Come the hot summers we used to enjoy on the six-week holiday from school, we'd climb up onto moored barges that seemed so huge and, at times, frightening.

I had wonderful parents. Dad was a hard-working man, never out of work, a man who had principles and virtues as numerous as the petals on a daisy but was never strict. He took great care with his appearance and was always very smart, probably influenced by his army training, but on many occasions, I saw him lose his temper when trying to fix the studs on his detachable pure white shirt collars which were in vogue at that time. While I was growing up and going out with the boys and to parties, I always enjoyed the compliments regarding my sartorial elegance ("Dapper Dan", "Lord Dunabunk", etc.). I remember hanging my jacket once on the back of a chair, in full view of Dad. "That's not the place – in the wardrobe!" said he. I still do it to this day (hang it in the wardrobe, I mean!). I owe all these habits and many more to my dad.

I used to love it when he would regale me with tales about his army days in India. He showed me how to "ball up", that is, spit and polish the toecaps of your shoes so you could almost see your face in them, as he would do when inspection was called or he was on the parade ground. And when firing a rifle, an old trick was to hold a lighter or match with the flame on the forward sight, which would blacken and allow you to see the target more clearly and therefore shoot with more accuracy. I would sit enthralled when he told me about his early life before his years in the Army and the colourful characters whose names I still remember: Blood Alan, Jackie Bolly, Charlie Lyons, and many more. He taught me so much about life for which I am so very grateful. I often find myself repeating phrases he would use, and I don't have to look for them; they are expressed without thinking because they are so ingrained in my psyche.

My dad was more than "a bit of a rough handful", as the saying goes, in his young days before he mellowed with age, but still a no-nonsense guy. One of my relations, who was about my dad's age, told me of an incident when Dad lived down the "Bass" and had a terrible fight with another guy. He knocked the guy out, grabbed him by the neck and dragged him across the tramlines for a tram to run over him. Once, Dad and I were on a bus heading for Highbury Corner, Islington. We were sitting on the long seat just inside the door where the conductor stood, and on the seat next to me was a small, empty paper bag that was used for copper coins. I had picked it up and was looking at it when the conductor came along and asked me, "What are you doing with that?" I did not know what to reply, so Dad said to him, "Is there a problem?" "Does he usually pick up things that don't belong to him?" asked the conductor. Dad made him aware I was no more than a child and, after more altercation, stood up, grabbed hold of him and almost threw him off the bus while it was moving. If this had happened on more solid ground, I feel sure the guy would have finished up in the Great Northern Hospital in Holloway Road, all because of an old copper bag that had been used time and time again. This conductor just wanted to assert his authority.

Pubs, in those days, were central to the community. Friends and family would meet there on Friday and Saturday nights, and at "last orders" would order much beer from the Governor and carry it out to have a Moriarty (party) in someone's house (often ours). The pub's resident piano player would be engaged to attend the party, kept in beer and given a few quid to play all the old songs. The player in question was a certain Sonny Adams, who was a friend of Dad's and lived in Ivy Street, which was just around the corner. The piano was the only entertainment available in those days, long before the coming of television and radiograms. Neither Dad, Mum nor I could play the piano, but Dad decided to buy a piano from a company named Jelks up Holloway Road, in anticipation of the parties we used to have in our house. Dad was the best I have ever seen at playing the spoons, a craft he had learnt in the Army, and would at times accompany the piano player. (I never could get the hang of them, try as I might.) He would also play the mouth organ and sometimes sing his favourite song, "Come to Me, My Melancholy Baby". Dad won many a competition taking part in talent nights whilst on holiday with Mum.

After some time, Dad left the Hoffman Pressing job, mainly due to the travelling back and forth to Victoria from the East End, and applied to British Rail for a job. He was assigned to LNER Railway Yard at Spitalfields Depot in Valance Road, Bethnal Green. He used to cycle to work in the morning and also at night when he had to take a turn at night shift. He had trained as a capstan operator and loved the work, which must have helped him to secure the job. He was very happy working for the "Rail" and was there many years, becoming an official for the National Union of Railwaymen (NUR).

He also organised the annual Beanos for all the guys he worked with, as well as other railway employees from the large Bishopsgate Goods Depot, which was at the top end of Bethnal Green Road. Every year, we went by coach down to Margate, a proper jolly boys outing, lots of singing, lots of booze. Most people were Oliver Twist (pissed) before we even arrived in Margate. On the way home, we'd stop at Halfway House and have a good sherbet (drink) with all our good friends. I have so many lovely memories of these outings and many photographs to keep the memories alive; they were so very special, thanks to Dad's fastidious planning and organising.

Mum was a good mother, a stay-at-home mum who cared about me, worried about me and did everything for me when I was still an only child. So-called child experts have often debated what makes a "good" or "bad" mother; the views may vary as often as the English weather. Child experts were invariably men, and women were told to surrender their motherly instincts. "Father Knows Best" was the watchword of the day. If the mother picked up the baby when it cried, to kiss and cuddle it or take it into her bed, which is perfectly normal, she would probably be denounced. No wonder the street urchins and ragamuffins grew up with the belief their parents didn't love them. Thankfully, none of that nonsense applied to me. My dad's idiom was wholeheartedly "Mother Knows Best."

Situated in Old Street, next to Moon's Motors, was Arthur Burton's, a large factory that manufactured bandages, dressings and medical equipment for soldiers who had been wounded in the war. Many women did piece work, working for this company from home. Mum applied for a position and was accepted. On our first day, Mum and I pushed an old pram all the way to Arthur Burton's and were loaded up with bags of brown bandages which reminded us of sausages when they come out of the machine. I often wondered why they were coloured brown as opposed to the usual white; maybe it was because blood doesn't look so stark and frightening on a brown bandage! The bandages from a long string could be snapped off by hand and then packed, which we would do whilst listening to the wireless to while away the drudgery. It was for a very worthy cause, though, and you felt you were doing your bit.

A pram load of unpacked bandages collected from Burton's would keep us going for a couple of days; then the journey would be repeated. The payment was a pittance, which was the case for most home work. We did this until the war came to an end; all this time, Dad was on night work.

During those years of rationing and deprivation, the old adage of "mend and make do" applied to most things. Mum thought she would further help by becoming an early-morning office cleaner and started work at a bank in Gresham Street in the City. It entailed dusting, sweeping, cleaning and emptying waste paper baskets. She would leave home at 5 am, trudge up to the bus stop in New North Road, meet other women cleaners there and catch the bus to work. She would return home about 8 am, get me up for school, cook me a breakfast and do me a packed lunch.

When I arrived home from school, Mum would do my tea and then at 5 pm set off to clean offices for another firm in the city, returning home at about 8 pm. She did two jobs a day five days a week for thirty years or so, in all weathers and never complaining. Eventually, Dad said he wanted her to pack up the office cleaning as our finances had improved, but I know she enjoyed the job and the camaraderie with the other women, so Dad relented and she gave up only the evening job. Mum was not necessarily big and strong in stature but certainly in resolve. She continued those jobs into her fifties until we did not need the money anymore. Dad was earning good money, and by this time I had started work and was giving Mum some of my wages, so things had started to look up, and as a family, we were coping quite well. I will never forget how much she did to help Dad and me. We were the first in our street to have a television, albeit you needed a pair of binoculars to watch the nine-inch screen, and were the first with a radiogram, a Portadyne. The first record I bought was Guy Mitchell singing "She Wears Red Feathers", followed by "Singing the Blues", which were big hits at the time.

One of my favourite forms of recreation was constructing a cart. It was made up of a five-to-six-foot length of floorboard with a wooden box set about a foot in from the end of the floorboard. The front end would have a wooden axle with a rubber pram wheel on each end, the same as the back end, situated under the wooden box that doubled as the cockpit where the driver sat. A pair of reins from the front axle sat in the hands of the driver, who controlled the direction of travel. Alternatively, the cart could be steered by your feet. On the back stood the pusher, who pushed hard to get sufficient motion and speed and when that was attained jumped on the back and also got a ride. This is the reason why the box was set a foot from the end; it allowed a small platform for the pusher to jump on.

Another favourite of mine was making a scooter from two pieces of wood, one piece upright and a piece you stood on, held together with two screw eyes. A piece of wood across the upright piece acted as the handle bar, and two ball bearings were the wheels. This mode of transport would be decorated with bottle tops from beer bottles.

We also enjoyed collecting autographs of the British film stars who came out of the famous Gainsborough Studios in Poole Street. We would wait outside the studio, sometimes for hours, to catch a glimpse of the stars, with our autograph books at the ready. Some of the stars we saw were John Mills, Patricia Roc, Alec Guinness, Rosamund John, Stewart Granger, and singer Gracie Fields, as well as James Mason, whose adaptation and portrayal of the German Field Marshal Erwin Rommel as the Commander of the Afrika Korps in *The North African Campaign* was outstanding and never bettered.

The Gainsborough Film Studios were built in 1924 and closed in 1949. For decades they remained sadly derelict, except for an occasional production of a Shakespearean play. The Studio's opening logo was of a smiling lady in a beautiful Georgian-era dress sitting in an ornate revolving frame. In 2004, the studios were converted into luxury flats that back onto Regent's Canal; no doubt the view of the canal and the boats that slowly meander by demands a premium price. Our pleasures in those long-ago days were effective, simple and much loved, a far cry from what's on offer to the children of today.

Our six-week holiday from school was a time for roaming around, fishing, exploring and playing football in the street. The summers seemed always to be sunny and hot. My mum and her friend Ivy Gordon, who had two children, Lenny and Joanie, and lived opposite us in Northport Street, would take us to Highbury open-air pool or on the trolley bus to Tottenham Lido. Mum and Ivy would make a packed lunch of cheese and pickle sandwiches and a bottle of Tizer or Cream Soda and it would be a lovely day out. But the adventure that possibly topped them all was a trip to the city, the Moorgate area and London Wall, which had been heavily bombed. Large buildings were razed to the ground and some banks reduced to rubble, with their steel strong room doors fully on show. On our way there, we would pass the barracks which were next to Moorgate Cemetery, which is quite famous for a few of its residents, namely, the poet John Bunyan, Daniel Defoe, who wrote *Robinson Crusoe*, first published in 1719, and the writer and poet William Blake. Moorgate Cemetery is also known as Bunhill Fields.

Our nearest park was Clissold Park in Stoke Newington. Mum and I would have a day out over there in the summer months, taking our sandwiches and lemonade. There were many animals in enclosures (rabbits, deer and peacocks), a miniature railway train that you could ride on and a large paddling pool no more than a couple of inches deep. I always thought Clissold was a nicer park than Victoria Park, which was over in Bethnal Green, maybe because Clissold was opposite the Arsenal Stadium which was our team, but Vicky Park, as it was known, had the edge on us because it had a large boating lake.

As the war came to an end in 1945, there were large celebrations and street parties across the country, especially in the East End. There were tables in the streets, bunting, flags and people dancing. All the women pitched in to make sandwiches, apple pies and custard, jam tarts and lemonade. Each street would have its own party, and everybody was ecstatic that the war was finally over.

My dad had three younger brothers, Arthur, Freddie and Ernie. Ernie had his own small asphalting business, and his equipment would be carried on the back of an open lorry. One day, Mum and Dad told me we would be going away for three or four weeks to Kent, wherever that was, to a place called Faversham to pick hops with Uncle Ernie, Aunt Rene and all my cousins, young Ernie, Anita, Kenny and Jeanie. I had no idea what hops were; I didn't know a hop from a pineapple. One morning in early September, Uncle Ernie turned up at the front of our house in his lorry with a makeshift canopy erected over the open back. Everything we needed was packed into suitcases and bags, our dog Trixie was lifted up onto the lorry and we were off! Thinking about it now, that 1949 film *The Huggetts Abroad,* with Jack Warner, Kathleen Harrison and Petula Clarke, springs to mind.

Little did we know what primitive hardships lay ahead for us, but after a while, we accepted that, like that lovely old song recorded by Tommy Edwards, "It's all in the Game."

My lovely mum, aged 12 in 1923 - a real Charleston flapper

Mum and Dad on their wedding day August 2nd 1936. Dad's sartorial elegance was Passed on to myself - down to his shiny shoes

Mum, Dad and I, with me looking like 'Frank Spencer' approx. 1939

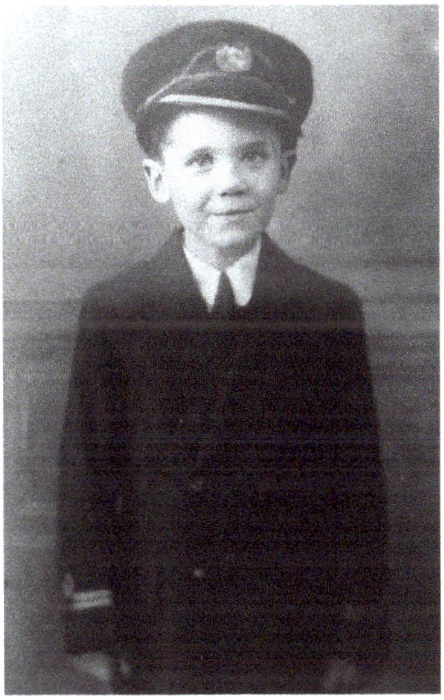

Myself aged 6 years as a pageboy at my aunt and uncle's wedding

Myself with a rascal's face aged 12 years old

Hopping days.
From left: My dad, mum, aunt Rene, sister Mary and uncle Ernie

Myself at 18 years old

Myself at 18 years old in Faversham, Kent with my Dad's Standard Vanguard car, in 1955

My Dad at work in his railway depot.

My two good pals, Frankie Hudson and Derek Adams at Southend in 1958

Me in the three piece suit with my old pal Frankie Hudson. A Sunday session in our local pub

Some of my old pals from the 1950's. Far left, Lennie Myring, Frankie Hudson, myself, Lennie Cluff, Terry Myring and Michael Isaacs

My lovely Mum and Dad in a reflective and pensive moment

CHAPTER 5

HOP PICKING

We arrived on the back of the lorry at a place called Harefield Farm in Selling, which is a market town within the borough of Swale in Kent. We had already been given our instructions in a letter from the owner, Mr Alan Bruce Neame, regarding where our accommodation was situated, so we pulled onto the designated field and could see nothing other than some rather dilapidated cow sheds. Within minutes, a yokel arrived and told us these sheds were where we were supposed to live for the next four to five weeks, which was the usual period required for all the hops to be harvested.

Upon inspection of these most primitive abodes, my mother and Aunt Rene almost keeled over. The black corrugated huts were devoid of any home comforts except for old rough-sawn wooden beds in two of the huts. These were to act as the bedrooms, one for Mum and Dad and one for Tony and me, and we were allotted an additional hut which was used as a kitchen and dining room. The same accommodation was given to Uncle Ernie and Aunt Rene's family, so we had three huts each, which must have been a bit of a squeeze for them as there were four children in their family, as opposed to just my brother Tony and myself. These old wooden beds had no mattresses, but we were told by other hopping families that we needed to take our palliasses and fill them with straw, of which there was no shortage on the farm. We finally realised the purpose of the string-bound bundles of straw lying on the damp ground, so it was down to the farmyard just at the back of our huts, and the barn holding dry straw was promptly raided.

The huts were alive with all kinds of creepy crawlers, mainly spiders and earwigs. I remember Uncle Ernie standing on one of their beds with a bowl of water, knocking all kinds of insects into the water, which would then be thrown outside into the field. Well, that was the intention, but he lost his balance on the soft bed and the bowl of insects was dropped in the middle of the bed. They quickly scattered in their newfound freedom, the bed was soaking wet and the palliasse had to be filled again with fresh straw. Uncle Ernie was not a happy bunny, unlike the wild cousins that scampered about on the sweeping slopes of the beautiful valley behind our huts.

On Monday morning, we made our way to the hop gardens at 9 am and were directed to our pitch. We learnt that the hop plants grew on vine-like stems known as bines to a height of eighteen to twenty-five feet. Hop pickers would usually give the bine a sharp, strong pull, the string at the top securing it to overhead string lines would break and the plant would come tumbling down. In the early morning, when it was covered in dew, it would soak you as if it was raining. If, after continuous pulling of a bine, the string would not break, you would call out for a pole puller who, with a large pole with a knife bound to the end of it, would cut the string for you and allow the bine to fall. Hops are a classified as a vegetable. The hop flowers form soft, pale green, cone-like structures that are usually two to four inches long and have thin, soft petals that turn yellow when ripe. The glands of the plant contain oils and acids that give the bitterness and flavour to beer and are also used for medicinal purposes, to treat insomnia and upset stomachs.

On fine days, we would work till about 5 pm, when the pole puller would call out, "Pull no more bines." Mum and Aunt Rene would leave a bit earlier to get the tea ready for us when we came home. At the start of the season, each family of pickers was given a small booklet in which the amount that you picked was recorded, not in weight but in volume, namely bushels. We were paid in cash at the end of the season. In our first year, we picked hops into one-bushel baskets, which were tipped into a long hessian bin with wooden handles at each end. The tally man and a couple of helpers would empty this into a large sack and hoist it up onto the back of a horse-drawn cart. In our second year, these had been replaced by huge, round, six-bushel baskets, which were much better. Up the inside of these large baskets were markers showing the volume of hops in the basket. Just prior to the tally man arriving to record our pickings, there would be just five bushels in the basket, but hops being so light, Dad would put his arms right to the bottom of the basket and lift the hops up to the six-bushel marker, thereby getting an agreement from the tally man that there were six in the basket. This was an old trick also practised by Uncle Ernie. Maybe we needed this little trick when you think of what pickers were paid: one shilling and sixpence per bushel (about 7½p). A substantial amount of leaves also went into the six-bushel basket, and we heard that some pickers included a whole bine and pieces of string, which was illegal. This would only be discovered when all the hops were taken to the oast house (drying kiln).

If the weather was half-decent, which it usually was, Mum would cook outside the hut on a fire which Dad would get going with faggots, which were large tied bundles of twigs delivered daily by an employee on a tractor. Over the fire stood a small metal tripod from which hung a kettle, and hot water for tea and washing was boiled in this way. On either side of the fire was a small row of bricks with a metal rack across them that would be used when a saucepan or pot was boiled for porridge or for washing. With constant use over an open fire, all receptacles became black with soot. Not once did I hear the pot calling the kettle black. In inclement weather, Dad would get the primus stove going, but it was very small and had to be constantly pumped by hand, with a small plunger on the side, or it would lose heat.

About fifty yards from our huts was a free-standing tap where we would fill our kettles and water containers. In all the years we attended hopping, I can't remember seeing my dad wash in hot water. He would walk up to the tap in his vest, with a towel over his shoulder, and would wash his face, arms and back of his neck all in cold water, although some mornings were icy. Mum did Dad and me some breakfast, after which we pickers made our way to the hop garden, carrying flasks of tea and sometimes our Primus stove to boil up a kettle and make a cup of tea mid-morning and dinner time. Mum and Aunt Rene stayed behind to tidy up and make sandwiches to take up to the field for dinner. We soon learned how to pick hops, and other families who were well-seasoned would always help out if we needed to ask about something. The Londoners, mainly from the East End and South London, all shared a common bond, but the non-Londoners did not take kindly to us. These were known as "home dwellers", and their resentment was clear to see, why I'm not sure. Their accommodation was far superior to ours; they had small red-brick cottages with wooden doors, unlike our old black tin huts that were very cold at night.

In the nearby lane was a very old village store owned by an elderly

this so-called examiner. Dad then bought another car, a lovely Standard Vanguard with column change gears. I waited the customary period and applied again, this time sailing through. The year was 1957.

My years in Faversham picking hops with Mum and Dad were from about age ten to when I was twenty and the dawn of the permissive Swinging Sixties was just around the corner. Those of us like my family were regarded by some as unfortunate, or even poor, as well as quaint, to have to lower themselves to that level of working holiday with all its primitive conditions. However, I would never have changed them. They have a special place in my heart – the camaraderie with all my cousins, endless things and places to explore, seeing cows in fields for the first time, rabbits galore running about in the valley, the fresh smell of the straw in our palliasses and the flickering flame of the oil lamps as the daylight faded.

When it all came to an end in the middle of the last century, a period of Kent history drew to a close. Mechanisation replaced manual labour, farmers found it cheaper and more reliable to use the hop-picking machines and rain would never stop play, so to speak, but the writing was on the wall that hand-picking had run its course. When the season started in September, Dad had to take time off from work, without pay, and children were just taken out of school. It meant missing four to five weeks of education. As working conditions across the country improved and people, with more money in their pockets, took holidays in caravans at the seaside, working in the hop fields started to pall as a way of earning a few quid. Young girls and guys looked to other ways to enjoy themselves, and American music broke on the scene: Elvis, Bill Haley, Gene Vincent, Eddy Cochran and Chuck Berry, to name but a few of the singers. For our family and thousands like us, it all came to an end.

It was a special time in my life, and I would dearly love to be given the chance to do it all again. Those memories fill me with an overwhelming melancholy, but I am fortunate to have an abundance of photographs to bring it all back. I have at times revisited the places where the hop fields were and are no more; some of our huts are still standing but rusting away, and the beautiful valley in all its majesty still lifts my spirit to another plateau. My brother Tony and I took our mum back there some years ago when she was in her nineties to just relive some of our memories of the wonderful smell of hop fruit and flowers, the cattle in the fields and the village store where we used to shop, marvellous magical memories of a vanished way of life that I long for with an aching heart. In that same heart, hopping has become part of a pastoral golden age, a kind of utopian past. I find myself ensconced in warm nostalgia, a powerful alternative to the present that offers an escape to sunnier days when life was less complex and querulous times rarely showed their face.

I took my daughter Gretchen there too, after telling her all about it. She had packed a nice picnic of sandwiches and pop, which she laid out on a large colourful blanket. Watching us nearby were a whole herd of cattle, which are very curious creatures. I said, "If you approach them and lie still on the floor, you will experience something quite magical," which she did, albeit a bit reticently at first. The cattle formed a complete circle around her, sniffing her face, her feet, so very gentle. When she made a move to get up after ten minutes or so, they moved away; she couldn't believe what she had just experienced. I told her they were placid creatures and probably knew we were both vegetarians. At the time of writing, I have been a vegetarian for about thirty-five years and feel much better for it.

Over the years, I have travelled extensively across the American continent, through Yosemite National Park, the Mojave Desert and reputably the hottest place on earth, Death Valley. I've seen the wonders of the Grand Canyon in Arizona, the lovely city of San Francisco and Alcatraz across the Bay, New York, Florida, Chicago, Las Vegas and Boston, Massachusetts, but for me, they pale into insignificance. My heart belongs to the hop fields of Faversham, a rustic paradise, where my childhood was spent in a world that has now been relegated to antiquity. We had nothing, but we had it all.

Roy Wild

CHAPTER 6

THE BLACKBOARD JUNGLE

At age eleven I started secondary school at Pitfield School in Pitfield Street. There are two schools of thought regarding the origin of the name Pitfield. One is that it is named after Charles Pitfield, who bought a large moated mansion nearby in 1648, and the other is that it comes from a large pit that was dug in a nearby field to bury the dead from the Great Plague of London. The latter sounds more plausible; local authorities probably sugar-coated it so that as memories faded, people would never know their properties were sited on dead bodies.

My first day at Pitfield School was overwhelming. The school housed boys from age eleven to fifteen, and the fifteen-year-olds seemed enormous to me. Some were as big as grown men and with the same amount of aggression. I was assigned to Mr Balin's class. He was a short, bald man with a laurel wreath of ginger hair growing around his head. His pet subject was the Roman Empire. None of us had ever heard of Marcus Aurelius or Julius Caesar or famous Roman generals, but as our teacher, he was very easy to get along with, too easy in fact. He could not maintain order in the class, and boys will be boys. Things would be thrown about, including ink pellets made of blotting paper soaked in ink. There was an ink well on each desk, which again was something new to us. It was two boys to a desk, and I sat next to my old pal from Northport Street, Michael Isaacs. From a bendy ruler, an ink pellet would be fired across the room, and then retaliation would occur and mayhem settled in for a while until Mr Balin would send a pupil for the Headmaster, a certain and much-feared Mr Nesbit, to restore order.

Fortunately, I was good at English, and it spared me from many a scrape. I was made ink monitor, filling up the ink wells on each desk (what an honour?), as well as milk monitor. All pupils, by government decree, were given a third of a pint of milk every morning, and I would hand the milk out.

One of our subjects was Woodwork, taught by Mr Brewer and Mr Riches. Mr Brewer was a nice guy with lots of patience and would explain things thoroughly; I drew the short straw and was assigned to Mr Riches, who was horrible, always criticising and short-tempered. We made things like towel rollers and small briefcases. I was quite adept at these manual tasks. Another morning we would be taken for Book Binding by an elderly Irishman, Mr Watson. Teaching book binding to a class of East End boys was completely futile; we had no interest whatsoever. Mr Watson was another tutor who could not maintain order. While his back was turned, the boys would throw a heavy blackboard eraser at him, and he nearly jumped out of his skin when the eraser thudded into the blackboard next to his head. Then in a rich Southern Ireland drawl, he would utter the immortal words, "There will be no more Book Binding for 2B." We thought, "Thank God for that. We never wanted it in the first place!" Enter again Mr Nesbit to straighten things out. "OK," said Mr Nesbit, "who's responsible for throwing the eraser?" only to be met by thirty innocent faces. "Right," said he, "you will all be kept in during playtime until we find out who threw it. It could have knocked Mr Watson out or done him serious damage!" I'm sure the boys were thinking," That was the whole idea – then no more book binding!" The following week, Book Binding was on again, and I thought, "This calls for a different strategy."

I soon became acquainted with school life at Pitfield and made some friends. I was good at football, as I have previously mentioned, and would play against an opposing team in the playground before the bell went in the morning to start the day's lessons. At lunch time I would come home where Mum would prepare something to eat, then I would head back to school to get in a game of football before the bell went again to start the afternoon lessons. I hooked up with two boys, Terry Hiscot and Terry Robbins, the latter being a very good footballer. He had a cousin whose surname was Brown (his first name escapes me), and I had seen him and a pal bully younger boys. Before I set off for school each morning, Mum would make me a couple of sandwiches to eat at playtime, which was about 11 am. They started to demand half of my sandwiches, and Terry Robbins never gave me any backup, blood being thicker than water; neither did Terry Hiscot. In the next street to Northport Street were many prefabs that had been erected by the local council as temporary accommodation for families that had lost their homes in the recent bombing. Living in one of the prefabs were Mr and Mrs Rainer and their twin boys, Dougie and Dennis. These two were fearsome fighters, and everyone stood aside when they were in circulation. It just so happened that Mum and Dad were quite friendly with the parents of these two tearaways, as I was myself with the twins. I had told the twins about Brown and his sidekick demanding part of my lunch every day, which I had refused, and the twins said, "Roy, don't worry about it. We will see to it!"

One day, when the two bullies again demanded part of my lunch, watching from a distance were the terrible twins. They wandered over, collared these two and frightened the life out of Brown and Co, who were promptly put on a warning. Dougie and Dennis were the precursors to the later notorious "Brothers Grimm", twins Ronnie and Reggie Kray. All aggravation ceased from Brown and Co, and he tried to become quite pally, but that didn't work. You never really get over being bullied when you were young, and if I met Brown now, and I sincerely hope I do somewhere along the line, I don't suppose he would recognise me. I would remind him what had happened and then bust him right in the mouth, even after all these years.

At Pitfield, we had a metalwork room run by Mr Sparks, who was a long-haired hippy type, mad as a March hare but harmless. We would make brackets and all kinds of things that were totally useless, but it taught us how to drill with various drill bits and how to use a hacksaw and other metalwork tools. We used to see old Sparksy roaring away after school on his motorbike, in his tweeds and with his long hair billowing out behind, amid cheers from the boys.

Another teacher was Mr Arden, who took us for music. He was another long-haired, arty type who reminds me now of Christopher Lloyd, the American actor who played the part of the eccentric scientist Dr Emmett "Doc" Brown, inventor of the time-travelling DeLorean Automobile in the film *Back To The Future*. Mr Arden would give us singing lessons amid cat calls, raspberries and various other noises whilst he was playing the piano. He took his job very seriously, but to the boys it was all a lark. I think when it was our turn to be taken for music lessons, he would mop his brow in dread and couldn't wait for it to be over. The much-feared and talked-about 2B… One day we all filed into his classroom after playtime and found him all pumped up and smiles. He informed us that he had written a song for the school entitled "Strive to Make Pitfield the Best School Of All". The boys looked at each other and thought, "We'll soon see about that!" He gave us a quick run-through, accompanying himself on the piano, and then tried to get us all to sing with him. That was the trigger we were waiting for: boos, catcalls, and much laughter, not forgetting the raspberries.

This behaviour was not exclusive to our class; most classes were out of control. I saw a fight in the assembly hall between a big fifteen-year-old boy and the Headmaster, and old Nesbit was coming off second best. The sports master, Mr Bayliss, and Mr Dawes were called to assist as they were two of the younger teachers and fancied themselves able to bring law and order to the school. I think the boy was expelled.

Our Geography teacher was Mr Johnson, who was old school (no pun intended). It is hard to attach any kind of age to him; at our age, anyone over thirty-five or forty was ancient, but I would say he was more than sixty years of age, with a shock of almost white hair. He was a Mr Pastry look-alike and no nonsense given or taken. He was known as "one eye and a whelk" which is an old East End observation for somebody who has an eye affliction. Mr Johnson's eyes did not look straight ahead; only one looked straight ahead and the other one looked to the left, so you could never tell who he was talking to. If he caught one of the class larking about or talking, he would say, "Right! Come out here, you," and the boy would leave his desk and approach the teacher's desk. Old Johnson would say, "Not you! Sit down!" and then point to one of the other boys to come forward. It was hilarious at times.

There was a cat that used to wander around the school, and the boys would make a fuss of it and stroke it. One day, a couple of the boys during playtime crept into old Johnson's classroom and put the school cat into the cupboard where he kept all our exercise books. When we were seated for the lesson, breathless in anticipation, he opened the cupboard and out jumped the cat with a squeal. It scampered off into the main hall and down the stairs to freedom. Old Johnson was beside himself with rage and demanded to know who was responsible. He went round the class asking each one of us whether we knew anything about who had put the cat in the cupboard. Thirty pairs of innocent eyes returned his glare and we all denied it.

When the cane was given by any teacher, it was taken on the hand – unbelievable, now. It was violence to children, and many a parent was seen at the school having a row with a teacher. Some teachers would bring the cane down with more force than others, and teacher and child might have to go to hospital. Mr Johnson believed in giving the cane on the Khyber Pass (arse), and boys would slip something thick, such as an exercise book, down the back of their trousers to take the sting out of the blow.

After a time I was promoted to 3B, where Mr Dawes was the teacher. I excelled at spelling, reading and writing composition, and I loved history. Another boy in our class, Bobby Jewell, was also very good at spelling. Once a week we would have a spelling test, which consisted of twenty questions. One week I would get nineteen right and Bobby Jewell would get eighteen, and the following week the results would be reversed. For our final examination, we were given fifty spellings to complete. On this occasion, I reigned supreme with forty-nine right, and Bobby came a very close second with forty-eight. I was still sitting next to my old pal Michael Isaacs, who was quite good at maths but not so good at spelling. He would copy my spelling sometimes, and I would copy him in maths. One day Mr Dawes gave us five sums to complete, long division and a couple of fractions, and that was the day that Mike didn't turn up for school. Mr Dawes gave us an hour to complete the sums, and finally he looked up and stated, "Time's up. Pens down!" He knew I was no good at maths and sorted me out first. "Number one, Wild," said he. Wrong! Number two, Wrong, Number three, got that right. Number four, Wrong, Number five, Wrong. He told me to stay behind at the end of the lesson then sent me to the Headmaster's office to fetch the cane and book. The Head's office was on the top floor, so after a slow walk up the apples (stairs), I knocked softly on his door. "Enter," came an unmistakable gruff voice, and in I went. "Yes?" he said after addressing me by one of his favourite expressions, which was "you half-baked rogue". The other one he frequently used was "half-baked scoundrel". Thinking about those expressions now, what a lovely turn of phrase! "Who is the cane and book for?" "Mr Dawes, Sir," said I. "No doubt misbehaving yourself," said he. I stood there silently until dismissed. On my return, I steeled myself for the lecture that I knew would be forthcoming. "You are a bright lad, Wild, and can do better than this," Mr Dawes said, pointing to my book. I always liked Mr Dawes. He was a smart man, dress-wise, always wore a three-piece suit, had a mop of well-groomed black hair which matched his thick black moustache and could be quite funny, throwing in a few jokes now and again. "You are the best in my class at spelling and writing as you were in your previous class, according to Mr Balin. You just need to brush up on your maths." He told me to return the cane and book to the Headmaster and be thankful that the other lessons I'd excelled in had got me out of trouble. I knew he never really had the heart or inclination to use the cane for my benefit. It was nice of him to give up his free time when he could have been relaxing in the Common Room with the rest of the teaching staff.

That brings me to another misdemeanour the boys got up to. Just before the bell was rung for the morning and afternoon playtime, a prefect would make cups of tea in the Common Room for all the teachers. A couple of the boys would get in there just before the teachers and would drop lumps of broken chalk into the cups of tea. I never had a problem with that, as long as it was directed at some of the tyrants that taught there. Mr Dawson hardly ever used the facilities of the Common Room and very seldom did I hear of him using the cane. I don't think he was an exponent of that type of discipline. Then suddenly Mr Dawes was no longer at the school and I was told he had left teaching and joined the Police Force. I wish him well if he is still on this mortal plane.

I was caned many times for various offences at Pitfield: playing dice under the shed, which was gambling and not allowed, fighting (twice) and smoking in the toilets, until we got wise and posted lookouts at each end of the playground toilets, which had an archway leading in and out. Sometimes a teacher would come rushing in hoping to catch us before the fag was extinguished, but it would be thrown straight into the urinal and a line of boys would just be standing there pretending to have a Fraser Nash (slash). A couple of times I was caught smoking under a large shed in the playground where we sheltered in the event of rain. Just along the road from our school was a tobacconist who would sell the kids a single fag for tuppence, so there was always a ready supply. Caning in British schools was outlawed in 1986. Caning was permitted because the idea of *in loco parentis* meant that teachers were seen as authority figures and were granted the same rights as parents; they could more or less dish out any punishment they saw fit. Some boys expecting a caning would rub a piece of orange peel on the palm of their hand so the cane would slide off and the pain would be minimized. Receiving the cane hurt like hell and one would wear the red weals for quite a few hours afterwards. When holding the hand flat, you had to make sure your thumb was low because a teacher who was less than accurate would bring the cane down on the thumb, which could break it and a trip to the hospital could ensue. Depending on the sculduggery you were involved in, it was an occupational hazard! It is hard now to believe this could have been sanctioned by the government. It was a total assault on children.

Our History teacher was Mr Bayless, who, in his spare time, was a steward at the Arsenal ground at Highbury. He was known by the boys as "Boot Bayless" because he had a rather large hooter or "I suppose" (nose). He was also the sports master and taught boxing. He and I would sometimes speak about the Arsenal team, and somewhere along the way, I mentioned to him that my dad had been a regimental champion boxer in the Army and had fought in the All India Finals, which really impressed old Bayless. He told me that at lunchtime in the lower hall, he and a couple of the boys set up a boxing ring that the school had purchased and he was teaching boxing with a view to setting up a school boxing team to compete against other teams. Would I be interested in setting up the ring and starting training? I had always been interested in boxing, and Dad and I would sit around our radio at home and listen to world title fights with the likes of Bruce Woodcock and Freddie Mills, as well as the American fighters, so I took up Mr Bayless's offer. As the school bell was heralding dinner time, I would pop down to the lower hall and with a couple of boys set up the ring. If I remember correctly after all these years, it was an eighteen-foot ring, which I think is full size. With the ring set up, I would scoot home to grab something to eat that Mum had prepared and then charge back to school to start training, with some guidance from Mr Bayless. After a couple of months, I was doing very well as I was slim and wiry and fast. Once when I was in the ring sparing with another boy, old Bayless intervened. He told us to stop boxing and asked the other boy to step out of the ring. He then entered the ring himself and said, "You are doing very well, Roy, you are a good defensive boxer, very fast, but you have to dish it out as well as avoiding being hit." With that, he slipped on a pair of gloves and said, "Ok, I'll show you what I mean." We started circling each other, and I was very apprehensive; after all, he was the sports master and I wasn't sure what was about to happen! I had seen him throw a wooden blackboard eraser at a boy and also, once, a bunch of keys, which was quite normal in those days. We started shaping up, and I was quite reticent in my approach. He suddenly dropped his hands and said, "Roy, don't worry. Just treat me as another opponent." We started again, and he tried to catch me with a couple of shots. I jabbed him twice and then slung him a shot with my right hand which landed on his rather big hooter and probably increased its size even more. He stopped boxing, and I offered my apologies straight away. He said, "That's OK," through watery eyes, and the sparring stopped. As he said, I was very fast.

This training and setting up the ring every day finally lost its appeal, and I told him in his classroom one day I would not be continuing as I preferred to carry on with my football. This did not go down at all well with him, and he remarked that he wanted to enter me into the schoolboy federation, but I stood firm. He said as long as he was in charge of the boxing team, I would carry on. When I told Dad what I had decided and what Mr Bayless's response had been, Dad said, "Whatever you want, son. It is your decision. I will be up there to see him tomorrow." The next afternoon, Dad and I went up to the classroom where Mr Bayless was having his cup of tea. "I understand there is a bit of a problem with Roy not wishing to continue with the boxing," Dad said with a look in his eye that said, "This is a guy you don't really want to argue with." Mr Bayless probably thought discretion was the better part of valour and decided to butter Dad up to avoid a sticky end. He asked whether there had been any boxers in the family, knowing full well Dad had fought successfully in the Army. Dad was too old in the tooth to listen to that bull###t, so he said, "Roy has finished with boxing and will continue with his football." "Of course, Mr Wild," came the response, and so boxing at the school came to an end for me, as well as the friendly attitude. Prior to this meeting, everything used to be Roy this, Roy that, but now Mr Bayless referred to me only as Wild; he certainly had the hump with me. I had always liked Old Boot; we had many nice chats about boxing and Arsenal. He always reminded me of the Hollywood star William Holden. Rest in Peace, Boot. I say that with great affection because a few years ago an old friend from Pitfield told me that Mr Bayless had died at age ninety.

In1951 the festival of Britain was launched on the South Bank of the River Thames showing the advances Britain had made in the fields of science, technology and industrial design. Our class was one of many classes taken to the exhibition. In the large halls were various stalls displaying their wares that were eagerly anticipated by the bunch of rascals and tea leaves from class 2B. When we left in the late afternoon, everyone had enjoyed a field day of hoisting, and even the carrier bags that were used to hold the hoisted gear were nicked! I imagine that when we left, the organizers were mopping their brows, and when stock levels were checked, they must have keeled over. The pupils portrayed in the British film *Please Sir* were like something out of an Enid Blyton novel compared to the bunch of wayward rogues whose second home was Pitfield Street School.

At the top of Pitfield Street sat Charles Square, in one corner of which was a company warehouse that stocked thick comics known as Jumbo Comics, which were quite in demand at the time. My old pal Michael and I were a couple of opportunists, always looking to make a few quid, and one evening we decided to case the Jumbo warehouse. We made an entry through a very small toilet window and were amazed and excited at the thousands of comics piled up everywhere. All boys loved comics, and we were used to just the usual ones that we would swap with other boys, such as Beano, Dandy, Wizard, Rover, Hotspur, and Adventure. We found a couple of old sacks and filled them with Jumbo comics, but they were far too heavy for us to lift. (We were about eleven years old.) We took just one sack and carried it home between us. We surfaced the following morning to much acclaim from the rest of the gang, and those Jumbo comics did the rounds among our pals. This was my entry into crime, albeit on a minor level.

Running across the top of Northport Street was Mintern Street, where about forty terraced houses owned by the local council had suffered substantial bomb damage. All the families had to move out, taking only what they could carry. People had made numerous visits to collect essential items and whatever personal belongings they could rescue. One day, when Mike and I were playing in these old houses, we noticed that some of them had no staircases to give access to the floor above. Because boys love climbing, we managed to make our way to the upstairs rooms, and on a mantle shelf stood a radio, which, in those days, most people hired from a company by the name of Radio Rental. Obviously, the radio we found did not work as the gas and electricity had been turned off, but we took it anyway because the word was the houses would be demolished. Walking back to our street, we were stopped by two police officers and asked where we had got the radio. We explained it did not work and would be buried under the bricks and rubble when the houses were demolished, but they were not having any of it. We were taken to Old Street Police Station and charged with theft. We were escorted home in a police car and bailed to appear at Toynbee Hall Juvenile Court at a future date. When the day came, we were ushered with our parents into a beautiful wood-panelled room where there sat a couple of men and a woman to decide our fate. What should we do? Was this the time to say farewell to our parents as the hangman's noose was beckoning? I'll bet it made their day, these two pieces of rubbish that nicked us, CID's finest; they would have nicked us if we had been caught taking home a house brick. This heralded our second entry into the world of crime. What next? The crown jewels?

One thing that is different in schools today is the absence of assembly. All pupils would meet in the central hall and then be divided into four groups or houses, named after famous English Sea Admirals: Drake, Nelson, Grenville and Anson. We would line up in formation and the Headmaster would start his inspection of cleanliness and presentation. He would walk up and down the lines, checking for clean shoes (unlikely after kicking a ball about in the playground before the bell went for assembly), the crease in your trousers, well-groomed hair and clean fingernails. At the end of it all, points would be given for the cleanest house. We would also line up like this on the annual prize-giving day. I remember once my name was called out and I won a book. If they had handed out prizes for skiving and pulling strokes, I probably would have swept the board.

I stayed at Pitfield until I reached the age of fifteen and then left to make my way into the world, which starts another chapter in my life.

CHAPTER 7

FUN TIMES

At fifteen, I was getting about with a crowd of about twelve guys and the same number of girls, all of us good friends. At the top end of Northport Street was Colville Estate, made up of various blocks of flats bordered by a low brick wall. That was where we would all congregate of an evening. The 1950s were a never-ending round of Saturday-night parties where we danced to the music of Bill Haley, Elvis, Gene Vincent, Little Richard and Chuck Berry. The parties we enjoyed the most were staged at the home of our pals, Lennie and Terry Myring. Their dad never said no to a Moriarty up in the flat and would make it really nice, with coloured lights around the walls. One incident I must mention was rather funny, if not bizarre. My good pal Frankie Hudson and I had pulled a couple of mysteries (girls) during the week and invited them to a party at the house of one of our pals, Tucker Wade. Tucker's house was next door to Jackson's Undertakers on the corner of Hyde Road and Pitfield Street. I was with a girl called Josephine, and after a few drinks and dances, we thought we would get better acquainted by popping down to the bottom of the house. We found ourselves in a large cellar, shared by Jackson's Undertakers, which I was not aware of, and stacked up against the walls were rows of coffins. Josephine gave a scream and dashed up the stairs in a clatter of high heels. Any thoughts of romance went into rapid decline, followed by oblivion. Magical times!

My pal Frankie Hudson worked for *The Evening News*, and I used to see him delivering papers to local newsagents in Hoxton. He rode what was known as a butcher boy's bike, with a square metal frame over the front wheel to carry his newspapers. We soon became on nodding terms, and one day he stopped and we spoke and exchanged what we did of an evening and at weekends and in no time became good pals. I would see Frank during the week when he had finished his rounds, and I would ride in the carrier with my legs dangling over the front wheel. Frank lived a couple of minutes away in Nicholas Street with his mum, dad, sister and Nan, whom I came to know as Mrs Skeets. When I mentioned to my mum and dad that I had a new pal in Frankie Hudson, they told me they knew his parents from the Ivy House pub that was just round the corner. Mum had also worked with Frank's old Nan some years previously. Frank and I shared a love of music, both of us total Sinatra and Mel Torme fans, and we would sit up into the early mornings listening to AFN (American Forces Network). We were both into Glen Miller music and loved dancing, and Frank was a very good singer in the Sinatra and Tony Bennett Style. We also prided ourselves in being the smartest (clothes-wise) in our group of guys and received many compliments. My suits were all made to measure, and our top smothers (overcoats) we would purchase from a tailor in Hackney Road by the name of H. Sole. I once remarked to Frankie it was a good job his first name wasn't Richard. We also wore a yellow scarf with matching turtles (turtle doves, gloves) that really completed the look.

Frankie was given a new area to work and was moved from Hoxton to East Finchley, which was in North London and covered Muswell Hill and up as far as Tally Ho Corner. One day he said to me, "Do you fancy us having our own paper pitch? We can open a pitch at the bottom of Colney Hatch Lane." Frankie had a word with a butcher who agreed we could stand in his shop doorway after closing, and should it be raining he would leave the blind down to give us some protection, all this with a proviso that all the loose change we would take on the paper pitch Frankie would hold on to until Monday morning and then the butcher, who always needed change, would convert it into notes. At that time, we sold three papers, the *Evening News*, the *Evening Standard* and *The Star*. We agreed that I would work the pitch while Frankie was delivering evening papers to the shops, being driven around by his driver, a certain Albert Price. We opened the pitch about 5 pm and served until about 7 pm, after which Albert would drop us back in the East End and we would get ready for a night out with our pals.

There was a lot of competition between the various newspapers to get their papers into the shops before their rivals. For us, the competition was *The Star* and *Evening Standard*, especially for the Classified Results. Albert was a very fast driver, and I remember once when we were speeding along to deliver the late-night papers before anyone else, we had to pull over briefly as an ambulance needed to get past in an emergency. Albert pulled up close behind and we followed it as it was making a path for us to follow. Albert's vehicle, like most of the *Evening News* fleet, was a Humber Snipe, noted for being a bit swift. Albert was always singing as he drove along and taught Frankie and me the words to quite a few songs, some of which I remember with reverence and nostalgia, "My Mother's Eyes", "Little Pal", "Goody Goody" and "Bye Bye Blackbird", to name but a few. We worked the pitch for about six months and then decided to give it up. It made us later and later getting home, and all we wanted was to get out on a Saturday night for the parties or dancing at the famous Tottenham Royal or Barry's Dancing Academy in Mare Street, Hackney, which were very popular at the time. Frankie carried on working in East Finchley and would get home about 6.30, without having to rush about to get ready for the evening.

Every year, Frankie would get us two complimentary tickets to the Poll Winners' Concert at the Royal Albert Hall. This was put on by the New Musical Express, and the tickets were provided by *The Evening News* to their employees. Awards made according to the votes would be presented to best male/female singer, best band, best instrumentalist and so forth It was always a fabulous night out and made a change from all the parties we attended. Frankie and I and a few of the gang could be found wandering homewards during the early hours of the morning singing, "We are three little lambs who have lost our way, Baa, Baa, Baa. We are three little sheep who have gone astray, Baa, Baa, Baa, Gentlemen songsters out on the spree, doomed from here to Eternity, Lord have mercy on such as we! Baa, Baa, Baa." Invariably, that would be followed by someone opening their window and shouting, "Do you mind? Some of us are trying to get to sleep!" Indelible memories, and how safe it was in those 1950s...

One of the girls in our crowd, Iris, liked Frankie and me and made it quite obvious by flirting with us, so we decided to stage a mock fight for her favours. I asked her out in front of Frank, who said, "Hold up a minute, I was about to ask Iris out!" and we made it escalate from there. Frankie then offered me outside, so we both stepped outside, with Iris imploring us not to fight! What girl doesn't want two guys to fight over her? We stood outside for a couple of minutes laughing and then stepped back in and told her it was all a wind-up, for which she gave us both a shove and took it all in good part.

Another good pal of mine was Frankie Shea, who came from the other side of Kingsland Road. He lived in a small street behind the Geffrye Museum but still regarded himself as a Hoxtonite. I would call round for Frankie at various times and the door would be opened sometimes by his younger sister Franie. Frankie had an old Humber car which he was thinking of selling, and Frankie Hudson was showing some interest in learning to drive as he had seen me driving my Dad's cars and also driving on the railway, so Frankie with the car sold it to Frankie who wanted the car, and I started to teach Frankie Hudson to drive. He was very impatient and went up the kerb more times than I can remember, with great admonishments from me as at times I felt my life was in danger. He could never find the right gear and would always blame the car; the noise from the gears grating would cause people to stop and wonder what was going on. Frankie finally gave up the driving business and went on to other things.

Frankie Shea would occasionally give a lift to the Kray twins, but contrary to certain people's belief, he was never their regular driver. His young sister Franie later married Reggie Kray, which I will elaborate on in a later chapter.

At this time, I was working on the Railway (LNER) at Bishopsgate, and my work pals came mainly from Forest Gate, Leytonstone and Romford. They would ask me, "What do you do of a weekend? We only see you during the week." I explained that I had another crew of pals in the East End who I spent my weekends with, so it was suggested that we all meet. I stuck this up to my pals back home and we all went off to Leytonstone on our first meeting. I did the introductions and the two crews really hit it off. Our first foray was up the dolly mixtures (pictures) to watch a couple of films at the Rialto in the High Street, and we rounded off the evening with fish and chips. These visits became a regular thing, once a week to Leytonstone. Perfect.

One particularly funny incident that I must relate occurred on a visit to the Rialto. I was sitting a couple of seats away from Frankie with a young lady I had secured a couple of weeks previously, and Frank was with a bird he had given a John Bull (pull) just recently. When another picture goer saw what was going on with Frank and his young lady, she started shouting and the usherette came running down, shone her torch on Frank and immediately called for the house lights to be put on. The film we were watching was stopped, and our crew, as one, started cheering. Frank and the girl were given a warning that if there were any more shenanigans, they would both be evicted from the cinema. At this point, Frank's ardour had been severely dampened, if not dented. Maybe if we had been watching Marilyn's *Some Like It Hot*, Frank could have been forgiven! So here endeth the first lesson.

CHAPTER 8

THE SWINGING SIXTIES

Then suddenly the Swinging Sixties were upon us, more magic with the Beatles, Mick and the Stones and the Mersey Sound. From Monday to Friday, we would all sit on the wall talking and laughing and discussing music and fashion until about 11 pm, then gradually drift away home. This was sometimes interspersed with a trip up to Dalston where all the picture houses were located. Come the weekend, the girls would all disappear, and when questioned, they said that on Sunday evenings they went to "Saints". They explained it was a club at St Peter's Church in De Beauvoir Town, which was just up the road, roughly twenty minutes' walk away. The Vicar, Father Perry, a tall, imposing guy with a very nice demeanour, had formed a club downstairs in the crypt, and all were welcome as long as you attended church for the evening service. Our motley crew all turned up on the front steps of the church and were welcomed by Father Perry. We sang a few hymns and listened to the sermon, which took about an hour, by which time we couldn't wait to get down to where the action was. At the rear of the pulpit was a concealed winding stone staircase that led down to the crypt, so when all the local parishioners had filed out of the church, the young people filed down into a large room where music was playing and there was a small bar that sold soft drinks, Mars Bars and various types of confectionery. It was a lovely atmosphere – we were amazed! A young guy was in charge of the turntable (in those days music was on vinyl), and suddenly on came Elvis singing "Don't Be Cruel". Lo and behold, Father Perry hitched up his cassock and jived with one of the girls – he was quite good at it. When the BBC got to hear of it, Father Perry was approached about televising our club, and it was featured in a TV programme. For old time's sake, I went back to St Peter's a couple of years back, when I was eighty years young, and sat in the church on my own. All the memories came flooding back, as well as the tears, as they are now at the time of writing.

You're young for a Golden Moment, and too soon it becomes "remember when"! Take hold of that Golden Moment, for when it's gone, it never comes back. You cry, and still it doesn't come back! It's gone and never comes back again.

So that was our Sunday nights taken care of for the foreseeable future. We loved it! Saints finished at 10 pm, and I remember with great affection walking home one winter's night through heavy snow, with two of the girls, one on either side, holding my hands in my overcoat pockets. They were Maureen Dean and Maureen Major. I have often wondered what happened to them and the rest of the girls. Where are they now? On leaving the church after my visit in 2018, and still feeling emotional, I met the current vicar, who was a woman. I introduced myself and told her about the club all those years ago. She asked whether I was one of the originals, and I assured her I was and it was in the church records. She said she had heard all about what Father Perry had done and he was now retired and well into his nineties. She told me I was always most welcome at St Peter's, but then sentiment overcame me and I had to leave. She looked at me, and I knew she understood how the memories of those lovely times had affected me.

Next door to us in Northport St lived Flo Jones and her family, and the next property was owned by City Electrical, a fair-sized company that employed various electrical engineers who would be dispatched to companies to solve their electrical problems. The governor was Mr Tom Sayers, who was quite friendly and would stop and chat with my dad on various subjects. As I had not yet decided what I wanted to do in terms of work, Dad asked him whether I might find something in his company in the way of employment. He said he would see what he could sort out for me and would soon be in touch. Tom knocked on our door soon after and said that one of his electrical fitters was looking for a mate, who was like an apprentice. A mate would work with a fitter for maybe three or four years, carry his tools and learn the trade. One day, the fitter would be satisfied that he could teach his mate no more and would relay to the management that, in his opinion, the mate was ready to take out the tools, as it was known. I was assigned to Mr Sid Greenhill, who was a young guy with a twin brother, Ernie. They were both fitters and usually worked together on various projects. Ernie had his own mate, Bob, who was looking forward to taking the tools out himself soon and having his own mate.

Bob lived close by and helped me a lot in this brand new electrical business. I just about knew how to switch the light on in our house, but I was a quick learner, never academic, but always good at making things manually. First thing Monday morning, I reported to the depot next door where Sid Greenhill was waiting for me. He informed me we had a small job to do somewhere in Clerkenwell, and after collecting what we needed from the stores, we set off by bus. By bus? Yes, by bus! Not many people in those far-off days had their own car. We had only a few small items for that first job; anything bulkier or heavier would have been dropped off by one of the company's delivery vans. For the first few months, we travelled about mainly in the London area, carrying out small jobs which I enjoyed and learnt a lot from.

Then we were assigned to a very big contract in Crawley New Town, West Sussex. It was to carry out all the electrical work in a large new building owned by Lloyd's Register of Printing. We were to carry out all the electrical work pertaining to lighting and the machinery, mainly German printing machines. I think they were called Heidelberg Printing Machines. There were another couple of fitters with their mates also assigned to this rather large job. We were told we could be there for another two years. My wage at the time was £2 40d per week, and we received travelling expenses of bus and train fare to and from Crawley.

To boost our wages, we would catch the early morning workmen's train, for which the fare was much cheaper, but book the full fare for the weekly time sheet. The only downside was that I had to get up much earlier every morning to catch this train. I rose from my bed at 5 am, trudged up to Kingsland Road and waited, often in the snow or the rain, for the bus to take me to London Bridge Station. Our train would take us as far as East Grinstead where we had to change onto another line that would take us to Gatwick Airport. We would then wait outside for a bus that would take us to Lloyd's. On entering the shell of the building, we'd change into damp overalls and start the day's work.

At the end of sixteen months of this repetitious, early-morning start, I decided I was not having much more of it. I explained to Dad how unhappy I was with all the travelling, which would continue for at least another eighteen months, another winter! He asked me whether I'd be happy working with him at his depot of the LNER, and of course the answer was yes. After making enquiries, he found that there was nothing going at his depot, which was a rather small railway yard, but he could get me in at the main depot, which was Bishopsgate Goods Depot in Shoreditch High Street, as a van boy in the cartage department.

On the first day, I was given a number (1917) and told I would have to clock in at 8 am every morning at the time clock and clock out at the end of the day. A card with my name and number on it would be in the rack. I was told to wait in the canteen for my driver who would come looking for me. The canteen was at the other end of the depot and rather antiquated. It was due to be closed and a brand new canteen built to accommodate up to five hundred people. I didn't know a soul, there were dozens and dozens of van boys, drivers and railway vehicles everywhere, and I was just sitting there, a bit apprehensive, waiting to foray into the unknown. But never a shrinking violet, I'd begun chatting to a group of friendly boys when a pleasant-looking man with a kindly face, by the name of Dick Wiley, arrived to fetch me. He was to be my driver for the foreseeable.

Dick's vehicle was waiting outside. It was a three-wheel Scammel Scarab with a trailer. There were hundreds of these all over the country, delivering goods in their red and white livery, usually referred to as blood and custard. Each railway region had its own delivery vehicles: London North Eastern Region, Great Western Region, London Midland & Scottish, and Southern Region. These vehicles replaced the horses and carts that the railways had always used. They were known as Mechanical Horses and with just one wheel in front could turn on a sixpence. They were very primitive, and some had only one windscreen wiper and one side mirror. In winter time it was freezing inside the cab; if there was any consolation, it was the radiator that sat behind the driver and passenger seats, so sitting on the left of Dick, I could keep only my right hand warm.

When we first reported for work and clocked on, the first port of call was the canteen where all the drivers and van boys would meet for breakfast. After a while, your driver would come looking for you, after he had been to the cartage office to pick up the delivery notes. The deliveries ranged usually from fifteen to twenty-five, in different areas of London. When all deliveries had been done, we would stop for dinner in a railway yard in Manor Road.

Trucks were shunted into this small depot and unloaded, and railway vehicles would transport the goods to Bishopsgate, also known as B.Gate, to be sorted and delivered. After we had finished our break, we would continue in our own area collecting items from factories and small businesses that would be sending their goods and orders all over the country. These were our regular customers and I got to know the area well.

Our area was N16, which was Stoke Newington, as well as Highbury and Hackney. The Manor Road depot was overseen by an elderly man in full British Rail uniform, with his hat sporting the British Rail logo, the lion on top of a wheel. He went by the name of Fred (I never did learn his surname), and Dick and I would sit in his office to have lunch. Fred would put the kettle on and make us all tea.

One interesting job was moving all the equipment of Billy Smart's circus from the old Haringey Arena to a new venue in South London. Our articulated vehicle was loaded up with cages of lions and tigers and circus paraphernalia. The cages were all covered over with heavy tarpaulin, which did nothing to stop the animals roaring whilst in transit. I wonder what the members of the public thought as we passed!

At this point, I would like to explain how my first driving experience came about. When a driver had booked his annual holiday with the cartage department, a relief driver would be assigned to carry out his duties with the van boy, who would be familiar with delivery addresses and collections. The regular driver and the van boy would never be allowed to take their holidays together because the relief driver would not know the area. When Dick went off on his annual holiday, a relief driver was dispatched to take over the round until Dick was back on the scene. On this particular morning, I was in the canteen with the rest of the boys finishing off a breakfast that was very popular with drivers and van boys alike, Bubble & Squeak, which consisted of a vegetable and potato fry-up with a fried egg on top. (God, my mouth is watering just thinking about it.) Suddenly, standing at the top of our table was a young guy named Charlie Boreham, who introduced himself as the relief driver. He was known as Oats (as in oats and barley, Charlie), and Oats and I got on fine from day one. I learnt later he had only recently gained his licence to drive these articulated vehicles. One day when we had finished our lunch in Manor Road, Oats asked me whether I was ready to leave. I of course replied, "When you're ready!" He said, "As soon as I've finished this cigarette." I said, "Shall I be turning the motor round?" as it was facing down the yard. Oats said, "Is that what you usually do for Dick?" I replied, "Yes, always." "Ok," he said, " be doing it!" I had never driven any vehicle in my life and was dying to drive. This was no small car, it was a big commercial vehicle with a long trailer and articulated motor. I entered the cab, switched on, released the handbrake, put it into gear, let up the clutch slowly as I had seen Dick do a thousand times and suddenly we were moving, little old me driving this monster, totally thrilled and beside myself. It was a long way from my old cart with the pram wheels from a few years back. I took our rig to the furthest part of the goods yard just to keep driving and then turned around and headed back to the office where Charlie was waiting. I then proceeded to take it out of gear, applied the handbrake, all very professional, and moved over to my side of the cab. Charlie said, "Everything OK?" "Fine!" I said, and that's what I did every lunchtime for two weeks. I was a born driver, but when Dick returned from holiday, my driving the rig was never mentioned. I'm not sure whether old Fred, the station master, told Dick after he returned, and Dick never approached me on the subject. I don't think he would have approved; he was old school. I will never forget, no more than my own name, the number plate of our artic, which was LUV 37. At this point, I am quite close to having some silver cascade down my cheeks as I think of those wonderful, far-off days.

CHAPTER 9

CISCO

I was with Dick Wiley for about a year and also friendly with another driver by the name of George Holman, whose swarthy complexion, black hair and thick Emiliano Zapata moustache made him look very Mexican. That earned him the nickname of Cisco, another Mexican hero who was featured on film and television with his partner Pancho. George had his own van boy by the name of Bobby Beeson, and they covered the area of Rotherhithe, in South London. They collected large bags of spices, nuts, rice and various incidentals from the Thameside wharves. It was noticed that large consignments had started to go missing, and the company called in the police. An investigation was initiated, and Bobby Beeson was found to have some knowledge of what had been happening. He was interviewed by the police and gave some information that was detrimental to those involved and brought about a conviction. I am not sure whether loss of liberty came about for the guilty, but loss of employment certainly did.

The bottom line was that Bobby had to be taken off the job for his own safety and installed with another driver. George asked whether I would be interested in working with him and Bobby could be Dick Wiley's van boy. I was happy with that. George was an ebullient person, possessed of great alacrity of wit and full of jokes, so we swapped drivers and the fun began. Unlike the three-wheeled Scammel that I had been used to, George's vehicle was a fixed-body Austin with an open back that seemed enormous and much more modern and comfortable. After completing our deliveries, George would drop me home for lunch and collect me again at 2 pm. He lived only a stone's throw from my house in Goldsmith Row, which ran down the side of the Queen Elizabeth Hospital for Children in Hackney Road. Sadly, due to cutbacks, the hospital has been closed for some years.

I enjoyed working with George but often thought about Dick, his calm demeanour and old-school ethics. We remained on good terms and would stop and chat in the canteen or various parts of the depot, but I still missed him. One day, when we were ready to head back from the wharves, George said to me, "You drive! Take us back to Bishopsgate." I said I had never driven a motor that big before, especially having to travel through Rotherhithe Tunnel with about two feet between your vehicle and the traffic coming towards you! He said, "Don't worry, you will be fine." He must have had a lot of confidence in my driving ability, although he had only seen me moving the vehicle a couple of feet forwards or backwards to accommodate the loading bay of the wharf. If I had been involved in an accident, George would have been terminated by the Railway and possibly faced prosecution by the police, as I would have done. We set off with me driving and eventually approached the entrance to the tunnel. I thought, "Here we go! Eyes down for a full house," and sailed through the tunnel. When we finally passed into bright sunshine again, George looked at me and said, "I told you so. You were fine!" Not a lot bothered George.

After about a year, George packed up driving and took another non-driving job within the depot. I was assigned to another driver and back to the old three-wheeled Scammel. My driver was Mr Bill Knight, who was quite elderly, as were many of the old railway drivers who had many years' service at Bishopsgate. Bill and I got on quite well. Being of large proportions, he could not mount the rear of the box trailer, so it was down to me every time to jump up and retrieve whatever it was we were delivering and hand it to him. Bill was a very slow driver and, before the mechanisation of the Railway cartage department, had been a car man, a driver of horse-drawn vehicles, for years. He was more used to a horse's nosebag and a set of reins than a steering wheel and a gear stick. A lot of those old drivers were called up out of the blue, given a driver's licence and told, "Your vehicle is waiting downstairs." They received no tutelage whatsoever in driving anything mechanical.

Late one afternoon, I saw Bill making multiple attempts to back our vehicle into the loading bank in between two other trailers. Finally, he alighted from our vehicle rubbing his shoulders and remarking how the steering of our vehicle was very stiff. He invited me to have a go at it, so

I jumped into the cab and with one shunt backed it in. Having watched this, Bill said, "The steering is stiff, don't you think?" I diplomatically said, "Yes, it is stiff, Bill. You should take it down to the fitters' shop and let the mechanics have a look at it." There was nothing wrong with the steering at all; Bill just did not have the ability to reverse it.

I had a couple of drivers after I left Bill: Harry Grafton, Dennis Povoas, Jimmy Green and finally a young driver of about twenty-five by the name of Bill Scola, who became a real pal and a friend of my family. Bill drove a three-ton Scammel, and I still remember the number plate, RGC 39. Bill was like Cisco (George Holman) but more so! He was forever larking about. He came from Morpeth Street in Bethnal Green and many times took me home with him to meet Edna, his wife, and their children; he, in turn, met my mum and dad and they got on well with each other. Bill and his family became regular visitors to us when we were down at Faversham hop picking.

Bill and I were assigned to night work, which entailed clocking on about midnight, making our way to Liverpool Street Station, loading up with parcels and delivering them to various other railway depots. Sometimes we would pick up a trailer that was loaded with fresh fish that had come by train from Grimsby for delivery to the famous Billingsgate Fish Market, which used to be next to London Bridge and is now in Poplar E14. This was a job neither of us relished. The fish were in wooden boxes on an open-back trailer, with all the slime running out of the boxes and a strong smell of fish that would cling to the clothes we were wearing. We had to stand on the back of the trailer, sometimes in the rain and snow, and lift the box or boxes up onto the flat hat of a porter, who, in turn, would give us a brass chit for each box. When the last box had been cleared, we would go to the office to receive a signature for the fish delivered and exchange the chits for cash.

At seventeen, I was riding my bike in Kingsland Road when suddenly a London trolley bus hit the back wheel of my bike and I was thrown onto the pavement and knocked unconscious. Fortunately, this was right outside St Leonard's Hospital, and I woke up in a hospital ward where I found out I had sustained various injuries. My right eyebrow was missing due to hitting the kerb, all the knuckles of my right hand were grazed and damaged, and an X-ray showed I had sustained a suspected fracture of the skull. I was kept in hospital in Shakespeare Ward for a further two weeks and then released with a proviso to return in two weeks for further observation, which proved no lasting damage. I claimed damages through the Railway Union, which took up the case on my behalf. The bus company, after interviewing their driver, came to the conclusion that some of the blame had to be attributed to me, but they were prepared to offer some compensation "without prejudice". It came to a paltry amount of £35 and a new suit. The person appointed by the NUR to represent me was totally useless; I would have been better represented by Laurel & Hardy.

Soon afterwards, I received from the war office my call-up papers for two years of national service. After a full medical examination at the British Army Offices, I was asked whether I had any scars or had ever had any accidents. I informed the Army doctor of my recent accident and the hospital that had treated me. Not long afterwards, I received a letter stating that based on the report received from the hospital, I would not be fit for national service. That later proved to be a bitter pill to swallow as most of my pals were called up and were deployed to various parts of the world, one in Malaya, two in Germany and two in Aden. Dad, being an old soldier with many years in the forces, was disappointed for me, but like all mothers, Mum was pleased I was not to be called up.

As far as security on the railway in the fifties and sixties was concerned, it was non-existent. There was no CCTV in those days, pilfering and thieving was rife and all the British Transport Police could rely on was good old-fashioned policing, catching people red-handed after lengthy surveillance from some covert hideaway. Drivers and van boys alike had a field day, as did most employees, especially those who worked on the loading banks. When trucks came into Bishopsgate for unloading, many goods were "damaged in transit" – large cartons of shoes from Lilley & Skinner, boxes of St Michael clothing, which was the brand name of Marks & Spencer, cartons of electrical goods, BMK carpets and just about anything one could name. So Bill and I, two East Enders thinking along the lines of "we're no angels", also helped ourselves. A guy we knew worked on the loading bank, and he would load the more valuable goods onto our trailer. We would couple up with our unit and show the pass to the copper on the gate. Most of them were elderly men and couldn't be bothered to check the load; they would just give it a cursory glance and wave us through, as easy as that. Some drivers would also fill their working vehicle with petrol from the supply at the depot and siphon it out into their own private car. There was no record kept or any way of knowing how much fuel a railway vehicle was consuming running about all over London.

One day, Bill and I were told to go to Fulham to pick up a load of cigarettes, which were known as vulnerable traffic and highly prized. At the depot, we backed our artic into the loading bay and started to load up. An employee of the company would load the cartons onto a roller conveyor belt and push them to us through a hole in the wall, counting the cartons as he did so, and we would count them onto our vehicle. At about 12.30, the guy said that they were going to break for lunch and would resume about an hour later. Shortly afterwards, Bill put his head through the hole, turned round to me and said, "Do you think you could squeeze through that hole and pass back a carton of those cigarettes?" I was much smaller than Bill and had always been slim, so I squeezed through and passed Bill a full carton of cigarettes, which he put into the back of our vehicle. It would not be missed until another vehicle was being loaded, either later in the day or week, and this would probably be put down to a miscount somewhere along the line. We finished loading, signed for the load and were off back to Bishopsgate, but not before dropping the carton off with a guy who owned a newspaper and tobacconist shop in the East End. We were paid for it immediately, so it turned into a sweet little bunsen burner (earner) for a couple of hours' work.

I approached someone I knew who worked on the loading bank and asked whether he could get me a job on the bank. He said he'd see what he could do, and by the end of the week, I had started on the bank. Bill and I were delighted with the thought of what lay ahead. Bill enjoyed the status of spare driver, who would deliver anywhere and step in if a regular driver was off sick. So first thing in the morning, Bill would be given a sheaf of delivery notes with the fleet number of the trailer and pass it to me in the canteen. I would then head for the bank to resume work, look for the relevant trailer and load it with boxes of Marks & Spencer goods, carpets, shoes and various other expensive items that were not on any delivery sheet. This practice was employed by many drivers, and the goods that were in excess would be sold on that day to various people who were always looking for a bargain. I was approached one day by two guys, Steve and Bobby, who also worked on the bank and had heard that Bill and I were a good team. They asked whether they could join us into one firm, so I ran it past Bill and he agreed. Two became four and we had a very nice earner. Bill would ferry the illicit goods to the buyer we always used in the afternoon, and the van boy would be told to take the afternoon off but not to mention it to anyone, otherwise he would have some pay stopped by the cartage department.

Bill was friendly with a cartage foreman who told him in strict confidence that the BTC police were watching various people who worked on the bank loading trailers with illicit goods that had not been sanctioned for that particular trailer. This was not said as a warning to Bill, he had no idea that we were at it, but merely mentioned in passing. I told Bill we should give it a miss for a couple of months if there was surveillance being carried out, and he, Steve and Bobby wholeheartedly agreed. It would be folly to carry on and have our collars felt now that our cards had been well and truly marked.

About a month after we had decided to give the skulduggery a miss for the time being, I was eating breakfast with a table full of drivers and van boys when I was suddenly lifted bodily out of my chair with my arms pinned to my sides by two guys who said they were BTC police. They said I had been seen loading illicit and unauthorised goods onto a trailer, which was totally ridiculous and untrue. I had just clocked on at 8 am and had gone straight into the canteen and lined up to be served. Numerous drivers stood up and said the police assertion was a complete and utter fabrication; I would not have had time to run up to the next level where the bank was, sort out various goods and race downstairs into the canteen to have breakfast. One of the drivers at our table was Mr Sid Green, a driver with many years' service on the railways who was in charge of the Bishopsgate football team. He was a man well thought of and of unquestionable character who immediately protested and vouched for me, all to no avail. I was taken across the road, out of the jurisdiction of the railway police and into a Metropolitan Police Station nearby in Commercial Street, and charged with larceny by the BTC police. Also charged with larceny were three other employees and friends I worked with, Stevie Hands, Bobby Goodwin and Connie Riley, who had also been in the canteen having breakfast.

CHAPTER 10

MY TRIAL

After five or six weeks, I received a letter from my solicitor informing me that I had been given a committal date and we were due to appear at the Quarter Sessions at Newington Butts, which was the other side of London Bridge in South London. On the day, I met my solicitor and a barrister who had been supplied by the NUR to decide how we were going to proceed: it was my first offence, there were many discrepancies in the police evidence and we had many witnesses to testify that the account given by the police was complete fabrication. My barrister put Sid Green on the witness stand, and after he had given his evidence, numerous other drivers took the stand and also said the police account was total nonsense. Finally, the jury retired and after a while returned to give their verdict: guilty. My dad and all my friends and colleagues were in a state of shock; they had been certain I would receive an acquittal. During his summation, the judge took into account it was my first offence, but it was a serious offence against my employer whose trust I had betrayed. I had been told by my brief that if it all went against me, I would probably be looking at a period of probation. I received a six-month jail sentence. Everyone was completely shocked – my first offence! The three friends also received a six-month sentence. Later in the day, we were all handcuffed and taken to Wormwood Scrubs Prison.

Roy Wild

CHAPTER 11

WORMWOOD SCRUBS

What a shock to the system! Upon arrival we were ushered out of the prison van and into Reception. We were told to strip, given a cardboard box in which to put in our personal possessions, which were logged in a large book, and ordered to change into prison-issue clothing, drab trousers, matching battle blouse, striped blue and white shirt and shoes that had been worn previously by other inmates. We were then taken to a prison cell. I was separated from the other three as I was nineteen and classed as a YP (young prisoner). I was taken to another wing of the prison.

The following morning at about six-thirty, we were awakened by a prison officer banging and opening the door and told to "slop out", which meant emptying the plastic pot that you might have used to relieve yourself during the night. On each wing, there was a recess where dozens of inmates lined up to empty their pots. The stench was unbelievable; it made you want to retch immediately. If you needed to do more than sprinkle, you had to use the bell to call the night screw to open up and escort you to the recess. That was highly embarrassing as the toilet door was only three feet tall so your head and shoulders could be seen; it was devoid of privacy. If you had to ring the bell during the night, it was usually ignored, possibly because the night screw was reading a book or asleep and couldn't be bothered to open your cell door. They stayed on the ground floor, known as the "ones"; the next landing was the twos and so on up to four. Having to use the pot for a pony (pony and trap, crap) was disgusting when there were two other inmates sharing your cell. There were nearly always three cons in a flowery dell (cell), never two because of the risk of homosexuality Sometimes two cells were knocked into one to house four cons.

I heard that in the notorious Wandsworth prison, the cell where a man was kept while awaiting to be hanged was knocked into an adjacent cell to accommodate four cons, after the death penalty was abolished. It was not much of a thought to relish if banged up in that flowery, and never once did I ever contemplate or wish to trade my life of freedom for the drab life of captivity.

I was put to work sewing mailbags, which was soul-destroying, and asked for a change of labour. I was then assigned to the GPO shop, dismantling old out-of-date telephones. A million and one nuts and screws and other bits and pieces had to be put into various little boxes. It was also soul-destroying but one up from sewing mailbags.

We were assigned to the bathhouse once a week for a shower or bath and a change of clothes. We then went to the canteen, which was just a hole in the wall where we could spend our weekly wage of about 1s 6d (7 pence). For that, you could buy a jar of jam, toothpaste, a Mars Bar, a packet of Spangles and Old Holborn tobacco, which was the currency in all prisons.

After a couple of months, I was taken to the Prison Governor's office and told I would be leaving the following day and transferred to HMP Eastchurch Open Prison on the Isle of Sheppey as I was classed as low risk and it was my first offence. The next morning, instead of the prison van I was expecting, there was a very nice modern car. When I asked the screw why, he said I was the only one leaving for Eastchurch and it was hardly worth taking a big prison van all the way to Kent for just three people. Halfway there, we stopped at a roadside cafe and had a cup of tea and a sandwich; these two screws weren't half bad. On arrival at Eastchurch, I changed again into prison greys and was taken to a wooden hut that housed eighteen boys, all about my age. The following morning, I was taken to see the Deputy Governor, who told me to behave myself and how fortunate I was to be an inmate in his prison. I was assigned to the Farm Party, and there were some advantages, I could see, to working on the farm. After breakfast, about thirty of us would be marched down to the farm, and maybe five of us would be given the job of cleaning out the deep litter from the chicken sheds. There were hundreds of chickens all clucking around you and eggs everywhere. Our trousers were tucked into gaiters, which allowed us to secrete many eggs down the bottom of each trouser leg at the end of the working day. When being marched back, you had to be very careful, otherwise the eggs would smash into each other and all the slime and yolk would run down into your boots and socks. You had to march back with a rather unseemly gait, making sure your legs never came into contact with each other.

We also had to pull a cart up to the kitchen behind the dining hall, pick up all the left-over food from the previous day, which was known as swill, and feed it to the pigs. Some of the guys in our hut would be assigned to digging up potatoes and spring onions and would bring some of those back to the hut. After lights out, we would have jacket potatoes, fried eggs and spring onions cooked on the large pot-bellied stove that was in every hut. This was the life of Riley compared to where I had come from. There were also some cattle on the farm, and I had the privilege of seeing a calf being born, which, for me, was a very emotional experience as I loved animals. I was also attached to the two plough horses that were used on the farm, beautiful Clydesdales called Marcus and Imogen. They worked so hard, without complaint, pulling the plough through the mud, soaking wet on cold, rainy days. You will always live on in my heart and mind. "R.I.P. Old Friends"

Finally, my fourth month was imminent, and prior to release I was granted a week's "home leave". This scheme is to assist prisoners to reintegrate into society and restore family links, after which they return to prison for the remainder of their sentence. Should I have decided not to return to Eastchurch on my given date, as quite a few inmates do after tasting a week of freedom, the local police would immediately have been made aware and the hunt would have been on, leading to an almost certain capture and then a return to the sombre confinement of a closed prison, which would have been Wormwood Scrubs.

Suddenly my EDR (earliest date of release) surfaced, and I was due for release after serving two-thirds of my initial sentence. Before I left, I shook hands with the rest of the guys and received well wishes amid cries of "See you, Roy, in such and such pub!" when it was their turn for release. At the gate, there were a small, square, brick building and a barrier arm that was lifted or lowered – no imposing oak door to impress first-time internees, which brings to mind the adage which used to be on the front of Reading Gaol during the incarceration of Oscar Wilde: "Abandon Hope All Ye Who Enter Here." Everything in an open prison is so much more relaxed; inmates, as well as officers, are specially picked for open prisons. Dad and his brother Freddy were waiting just outside the gate in Dad's Ford Zephyr that Freddy had driven them down in to meet me as Dad did not drive. The barrier went up and I stepped out into freedom, but not before the officer on the gate shook my hand, wished me well and said, "Behave yourself! We don't want to see you back." I answered, without a backward glance, "Not a chance!" The year was 1957. I was just twenty years of age and unaware of what the years ahead would bring, albeit of my own volition.

CHAPTER 12

BACK IN CIRCULATION

Thursday was my first day back at home with Mum, Dad and Tony. My old pal Michael Isaacs had kept in touch, and Mum had told him I was home, so Mike came round to see me and suggested we went out the following night for a drink to celebrate my homecoming. We headed for The Pegasus in Green Lanes, Newington Green, a pub we had used many times before that always had good entertainment. The evening wore on and the band had just finished a song when a young and rather dishevelled-looking guy approached the resident singer and asked if he could sing a song with the band. Over the microphone, the singer told the crowd what this guy had asked, and some people had a look on their faces that said, "Wait for it…" He told the band that he would sing Andy Williams' "Happy Heart", and then he started to sing! After the first couple of words, the crowd fell silent and could not believe what they were hearing. His voice put the resident singer to shame. He finished the song amid applause and cries of "Encore!" but he just stepped down, made his thanks to the crowd and could not be cajoled into singing again. It was certainly a pleasure to witness something so lyrical.

After a while, Mike spotted a couple of girls standing on their own, whom he had met a week or so previously at the famous Tottenham Royal dance hall. Shortly after introductions were over, the four of us moved on to another pub close by, the Clarendon, where the resident singer was a guy who sang country and western and was always kitted out in cowboy clothes, minus the six-shooter. His name was Hank, and he would always sing "Your Cheating Heart", a song recorded by the Hollywood cowboy Tex Ritter and later Frankie Laine. That evening, the crowd was waiting for Hank to turn up when there was a clatter of hooves and Hank breezed into the pub leading a large white horse all done up in Western saddlery. It stood passively by while Hank launched into Your Cheating Heart, to everyone's delight.

The girl I was with was June, who lived nearby in Stoke Newington, about fifteen minutes away. I had borrowed Dad's car for the evening, so I drove her home and arranged to meet her later in the week to take her up the dolly mixtures (pictures). This led to more meetings and we finished up a courting couple. At that time, I was working for Mears Brothers, a company that had the contract for repairing and re-building the dilapidated Victorian sewer systems of Shoreditch. My job was driving a small crane that hoisted a large metal bucket that was filled with the old crumbling brickwork being dug out and loaded by the sewer men down below. Standing beside my crane were two Bedford tipper trucks that I was also responsible for; the buckets would be tipped into them, and when they were full, I would drive them away to be emptied at a landfill site. I did, at times, have the opportunity to explore the sewer systems and marvelled at the way the Victorians had built them without the technology that was available to the company I worked for. In most sewers, you had to bend over double they were so small, but in the trunk sewers, you could walk upright. One had to be completely covered in oilskin protective clothing, and before submerging into the depths of the sewers, one of the sewer men would test the air with some kind of meter to make sure there were no poisonous gases that could prove fatal. The Victorians, who had no such appliances, would take down with them a canary in a cage, much the same as the coal miners did all those years ago. If the canary lived, the air was safe to breathe. For anyone who had a phobia of rats, it was not the place to be. Some were enormous, as well as being albino, but they soon scurried away, and personally, I wasn't affected by them, probably due to my love of all God's creatures!

June and I were still seeing each other, and she was very miserable living at home with her family, where there were constant rows with her parents and siblings. Her father was a nasty piece of work, drunk on many occasions and abusive, and finally June had to move out. She found a room to let in a house in Stamford Hill that was owned by a kindly old Jewish lady, and she remained there for almost six months. One day, she told me she had found an upstairs flat in a house close to Dalston Junction which was much better and offered superior facilities. She agreed a date with the new landlord to move in, and on the day we drove back to the one room in Stamford hill to collect June's bits and pieces. We had to pass her parents' home where we stopped while June went in to collect some of her things. Whilst waiting outside for her (I had no inclination to go inside), aggravation in the shape of her father suddenly appeared beside me and started to become very abusive, telling me to get out of the car, which I did, amid shouting and swearing from him, backed up by "I'll fight you anytime!" I told him we were just there to pick up some of June's things, but he was intent on having a fight. Out of the blue, totally without provocation, he slung me a shot on the chin and split it open. I knew I was more than capable of meeting him in a one-to-one fist fight on the cobbles, but I wanted to hurt this no-good rubbish without damaging my hands, so I walked to the boot of the car and retrieved the car jack handle, safe in the thought that only one of us would spend the night in hospital, and it wouldn't be me. I walked round the car to where he was standing and was about to go to work when June came out with her mother, who was shouting and hooting. June pleaded with me not to attack him, not because of any feelings of concern for him but she knew what I would do. By this time, a couple of the neighbours were on their doorsteps wondering what all the commotion was about and giving their eyes a treat, so for her sake, I backed off and we drove to the new accommodation she had taken, all the while driving with one hand on the wheel and the other holding a handkerchief to my face where my chin was still dripping blood. I was fuming that I had been unable to make one with him and dwelt on how to get back at him.

Suddenly it came to me, although against my better judgement, that I'd nick him for assault. This is something I would never normally contemplate, but it was the only course left to me to get back at him. I went to Stoke Newington Police Station with my chin still bleeding and filed an assault charge against him. This was corroborated by June, and he was duly arrested and bailed to appear at Well Street Magistrate's Court in the West End. A month or so later, in an upstairs courtroom, I gave my evidence to the magistrate and again June backed up my account of the fracas. Her father was fined, given a dressing down by the magistrate and bound over to hold the peace. He was beside himself with rage, shouting and vowing all kinds of things. I thought, "Yeah! Let's have some – soon as you like!" Waiting close by the lift that would take us down to the ground floor was a uniformed police officer, and more for devilment than anything else, I explained to the officer what had just taken place in court and told him I thought June's father was going to cause trouble outside the court. I asked him if he could detain him just long enough for the lift to get us down to ground level, and as the lift doors closed, we could see the police officer holding her father's arm and talking to him. We laughed all the way home, and I thought, "How do you like those apples, you prat?"

I decorated June's new flat and there she stayed until one day she told me she was pregnant. I dreaded telling Mum and Dad, but it had to be done. They were not happy about it but still offered us the two upstairs rooms in the house I had grown up in, which allowed us to remain in my beloved Hoxton, so we took up their offer and moved in. After a while, we became engaged and decided to get married. I knew Mum and Dad were disappointed – they would have loved to see their eldest son get married in a church, with all the trimmings of a white wedding, but it did not seem right with June pregnant, so we got married at Shoreditch Town Hall, bypassing considerable expense. It was three half-crowns, 7/6 in and out, a couple of witnesses off the street, and twenty minutes later you were man and wife.

Afterwards, we went back to Mum's house and waited for the pubs to open. Later in the evening, we took some beer back home and had a Moriarty. Against my wishes and better judgement, we had to invite the rubbish who called himself her father and some of June's brothers whom I was totally against, but what can you do? In no time at all, one of my pals came into my Mum's kitchen and said, "Roy, you'd better get in the front room – it's going off!" Sure enough, June's brother had, had it offwith a load of nicked cigarettes, and June's old mother, who smoked like a crematorium chimney, wanted to know, "Where's mine?" That started the ball rolling. Then some more of the family got involved, amid lots of shouting. Someone got a drink thrown over them, and there were a couple of right-handers and various scuffles, and I wondered whether this was, like the title of H.G. Wells' book, *The Shape of Things to Come*. How right I was; this family I married into became to me an anathema. In 1961 our firstborn came into the world, and we named her Debra, followed two years later by Sandra, who was born in Homerton Hospital, Hackney.

I continued to work for Mears Bros, which was within walking distance, and I made friends with a guy named Vic, from Orpington in Kent. He would take over the crane while I was driving the tippers to the landfill. On one of my trips to the landfill site, which was in the Romford area, I backed up the vehicle to a large hole that had been dug for filling and set in motion the mechanisation for tipping the back of the vehicle so that the rubble and old brickwork could slide out into the hole. Unfortunately, I had forgotten to release the tailboard that opened from the bottom. I was still sitting behind the wheel in the cab when suddenly the whole of the front of the vehicle started to rise into the air due to the tremendous weight that had nowhere to go. I had to jump down from a height of eight feet in case the whole tipper fell back into the deep hole, but it had stabilised, and the problem I now faced was how to eject all the rubble. A couple of guys who were witnessing this farce suggested we get into the tipper with shovels and unload it by hand, which we did, and slowly the weight started to diminish and the cab came down, allowing me to release the tailboard and tip the rest of the load automatically. I never repeated my mistake.

Finally, the job with Mears Bros and the sewers of Shoreditch came to an end and I looked around for another job. There was a newspaper called *The Hackney & Kingsland Gazette*, which advertised all kinds of things for sale and, most importantly, jobs being offered. There were always columns and columns of "Drivers Wanted". In those days, you could terminate your current job on Friday and start a new job on Monday morning, so I answered an advert for a driver for a company called Rapley Hart, which was situated in one of the Railway Arches at the top of Hackney Road. This company had the contract for collecting sacks of paper from various banks, Nat West, Lloyds, Barclays, etc., and they would be taken to Bowaters in Stamford Street, Blackfriars, to be pulped and made into enormous rolls of paper that supplied the newspaper companies, *The Evening News*, *The Star* and *Evening Standard*. They were like large toilet rolls but probably weighed a couple of ton. It wasn't until one of the sacks that had been thrown into the back of my lorry burst open did we see what the sacks contained: they were full of customer statements due for pulping. You can imagine how the scammers of today would have revelled in all that information!

I reported for work one morning to be told that I had a new van boy named Harry. He seemed a friendly guy, somewhat older than myself, and we had been working well together for a couple of weeks when he asked me whether, if we finished a bit early, we could pop into Mile End, which was just the other side of Bethnal Green, as he had a small piece of business to conduct. I said it was not a problem, so later we stopped outside a venue in Eric Street with a sign above the door saying Billiard Hall. I followed Harry in, and he was obviously well-known as various people greeted him. Standing up against the bar were two well-dressed guys, suited and booted, who called Harry over and shook hands. Harry introduced them to me as Reggie and his brother Ronnie. Reggie was quite friendly and shook hands, and Ronnie just nodded. Reggie called for a drink for Harry and me, and Harry asked whether everything was alright regarding what they had spoken about a couple of days previously. They both nodded and said they would see Harry later in the same place. We finished our drinks, Harry offered them a drink but they declined, and we shook hands again and left.

On the way back to our firm, Harry said, "Do you know who they were, Roy?" I replied, "I've never been in their company before, but weren't they the Kray Twins?" "Yes," he said, laughing, "I'm doing a little bit of business with them." Little did I know that some years in the future, I would be in their company again, once for the right reason and once for the wrong reason. A couple of weeks later, I was relating this story to another driver on our firm, who asked me how well I knew Harry. I said I had only met him through our job and asked him why he'd asked. He told me Harry came from a villainous family who were friends of the twins and had assisted on various occasions when the twins needed some backup. But, he added, Harry was a good guy to have in your corner! Harry seemed to think a lot of me and said if ever I needed any help in any department or anybody should take a liberty, I was to call him and it would be straightened out, no doubt in no uncertain terms.

After some time, I left the job and started driving for a wallpaper shop owned by two Jewish brothers in Bethnal Green Road, delivering tins of paint and rolls of wallpaper within a three-mile radius of the shop. The vehicle I drove was a large, almost new Humber station wagon. What a difference from driving that old lorry for Rapley Hart! I really felt the business in this motor, wall-to-wall luxury and a better wage at the end of the week.

When I left the wallpaper delivery job, I became a spares delivery driver for a garage in Old Street. I drove a small, five cwt Ford van, and after doing this for about six months, I was asked by the manager whether I would be interested in becoming a breakdown driver. I had some knowledge of how a car worked, and he suggested I spend some time with one of the young fitters and gain more expertise, which I did. After a while, he thought I was ready to take out the breakdown vehicle, which was an old Land Rover, the type you see dashing about the Serengeti National Park filming wildlife. If a private vehicle broke down, the driver would ring one of the emergency services, the AA or RAC, and if they were busy, they would contact our control in the West End who, in turn, would call us. I would be dispatched to tow the vehicle into our workshop, that is, if I could not get it going by the roadside. I was then offered more money to work the weekends, as more people used their cars then than during the week. I was sitting in the office one Saturday morning waiting for the phone to ring when a guy walked into the garage and asked if he could have a service done on his car. I told him the fitters did not work weekends, but if it was just a straightforward service and oil change, I could do it for him. He agreed and I told him to come back in a couple of hours. I asked him whether he wanted some Redex put into the engine with the new engine oil, and he said yes. Redex was a fairly expensive engine additive that we sold at the garage that was advertised to make any engine run sweeter and last longer, which was a load of nonsense. You might as well have tipped a can of Pepsi Cola in the engine. I was always looking for a corner, and I could see there was some potential here! In those far off days, cars had grease nipples under the car, on the springs and at various other points. A grease gun would be pushed hard onto the nipple and the trigger pulled, leaving a tell-tale smudge of grease showing that the greasing had been done. All I had to do was put the vehicle on the hoist, squeeze a pile of grease onto my hand, scoop a small amount onto my finger and dab it onto each nipple, which made it look as if it had been done by the pressure gun. Next was the Redex. I would take an unopened plastic bottle from the store, empty the bottle into another container that I left in the office and leave the empty container near the car as if it had been added to the engine. I always changed the engine oil because you could see clean oil by lifting the dip stick from the engine, but you could never tell whether

Redex had been added. When the guy returned to pay and pick up the car, I showed him the empty Redex container, and should he look underneath the car when returning home, he would see all the nipples looking as if they had been greased. I informed him that he had been charged just half of the usual service rate but I had to charge him the full price for the engine additive. I also told him this was just between him and me; he was more than pleased with this arrangement and paid on. The empty Redex bottle was refilled and put back in the store, waiting for the next so-called service. The word soon got around and I was doing services every weekend; it turned into a nice little bunsen burner. I stayed at this job for about a year or so, and my reason for leaving was the manager was sacked for misappropriation, in other words, fiddling. How dare he! I then thought it was time for pastures new – I didn't need glasses to see the writing on the wall.

My next job was in East Finchley with a company by the name of Eyre Venables & Eyre, who had the contract with Heinz, the baked bean people, to supply their reps with a new car every eleven months due to the high mileage they would clock up. Each time we supplied a car, we would bring back their other vehicle, which would be cleaned up, serviced and sold from our showroom. Initially, I didn't realise the mileage that I would be covering and exactly what the job entailed and demanded. Heinz had a distribution depot in major towns all over the UK, so I delivered new cars to England, Scotland, Northern Ireland and Wales, but that more than suited me as I loved driving. This was before all the motorways we enjoy today that make journeys so much easier and safer, although, at times, more boring.

In Hoxton, an Esso petrol garage was opened in Whitmore Road by a well-known husband and wife team. I would often fill up vehicles there and would stand and chat for a while with the manager or the owner's wife. One evening, after about a year of delivering cars, I answered a knock on the door and found the manager from the Esso garage standing there. He told me the owner had got himself into some kind of trouble and was serving an eighteen-month sentence in "the Scrubs". His wife, Anne, was looking for a new manager as the current manager was moving on; should I be interested, would I pop round to see her? I talked it over with June and my Dad and decided to see what was involved. The wage offered was somewhat better than the car delivery job; it was also just a short walk from home and entailed opening the petrol station at 8 am, serving petrol and oil and motoring accessories, and closing at 7 pm. It was a breeze, so I gave notice and took the job as manager. The only thing I did not relish was when the undertakers in Hoxton, Hayes & English, who buried most of the people in Hoxton, pulled into our petrol station to fill up, with a very old Daimler Limousine hearse. The petrol cap was in the back of the hearse, and I had to crawl into the back, dragging the petrol hose with me, to fill the tank, ready to exit the vehicle as soon as possible. I often reflected that this was how we all finished up, in six bits of wood, in the deep six, with slow music! Anne would also spend time serving on most days, and once a month would receive a visiting order from her husband and travel to the prison where he was incarcerated.

My most favourite book of all time is Jack London's *Call of the Wild*, which is exactly what I was starting to feel after a year or so at the Orsman Filling Station. It wasn't so much the call of the wild but the call of the open road, so I gave notice that I would stay on until Anne's husband's release, which was now imminent as he had completed two-thirds of his original sentence. After he had been home for a week, I left the job and went back to car delivery, which was refreshing after such a static time in the petrol garage.

Roy Wild

CHAPTER 13

CAR DELIVERY2

My first job back was delivering a car to the Heinz depot in Newcastle. I met the rep there and handed over the new car, which he thoroughly inspected and then gave me the keys of his existing car for me to return it to London. On another delivery, a fellow driver, Robbie, and I had two cars to deliver to Heinz in Glasgow. We arrived about 6 pm, sorted out some digs for the evening and then asked the landlady what there was to do in town. She suggested a dancehall in Sauchiehall Street, which by all accounts was quite famous, so we had a wash and brush up, sorted out a small restaurant for something to eat and headed for the dancehall, only to be met by three minders on the door who demanded to search us. I enquired for what reason and, in a broad Scots accent we could barely understand, was told it was for any hidden bottles of drink, which was not allowed on the premises. We then paid the entrance fee and found ourselves in a very large ballroom with a live band (more like an orchestra) playing and an abundance of girls dancing and sitting around the perimeter of the hall. When on an assignment to deliver cars, we were always suited because of meeting the Heinz reps, and after we had eyed up the talent for a while, we made our way to the bar and ordered a couple of drinks. In no time we had a group of girls around us as they had heard our London accent and were totally mesmerised by it; they asked about the London scene, fashion, Carnaby Street and all things London. This was 1962, the swinging sixties, and for me, there has been nothing like it before or since. We continued to enjoy the rapturous attention from the girls, but the downside was we were getting some funny and aggressive looks from the guys. A couple of them came up to us and started to speak in an accent we couldn't understand, so I said to Robbie, "I think we should get out of here; things don't look so good. These sweaty socks (Jocks) all speak with a mouthful of marbles that we can't understand, so I think it is time to leave in one piece!" We had no problem understanding the girls, who had much softer voices, so we said our goodbyes, reflected on a chance missed and left. Later in the evening, we arrived back at our digs and the landlady asked us whether we had had a good time and where we had been. We told her about the dance hall and the attention we had received from all the girls. She looked at us incredulously and said, "You are lucky to be alive! They hate Sassenachs in this city, anyway, and what with grabbing the attention of all the girls, you are so lucky to be standing here!" I asked her why she had recommended that particular venue, and she said as it was a week night, she thought it would be quiet; it was always heaving at the weekend!

I was still living with June in the rooms at the top of Mum's house, but things were deteriorating and were leading to bad feelings and rows, which was wrong in front of our firstborn. I continued to deliver cars to many Scottish cities, Dundee, Fort William, Paisley, Garthanloch, Perth, Kinross, Pitlochry, Glasgow and Edinburgh. One of the trips I particularly enjoyed was the Dundee job. I would drive up the A1 to Queensferry, Edinburgh, and drive the car onto the ferry that would take us over the Firth of the Forth. We would then continue up the A91 into Dundee and return on the same ferry, which was replaced in 1964 by the Forth Road Bridge at a cost of £19.5 million.

Once, when I delivered a car to Dundee, I did the exchange at the rep's house. He kindly invited me into his home, where I met his wife and children and had a lovely meal with them. When I said it was time to drive home, he was shocked. "You have just driven 450 miles here and you're going to drive all the way back to London?" I assured him I would be fine, thanked him and his family profusely for their hospitality and left for London, driving through the night. I stopped a couple of times to rest and called in at an all-night café every hundred miles or so. I arrived home in Hoxton in the early hours of the morning and benefited by having the day off and keeping the cash that the company gave me for hotel accommodation.

When Robbie returned from a trip to Doncaster, he mentioned that he had met a girl who had just been crowned Miss Doncaster in the recent beauty pageant. He suggested that on our next trip up the A1 motorway, we could stop and say hello. A month later, we had two cars to take to

Wakefield, and he arranged with her that we would meet her at the Wishing Well café in Blyth, which was on the way. Cynthia was everything Robbie had told me, very beautiful and friendly, as, in my experience, most Northern girls are. We stayed and had a meal and then had to carry on to Wakefield, find digs for the night and wash the cars ready for delivery the following morning. Robbie promised to ring her the next time we were coming by. She said that it would be nice if she could bring her sister, which seemed a capital suggestion and would save me playing gooseberry. I thought if Robbie's beauty queen is to be used as a yard stick, the sister is probably out of the same stable! Two weeks later, we had two cars to take to Doncaster, and we arranged to meet her and her sister and spend the evening with them. Cynthia came walking over to our cars with sister Janet, who was about sixteen stone with a bike (glasses) on her nose and plaits. It couldn't have been worse if she had had a surgical boot and a number eleven on her top lip (runny nose). I said to Robbie, "I am not having that – I'll see you in Doncaster." He almost gave the game away by bursting out laughing, so we came up with the plan that we could not stay as we had to deliver the cars early that day and could not miss the rep, who was waiting for us. There were disappointed looks all round, including from me, so we bought them a meal and carried on to Doncaster. I later remarked to Robbie that if I had been pre-warned, I would have arrived in the company's tow truck, preferably the one with the crane on the back! I suppose it's some you win, some you lose.

Roy Wild

CHAPTER 14

ARLETTE

I was pleased to be back in car delivery, criss-crossing the entire country and unlike the drivers of some car delivery companies who drove on trade plates and then had to bring the plates back when the car was delivered. To earn a little bit more cash, they would stand on the side of the road thumbing a lift and keep the train money. Only once did I have to travel on trade plates with a view to returning by train. After a delivery to Dundee, I thought I would save the train fare and thumb a lift home. Never again! The first guy who stopped was only going twenty miles up the road and I had to get out. All in all, it took five lifts before North London was in sight, and three of those lifts were from commercial drivers in big old diesel vehicles that chugged along.

I quite often stopped if I saw a fellow delivery driver thumbing a lift. They always had their trade plates on show, and most drivers would feel safe stopping for them. I would also always stop for a soldier in uniform returning to his camp at Catterick. Suddenly there was a murder and rape committed on the A6 in Bedfordshire, and vehicles would no longer stop and give people lifts as the perpetrators had not been apprehended. Eventually, the police arrested a James Hanratty for the rape and murder of a man and his girlfriend, and he was duly hanged. A very dangerous incident I was involved in occurred when Robbie, Brian and I delivered three cars to Newcastle. On the return journey, we drove in convoy, with me leading. At Peterborough, on a dual carriageway, I was behind a heavily loaded brick lorry and indicated to those behind me that I was about to overtake him. Without warning, he swerved in front of me into the fast lane. The choice I had was to run into the back of him, in which case his tailboard and the rear of his vehicle would smash into my windscreen and probably decapitate me, or jump the grass verge in the middle of the carriageway, which was the option I took. Rising up on the middle reservation racing towards me was, of all things, a steel manhole cover on a six-inch brick mounting, which was impossible to avoid. The front of the car hit the cover, which went right under the front number plate and ripped out the engine and gearbox, as well as leaving the rear axle in a terrible state. Behind me were broken pieces of engine and gearbox and a stream of hot oil. The steering linkage had been locked left hand down, which was a blessing; if it had been the opposite, it could have thrown me into the path of oncoming traffic on the other side of the carriageway. Robbie and Brian travelling behind me were witness to the whole scene. The lorry driver had stopped and was about to be attacked by Brian, who was giving him a volley of vitriolic abuse and had to be pulled off by Robbie and me. The lorry driver said he was going to pull his vehicle off the road into a side street so as not to hold up the traffic and duly disappeared; none of us thought of taking the registration of his vehicle. We continued on our way, me in with Brian, trying to calm him down, and there was no police involvement. When we arrived back at base, we explained what had happened and I had to make out an accident report. The car was recovered and had to be scrapped.

The following day I was back on the road with a delivery for Swansea. We only delivered cars to two places in Wales, Swansea and Cardiff, where H J Heinz had their two Welsh depots. Without doubt, the best job was delivering cars to Belfast. We would travel to Heysham Harbour and book the cars in on the boat, which sailed at midnight; the cars had to be loaded by 11 pm. We would then drive to Morecambe, which was less than five miles away, and spend the evening in the famous Floral Hall, which was packed out with mainly young girls. We had to suffer much the same as we had in Glasgow. The girls crowded around us when they heard the London accent, and those Northern girls sure were friendly, but again, we were limited in our intentions. There were two very nice girls who were paying us quite a bit of attention, and Robbie seemed to think if they lived close by we could take them home and still be back in time for the cars to be loaded on the boat by eleven. While waiting in the foyer for the girls to get their coats, one of the security guys asked me which one I was with. When I told him, he replied, "You are not a bad judge. She is the most gorgeous girl that we have in here every weekend." I winked at him and said I wouldn't settle for anything less. Afterwards, we had to put our foot down to get back to the boat in time. The cars would be lifted by crane into the hold of the boat, we would be given our cabin, which was very small and meant for just one person, and in the morning when we awoke, we would be in Northern Ireland. The car would be unloaded on the quayside, and after a quick breakfast, we'd be on our way to the Heinz factory to deliver the new cars. This Heinz factory was the only one that would always give each of us a large box of assorted soups as a thank you. Yes, that sure was the best trip.

Things at home were going from bad to worse as far as my marriage was working out. It was not fair on my parents, with the constant rows and disagreements, and at times I thought it best if we parted.

On returning from a car delivery to Manchester and about to pull into the company car park in Fortis Green, East Finchley, I was held up in some backed-up traffic. Standing at the bus stop were two young girls waiting for a bus to take them to the underground station in the high street. They kept looking into the car and smiling, so I lowered the window and asked where they were heading. I offered them a lift and dropped them down at the station. The one sitting next to me was called Arlette; the other one had stepped out of the car to pop into a shop to buy something for their journey back to Wimbledon. I said to Arlette that I had a trip coming up in two days' time to deliver a car to Liverpool and suggested that she came with me. She said she would love to and gave me her phone number. I said I would call her the following night at her parents' house and make arrangements where to meet her. She lived at the top of Putney Hill so I had to leave extra early to drive to South West London. As I arrived, she was walking towards me, and with her was another woman, who opened my car door and said, "I am not at all happy with my daughter going all the way to Liverpool. She doesn't know you, or anything." I assured her my intentions were honourable, but she turned to her daughter and said, "I do not want you to go, Arlette." She replied, "I am going, Mother," and got into the car. I reiterated that she would be fine with me and I would return her safely. We arrived in Liverpool later that evening, sorted out a small hotel to stay in for the night and delivered the car to Heinz the following morning. Upon our return later that day, I walked her to the flat, intending to just stop long enough to say hello to her mother, and was invited in for a cup of tea. Her mother was grateful that I had kept her safe. Little did I envisage how this blossoming relationship would change my life.

Without wishing to make excuses, perhaps if I had been in a happy marriage this would never have occurred, but as the saying goes, "It takes two hands to clap." The more Arlette and I saw of each other, the more we fell in love, as I had never known. She was very continental-looking, the daughter of either a French or Belgian father and an English mother, and she always reminded me of the French film star Brigitte Bardot, with the same beautiful mouth. She worked as a hairdresser in Putney High Street at the John Cornell Salon, which had various salons across London. She told me that she occasionally cut the hair of the film star Oliver Reed, who lived close by. She was eventually moved from the Putney shop and put in charge of another of the salons in Queensway off the Bayswater Road. We would meet there later in the evening and spend many hours in the salon after it had closed, just the two of us, declaring our love for each other on the gowns that were put around the shoulders of customers having their hair done.

One Sunday, my witty friend Vic, whom I had worked with at Mears Brothers, invited Arlette and me down to his house in Orpington, Kent, for lunch. We were introduced to his wife, Iris, who was very welcoming and also very thin (flat as an ironing board!). Halfway through lunch, Iris started to cough rather violently and said through watery eyes, "Oh Vic, I will have to get something for my chest." Vic, as quick as a flash, said, "A pair of tits would be a good idea." At this point, Arlette had a mouth full of food and it exploded across the table. Iris threw something at Vic amid the hoots of laughter. I often think of that incident and it always makes me laugh – the greatest one-liner I have ever heard.

The work of delivering cars finally came to an end as the company found it was cheaper to use transporters to deliver cars, possibly ten or so at a time, and we were made redundant. My good friend Billy Scola told me he was going to apply to become a black cab driver, licensed by the London Carriage Office in South Lambeth Road. That appealed to me and I also applied but was refused, due to my conviction and incarceration a couple of years previously. I was very disappointed but was advised to see my local MP, who wrote to the carriage office and pleaded my case, explaining that I was now a responsible person and had always been in gainful employment. Two weeks later I received a reply stating that when a period of three years had passed from the date of my conviction, I could apply again. This time I was successful. At the initial interview, I was given what is known as the Blue Book, which has all the routes listed that I would have to learn, including the suburbs and finally the drive at Scotland Yard. Learning all that seemed, at first, a Herculean task, but as I got into it, London appeared to get smaller and smaller.

I bought myself a small motorbike known as a Mobylette, and Bill and I would meet up on our bikes and start to learn the shortest routes from one point to another. There was a lot of paperwork as well, recording our progress, and we would test each other. The more we covered London, the more the paperwork piled up. Things were no better at home between June and me, and I was all for moving out, where to I had no idea. Suddenly, June found out somehow that I was seeing Arlette and World War Three erupted. She refused to let me into the home, and when my Dad's sister Emmie heard what had happened, she said, "If you have nowhere to go, you are coming home with me." Aunt Emmie lived in North London with her husband Dick and two children, my cousins Brian and Ellen. I could not carry on learning the streets of London because all the paperwork and books that I needed were in the top flat of Mum's house which was now occupied solely by June, who, in spite of my requests, refused to release them to me. Mum called me one day at Aunt Emmie's house to tell me that June was out for the day and I might be able to collect some of my things. I found that the door of our flat had been locked, so I crawled onto the roof of an adjoining flat and by stretching across, I could just reach the window. It was not locked, and I managed to swing myself into space and climb through the window. In the flat were some bags containing all of my suits, shirts and jumpers that had all been cut to shreds. Two other bags contained what was left of all the work I had done towards becoming a cab driver. Everything was ripped up, a year's work destroyed. Also in the flat were about sixty Sinatra LPs that I had started collecting when I was sixteen or so and which were very dear to me. I managed to balance them on the window ledge and retrieve them, a couple at a time, until the complete collection was safe. Mum later told me that when June found out I had been there and retrieved some of my things, she went ballistic. Mum had replied, "He's my son and he only took what belonged to him." It became quite clear to me that this ship was sinking, and inevitably, a divorce followed some time after.

Arlette and I continued seeing each other, and occasionally the conversation turned to acquiring a flat and moving in together. I was still living at Dick and Emmie's over in the King's Cross area of North London, and Arlette was at her parents' home in Wimbledon, quite some distance away. By this time, I had given up all thoughts of becoming a London cabbie after all the work I had done had been destroyed; I no longer had the appetite or inclination to go through it all again. Our first flat was in the Dalston area of Hackney, where we resided for about a year. Arlette had started work in an estate agent's in Mile End where she made quite a name for herself, and after a short while, we moved into nicer accommodation, again in the Dalston area.

CHAPTER 15

WORKING THE SYSTEM

I made contact with Derek, another old pal of mine from Bishopsgate, who informed me that he was back driving for the railway. I asked how come because he had also been nicked at B.Gate and served a short sentence, and no way would he have been accepted back! What he'd done was apply to another region, London Midland & Scottish, as the regions worked independently of each other, and he advised me to do the same. I applied and was asked to attend an interview, which I duly did at LMS Camden Town. I sold myself and was given the job, to start in two weeks' time. On the first morning, I reported to the cartage foreman and was taken down to the motor pool. Standing there was a brand new Carrier Bantam and a new trailer loaded up with deliveries for the East End, which was to be my area. After deliveries were done, my regular collections were to be at Spitalfields Fruit Market, which suited me fine as I knew the area very well.

One morning at the depot, I was approached by another driver by the name of Billy Davis, who asked me my name and where I came from. I said I was from Hoxton, and he said, "You come to work dressed better than I do on a Saturday night out!" He then invited me and any of my pals to come for a drink in his regular two pubs which were in the Dalston area. It was there I met his pal, a certain Patsie Murphy, and a couple of their crew, which I will elaborate on later.

Arlette came from a different walk of life from me, different parents from mine, totally naive and everything above board. She thought the people I introduced her to were fascinating; she'd never met anybody like me or my pals, and I would regale her with tales of things I had been involved in, which she listened to in astonishment and awe. I was introduced to Sammy, a shrewd young Jewish guy who had a small shop in the market. He would buy fruit and vegetables from the wholesalers and sell them on to visiting shopkeepers who would frequent his shop. He approached me one day and asked whether I got hold of any other goods that we could do some business with. The security at the railway depot was non-existent, and it was a case of here we go again! I must have been mad after the last conviction, but old habits appear to die hard! Once again I became involved in villainy, supplying Sammy with all kinds of merchandise that we would agree a price on, and he would hold a sale in his cellar beneath his shop. It was like Aladdin's Cave, everything laid out very professionally like a Marks and Spencer store, which would be visited by a constant string of market porters all looking for a bargain, so everyone made a killing, so to speak.

At the market, I would be loaded up with fruit and vegetables that I would take back to Camden for distribution to various parts of the country. I would pull onto the weighbridge and the load would be weighed minus the weight of the vehicle; drivers would be paid according to the tonnage they weighed in with. The load included lots of mushrooms, and I would take a small handful out of each punnet and take them all fresh to my Mum for her to enjoy, as well as for Arlette and me.

One morning after clocking, the secretary told me that the Goods Agent wanted to see me in his office before I left for the morning's work. He sat me down and began by saying, "Roy, I am very pleased with the work you are doing here, and you bring in more tonnage than anybody else, but when you applied for this job you never declared your conviction concerning the incident in another region, namely the LNER at Bishopsgate, and the sentence you served. Our security has discovered this, and now it is beyond my control. I have to let you go, which I am very sorry about." In retrospect, it was the best thing that could have happened to me. I was looking adversity straight in the face.

One morning I visited Sammy to pick up some money that was owed to me and was introduced to a close friend of his, another Jewish guy, quite smartly dressed, who asked me whether I was interested in doing some business of another type. This was after Sammy had vouched for me as being twenty-two carat to work with, but this was something of a more dangerous pastime. This guy was a manufacturing jeweller and was privy to valuable items being moved around: gold, diamonds and very expensive watches. The first meeting with Martin, as I will call him, was in the West

End where he asked me to collect some money from another jeweller who wasn't honouring his debt. I said I would need a third of what I recovered, which was quite a substantial amount, took a small retainer from him and the following day gave the guy a visit in his shop. I introduced myself cordially and said I was working for Martin and we needed to call in the money that was owed. All kinds of excuses were given, but I said, "Please don't be fooled by my calm demeanour. I will be back in an hour. You will have all of the money here or there will be a visit to your home tonight. Should you be out, I will be back in the morning and the debt will have increased by 25%. You really don't want to see me inconvenienced by a return visit..." The threat was clear, and when I returned in an hour, the money was waiting in a brown envelope. I met Martin in a hotel lobby in Regent's Park and handed over the money less my commission, sweet as a nut! This initial meeting with Martin expanded into something quite big and beneficial to both of us.

After I'd been working at Camden about six months, I was given instructions to go to another railway depot in Bethnal Green, pick up a load of bananas and deliver them to a trader in Spitalfields. I was never very happy about handling bananas as they were harvested in the West Indies and there were often big spiders hiding in the bunches, or even snakes that had wound themselves around the stalk. I wore thick gloves that I carried in the cab and with the help of a couple of railway employees loaded up, on full alert for unwelcome guests. On arrival at Spitalfields, I backed the vehicle in and with the help of a couple of porters and a guy in a white coat who was the checker, we started to unload. As we got to the rear of the trailer and I had to bring the large stalks to the tailboard, out fell a live scorpion, which made me jump. As anyone knows, their bite is poisonous and potentially fatal, so I shouted to one of the porters, "Be careful, scorpion!" The checker in the white coat retorted, "It won't hurt you!" "Oh yeah?" I thought and kicked it off the tailboard. It landed in the middle of his white coat and he jumped up in the air, visibly frightened. "What happened to 'it won't hurt you'?" I enquired. Finally, the bananas were unloaded, and in the trailer, I found a single one that had fallen off a bunch. There was a horse and cart just behind my vehicle, so I jumped down to give the horse the banana. My jumping down must have startled the horse, which promptly bit my arm. The owner rushed up to the horse and was about to cuff it, but I said I had startled the horse and the fault was mine. By this time the horse had calmed down and accepted the banana. My thoughts were that if he had punched the horse, he would have been the one on the floor looking up at his faithful steed, but I was pleased it had not come to that as he could have taken it out on the horse back in the stable.

Martin called me one day for a meeting to discuss a certain piece of business and we met in one of his favourite places, Golder's Green Crematorium. He told me that a certain jeweller would take home with him all the valuable items in his workshop because he did not have a safe there. We had a look at the route he would take and decided where the hit would take place. We had two cars, and we pulled what is called a back and front manoeuvre on a roundabout. The car in front stopped, he was boxed in by the car I was driving behind, and out jumped two of my guys, one to mind the target driver's door and the bag man to grab the loot. We understood that the bag containing the gold was a brown holdall in the boot. It was all over in a minute. The bag was secured and both cars raced away. You very seldom get interference from the public; some think it is a film crew making a robbery picture, but there is always enough of a working firm to deter most busybodies. After returning to our manor in the East End, we met in one of the bedrooms while the wife did tea and sandwiches. We were ready to take inventory of what we had but discovered that the bag that had been grabbed was the wrong bag. It contained a pair of rolled-up overalls, and the bag with the gold was in an old carrier bag, we later learnt, which our bag man recalled seeing in the boot. This was relayed back to us by our man, so a shrewd move by the mark. Some you win, some you lose.

Another hit-to-be was when another jeweller in the West End went on holiday, leaving a young girl and boy running the shop until his return. This sounded like a breeze and required just three of us, the driver, the bag man and the minder. At 9 am, as the shop was about to open, I said I was going to walk to the top of the street just to make sure there was nothing unusual or suspicious. On my return, our minder asked, "Everything sweet, Roy?" I said, "There are three faces sitting in a car two cars up from us. Could be the RCS (Regional Crime Squad) and if so, let's get out of here, a bit lively." By this time the shop had been opened, and from the car with the three faces, out jumped two guys, leaving the driver behind the wheel as you did when you were making one. They rushed into the shop and no doubt secured what they had come for. We looked on in utter amazement; they must have heard the same news as we had and pipped us at the post. Again I said, "Let's get out of here," with even more urgency. Within a minute of the phone call from the shop, the police, aka the Odd Lot, the Filth or the Hurry-up Mob, would be there and we would be nicked, if only for sus, which meant suspicion This was rife in the seventies and eighties and allowed a police officer to stop a person for any reason he saw fit, "fit" being the operative word. You could be fitted up in the sixties, seventies and eighties for just about anything. There were a lot of corrupt "Old Bills" about in those days. A pal of mine leaving a pub to get in his car and head home was approached by a notorious DSI from the local nick who knew Terry was at it and a bit too clever to get his collar felt. He was asked by this DSI, "How are you doing?" The reply came, "Not too bad." "In that case," said the detective, "you could weigh me in with a few quid. You don't want us to find something in the boot, do you?" The inference was quite clear: Terry would be arrested and his car would be taken back to the nick and searched; lo and behold, some stolen property would miraculously be found in the boot, which up to this point had been empty. This is what being fitted up means. Terry parted with £30, which was considered a "drink" or a "sweetener" to keep the wolves at bay! This was happening all the time, and the "Sus" law was repealed in 1981 due to pressure and complaints about the police.

Another what we thought was going to turn out to be a nice little tiggle involved a small firm in the East End that made children's school uniforms. We knew the place had no screamer alarm, no bell system at all. In most of our criminal endeavours, we usually had someone on the inside who would mark our card and be willing to sell us some information. So, at about 9 pm on a cold winter's night, armed with a large pair of industrial bolt cutters, we approached the front door and noticed right outside on the corner was a street lamp, bathing the front of the premises in almost daylight. Fortunately, one of our firm knew how to switch off the street light; he opened up a small panel in the front of the lamp post and off went the light. We left it an hour before returning, in case anyone wondered why the light had gone off. Our bolt cutters made short work of a large monkey (padlock) that was on the door, and we were in and out in less than five minutes. Bundles and bundles of school uniforms took up half the space in our van, which we parked a mile away until the morning, when we would singly walk past it a couple of times to make sure the odd lot (police) wasn't plotted up and lying in wait. All was well, so we drove it to our "slaughter", which is where hoisted illicit goods are stashed and you have a chance to inspect the night's work. We did it all wrong this time! Every grey flannel uniform was for very young children, and all the trousers were shorts. We had a terrible job to "knock 'em out" (place them). We finally did, but at a give-away price.

CHAPTER 16

MICHAEL AND MOTOR CARS

As previously mentioned, Michael Isaacs was my oldest pal. He was a proper street urchin, "nobody's child", an "orphan of the storm" and a true product of the "Jago". His mother and father had separated soon after he was born, and he had been looked after by his gran. He was a nice-looking little boy with black, curly hair, mischievous and cheeky. His father had a newspaper pitch outside Whitechapel underground station, and every other Sunday morning we would walk from Hoxton to see him. He was an elderly Jewish gentleman who never showed any affection to Mike except to slip a shilling into his little hand. Mike lived in Myrtle Street, which ran off Hoxton Market, with his mother and a lodger that she had taken in, old Turner whom Mike loathed. Mike's mother, like a lot of people of the time, did love a sherbet (drink) and could usually be found in a local pub or putting a bet on with the street bookie. Betting in those days was illegal, and street bookies paid runners to keep an eye out for the police. If they were caught taking bets, they would find themselves up before the local magistrate in Old Street Magistrate's Court and the recipient of a hefty fine. When Mum, Dad and I decided to go to the pictures at the Hoxton Cinema, I would always ask, "Can Michael come, Dad?" I can't remember Dad ever refusing. Mum would wipe a flannel round Mike's face as well as mine, and Dad would pay for all of us, including the ice cream in the interval. I can still see Mike's little upturned face, his dark eyes and mop of curly hair! How could Dad possibly say no? Dad was too good a father for that. He thought more about this little street urchin than Mike's own father did.

At the age of seventeen, Michael and I bought our first car together, a 1934 Austin that had been a London taxi. It was blue with black mudguards, and we paid £35 for it. The back of it was like a baby's pram and on a nice day could be lowered. The rear of the cab was made out of some waterproof and hard-wearing material, but unfortunately there was a hole right in the middle of the roof. We put a square of old lino on the top to cover the hole against the rain, and we weighed it down with a house brick. The problem was that every time we went round a corner, the brick shot off. We were lucky nobody got brained by that brick! Oh, for super glue in those days. Mike could not drive, so it was down to me, and when we took delivery of the taxi, I sat Mike in the back and gave him a large la-di-da (cigar). I lit it for him and told him not to get ash all over the floor, rather flick it out of the hole in the roof and hold on to that brick! Mike must have thought he was part of the landed gentry without the tweeds and plus fours.

We used that taxi for everything, especially when I went to pick up some young filly I had pulled. In the winter of 1954, it was particularly cold and the engine of our taxi froze up. (This was before the days of anti-freeze.) Usually, when that happens, the ice will expand and split the engine block, and then the vehicle is fit only for scrap. One morning, we saw that our pride and joy was covered in snow and were trying to decide on a plan of action when a guy stopped and asked us what was wrong. He looked at the engine and asked whether we had any blankets available. I borrowed some of Mum's, and a neighbour gave us a big old army greatcoat. The filler for the water in the radiator was on the front of the taxi with a big chrome cap. This guy told us to put some salt in the top of the radiator, screw the cap back down, wrap all the blankets and army overcoat over the bonnet and front of the vehicle, start her up and not accelerate, just let her tick over for an hour or so. We did this and the problem was solved. We were ecstatic with relief; we could have lost her and she would have had to be towed away to the scrap yard. I mentioned to Mike that the guy who stopped and gave us advice and help was in line for a large la-di-da should we see him again!

We finally sold our taxi on, and how I wish I had her now. She would be worth a fortune as a vintage vehicle but worth much more in affectionate remembrance. In 2019 my son and daughter took me, as a Father's Day treat, to the London Transport Museum in Covent Garden, and there on one of the upper floors was a 1934 London Taxi exactly the same as the one Mike and I had owned. I was explaining one or two things about the taxi to my children, and starting to gather was a small band of people listening. Suddenly I became overwhelmed with nostalgia for the lovely times we'd had with that lovely old taxi when the world was a nicer place and our needs and pleasures were simpler, and I had to stop speaking. I'm sure most of the people understood my feelings.

Shortly after, Mike and I purchased a Wolseley Eighteen that was ex police and still had a chrome bell on the front bumper. It would have been rung loudly when in pursuit of another vehicle, although it had been dismantled when we took delivery of it. It was a long, sleek, black car that suited Mike better; at least it had two seats in the front and he could sit next to me. It was the last car we had together as Dad started to buy various cars for Mum and me and we started to get about, down to the south coast, to Dymchurch, and to Faversham in Kent, with me being the only driver. Mike continued to be my best pal and would accompany Mum, Dad and me on various trips to the seaside, as well as being part of our crew and a valuable member of our gang.

This was the mid-fifties, and during those years and the following sixties, it was one round of parties every Saturday night. The chaps would all be in suits and the girls in two-piece costumes. Tailors did a roaring trade as all the guys had made-to-measure suits. My tailor was Lew Conn of Kingsland Road, a very good Jewish tailor and a nice guy. I had thirty-four suits made by Lew, and I was quite friendly with his cutter, Stan. I would have two fittings for each suit, single or double-breasted, two- or three-piece, and guys in the clubs and pubs often asked me who my tailor was and complimented me on my sartorial elegance. Twice I strayed away from Lew to two other tailors, at the insistence of another old pal of mine, Mickey Day, who was a smart guy as far as clothes were concerned. I was measured for a suit at his tailors in Shoreditch High Street, Levine & Co, and then proceeded to Mick's other tailor in Old Street EC1, which was Alfred Myers & Co. Four weeks later, both suits were ready to try on and approve. I paid for both suits, but when dressed with all the accessories realised they were not in the same frame as my suits made by Lew Conn. I never strayed away from Lew again.

One Saturday afternoon, my other close pal, Frankie Hudson, and I were looking forward to the evening meet in our regular pub and then a party we had planned at the house of one of the girl's parents. We called round to Mike's house to arrange picking him up, but he told us he would not be coming with us to the pub and the Moriarty afterwards because his mum had pawned his shoes and suit at the local pawn shop that was in Cohen's Jewellers. That meant he had nothing to wear, so I loaned him one of my suits for the evening (we were about the same stature), as well as a pair of shoes. The pawn shop was on the corner of Hoxton Market and one of the worst streets in Hoxton, the notorious Essex Street. Legend has it that a police officer patrolling Essex Street was coshed and put down a manhole cover and died. It was such a terrible deed that the name of the street was changed by the Local Authority to Shenfield Street. Living in Hoxton seemed to give one a certain amount of protection and notoriety if you were out of your manor. When asked, "Where are you from, pal?" and you replied, "Hoxton," invariably people knew you were not the type to be messed with. The history of Hoxton goes back to the 17th century and beyond. Francis Tresham was arrested with Guy Fawkes in 1605 when they were about to blow up the Houses of Parliament. There is a commemorative plaque attached to the modern flats at the site of the home of William Parker, a local MP who was told not to attend Parliament that day because of the gunpowder plot that had been planned.

In the forties and fifties, there were many gang wars between the Hoxton Gang, the Angel Mob from Islington, the Boys from the Well, which was Clerkenwell (where Mum and Dad came from) and other small outfits, one of them being the Dalston Mob from Hackney. I remember as a child seeing some of the violent clashes, young guys fighting with knives, razors, broken bottles and pick handles, especially at the annual fairground that would be set up by the travelling people on a cleared bomb-damaged site behind the Roses pub, which is still there to this day but is now known as Macbeth's. When the older people of Hoxton discussed a recent fight, I never once heard that the Hoxton Boys had come off second-best.

On a bright and sunny morning walking through Hoxton Market, I came face to face with Mike's mother, who told me that Mike had been trying to make contact with me as he had moved and we had lost contact with each other. She gave me his phone number and we met up. He told me he was getting married and asked me to be his best man at his wedding. "Of course," I said. I had just taken delivery of another suit that Lew had made for me and that fitted in well with the wedding. Mike was marrying an

Irish girl, and the wedding was to be at Easter time in Tramore in County Waterford, Southern Ireland, which was not far from Dublin Airport. I tried to book a flight for Arlette and me to Dublin, but everywhere was booked solid. I was thinking I would have to tell Mike I couldn't make it due to circumstances beyond my control. However, later in the day, I received a phone call from Martin, our man on the inside, for another piece of business and started to tell him my predicament. He called me later that evening to tell me he had two VIP return tickets to Ireland for Arlette and me! One of the directors of Aer Lingus was a good friend of his and the tickets were complimentary, so we caught the flight to Dublin Airport, walked over to a waiting cab and asked to be taken to Tramore. Mike had told us it was more or less just up the road; just up the road turned out to be 117 miles and a two-hour drive away. The cab driver must have thought all of his Christmases had come at once. Finally, we were dropped at the address of Mike's bride-to-be and met the family. The next day was the wedding. I did my part as the best man and we all went back to a large hall for the reception. I stood up and made my speech and received much applause. They were a friendly crowd and only three of us were non-Irish, Mike, Arlette and I. Part of the tradition was that everyone, going round the room, had to sing a song. I thought, "No! That is not on!" I felt sure Arlette would sooner have been burnt at the stake than sing in front of all those strangers. I had never even heard her sing wandering about the home. I think she was a bit too refined for all that palaver, so when it came to the woman next to Arlette, Mike and I beat a hasty retreat to the Benghazi (toilet). On our return, we saw that we had been bypassed but had to suffer much laughter and jeering; we had been sussed! When we'd said our goodbyes, we were taken to our hotel to spend the night. In the morning, we came down to the reception to pay the bill but there was no one in attendance. I rang the bell a couple of times and called, "Hello! Hello!" but was starting to get wound up about the two-hour journey back to Dublin Airport. I said to Arlette, "We're out of here!" and we walked out with our cases, got into one of the cabs lined up outside the hotel and were taken back to the airport. Through no fault of ours, we had the night in the hotel free.

A couple of weeks later, we joined Mike and his wife in Wood Green for a dance in the local dance hall. We sat the girls at a table after taking their drinks order and were lining up when I turned around and saw three faces getting busy with our two girls. I left Mike waiting to be served, walked over to these guys and made it clear that these girls were with us. I walked back to Mike to help with the drinks, only to find these three idiots hadn't taken the warning. Again I told them to leave it out, and they finally drifted away but kept looking over all night. I think it was their intention to wait until the evening was over and cause aggro outside. At the end of the evening, people were leaving and mingling outside waiting for mini cabs, and next to the dance hall was a small building site where some flats were being built. I told Mike to keep an eye on the girls for a minute and squeezed through a gap in the wire surrounding an adjoining building site. I returned with two three-foot lengths of wood and said to Mike, "You take the guy in the grey suit. I will accommodate the other two." Mike was not interested in taking it further, but I was really wound up. He pointed out that there were three of them, but I reminded him that when their back was in front of you, it evened the score. However, the girls were getting nervous and I had to back off, but I was still in a terrible rage. I wanted to go to work on these guys, so we lost ourselves in the crowd and went back to Mike's house. Mike was not cut from the same cloth as me, and I respect that. Maybe discretion is the better part of valour.

CHAPTER 17

CLEVER!

Here is an incident of ingenuity that was regaled to me by an old friend of mine who has now passed on. I think it deserves a mention, if only for its resourceful inventiveness. He had been doing some business with a guy who, in turn, was doing business with a diamond dealer who had an office in France as well as in London.

This guy would make the trip to his London office every week from the Continent to carry out further business, and Lennie, as I shall call him, was given a description of the guy, the flight number and the day on which he would be arriving at the airport.

After coming through the barrier, the guy made his way to a well-known car hire company and hired a car to drive himself to his London office. Lennie followed him all the way back to London and noted that the hire car was parked on a plot of waste ground during the day. Early that evening, at roughly 5.30, Lennie stood at a bus stop just outside the mark's office, reading a paper and to all intents and purposes just waiting for a bus. After a short while, the mark exited his office, strolled across the road to his car, opened the boot lid, deposited his briefcase in the boot, locked it and drove off.

Here is the very clever bit I had to admire when told! At roughly 3.30 the following afternoon, Lennie rang the car hire company and told them in a quavering voice that he was on his way to his hotel and had stopped to buy a newspaper and his small terrier dog had leapt across and pushed down the small knob that locked the car doors and he could not get back into the car and the engine was still running, but close by he could see a car dealership of the same make as the hire car, and if they could give him the key number, he would quickly buy a key from the dealership and be on his way. The guy on the other end of the phone was making all kinds of sympathetic noises and said, "Of course, sir, that is not a problem." He promptly returned to the phone with the key number, after which Lennie found the nearest dealership and purchased the key.

At 4.30, Lennie went to the car, opened the boot, punctured the spare tyre and the off-side tyre and then adopted the same procedure of waiting at the bus stop reading the paper. On cue, at 5.30, the mark emerged, walked to the car, deposited the briefcase in the boot, got into the car and drove off. He soon noticed that there was something wrong with the steering, got out of the car and saw that the front tyre was flat.

This was either going to be a lovely night's work or the smallest detail would make it all go wrong. Lennie was thinking, "What would I do in his place? If I was immaculately dressed, with a bowler hat and suit, would I want to change the wheel?" But Lennie had punctured the spare wheel in the boot in case he did. This was all down to guesswork, and he guessed right. The mark decided to walk back to the office to get one of the young boys to come out to remove the wheel and get it repaired.

Success now depended on his next move: should he leave the briefcase in the boot as the office was less than a couple of minutes away? The boot was locked, anyway, and it should be safe in there, so he left it in the boot – bad decision! Lennie watched him walk back to the office, then he walked to the car and sweet as a nut opened the boot with the key. He retrieved the briefcase, caught a cab to an underground station, then a train to King's Cross station and deposited the goods in a left luggage locker, but not before checking the goods were all there. In Lennie's own words, "There they were, all shiny and new, smiling up at me." I said to Lennie at the completion of his story, "Not a bad day's work for a bit of fancy guesswork!" It was brilliant in its simplicity.

Meanwhile, Martin came up with another bit of business for the following week, but I had come down with flu-like symptoms. In the firm I worked with, we had an agreement that if anyone was not up for it due to unforeseen circumstances, you were still put in for your whack, so it went ahead with just three. A brief case had to be separated from a guy, but this time a chain was involved; a small pair of industrial bolt cutters soon ironed out that little problem. Soon after, I made my way round to meet the firm in one of their houses just as the case was about to be opened, giving us a chance to inspect the merchandise. This time, though, we blew out! Inside the case were a packet of sandwiches, two apples, a passport and two large boxes of chocolates. Liberty on the line for all this rubbish! One of the guys ventured an idea. "I wonder if he was smuggling diamonds and they are in the chocolates? Brilliant! So we bit open every chocolate until we were feeling quite sick and wound up with gornisht (nothing). But it was worth a shot, and this one was marked down to experience.

I would like to mention a robbery of a jeweller in North London that was very cleverly carried out. A young couple had gone into the shop and told the owner that they were about to get engaged and were looking for a nice ring. Congratulations all round, the young girl holding on to the man of her dreams, demure and eyes full of romance! A tray of rings was offered by the jeweller, but the couple didn't like any of them, so another tray of more expensive rings was shown. On about the fourth tray being shown, the owner of the shop had bent down to pick up a ring that the young lady had dropped and was then told that they had not seen anything they liked. The owner could see that there was a very expensive ring missing from the tray and accused the couple of stealing the ring. He wanted to ring the police, and the young man said, "Go ahead!" After a short while, the police arrived and searched the suspects, but nothing was found on either of them. To give it more credence, the young girl was in tears, her special day ruined. All clever stuff! The following day, a different young man called into the shop to enquire about a wristwatch strap. Running along the length of the display cabinet was a small lip where the glass met the wood, and under there was the very expensive engagement ring, stuck with a piece of chewing gum, which the young man removed rather deftly, then paid for the watch strap and left. No doubt he was paid a nice few quid when he handed over the ring. Nobody, including the police, had thought of checking it out. Well, you wouldn't, would you?

Roy Wild

CHAPTER 18

TURN-AROUND

I decided, at this point, to give up this lifestyle where my liberty was on offer at every illegal endeavour and go to work, which would allow me to sleep much easier without fearing a knock on the door late at night and being asked by the police to help them with their enquiries relating to a certain matter.

A friend of mine who was working in the asphalting business secured a job for me. I worked with him as a labourer asphalting roofs of buildings and private houses. I really enjoyed the job, working out in the open air, and the job took us to all parts of London, but the downside was that if it rained, you would earn no money because you can't lay asphalt in wet weather and you work on measurement. The more you lay, the more you earn. After six months or so, I'd made quite a name for myself as a good grafter and was promoted to a pot man, which means breaking up large slabs of asphalt, dropping them into a large steel pot that had an aperture at the bottom where a fire would burn, then cooking and melting the asphalt until it could be spread and laid. It was hard graft. I had to be on the site at roughly 6 am to light the pot and get it ready by 8 am when the two spreaders I worked with were ready to start work. The pay was very good, but you had to rely on how good the spreaders were, as well as the weather. Our company secured a large contract in Bournemouth asphalting some newly dug swimming pools, which would be a good earner. All sides of a swimming pool have to be asphalted to make it leak-proof, and vertical spreaders are paid much more than those laying it on a flat surface. Joe and Roger, the two young spreaders, and I expected to be there for almost a month. I would get up about 6 am, borrow Joe's car for a short drive to the site, light the pot, fill it with the asphalt blocks and return to our lodgings where all three of us would have breakfast and then return to the site, ready to start work. We would work until 1 pm, and by 1.30 we would be on the beach, finished. It was an ideal situation and a very good earner, and we were more like three good pals. In the evenings, we would go to a popular music pub that was always busy with young people, including guys from London who were also working in Bournemouth whom we saw regularly and became friendly with. So, a good social life, a good earner with the job, bundles of sunshine, every day on the beach and all was right with the world.

CHAPTER 19

VALERIE

One evening, an incident occurred that would change my life to some degree. I was approached in our regular pub by a rather lovely young lady by the name of Valerie, who said she had heard me speaking and asked where I came from. "London," I replied, and we started a conversation about this and that. She said that she lived in Boscombe, which is a couple of miles from Bournemouth, and The Fox was her regular pub. She then drifted back to a couple of friends she was with and said she hoped to see me on another night. Joe, Roger and I were back in the pub the following Saturday when Valerie separated herself from her friends and came over to say hello. Joe and Roger were in the process of giving a couple of young birds a John Bull (pull). Did I swim, she asked. I said yes, and she asked whether I would like to go for a midnight swim the following night from the beach. The following night, we met in The Fox, left at about 10.30 and headed for the beach. It was a very warm night. We stripped down to our swimsuits, lay on the beach for a while, then ventured into the sea, which was so warm. Thinking about it all these years later, it conjures up that scene where Burt Lancaster and Deborah Kerr were on the beach in that controversial sequence in the film *From Here to Eternity*. That was us! This was by far the most romantic interlude in my life. Along the sea wall behind us was a line of coloured changing huts. One of them was open, and there we stayed until the sun crept over the window sill. We were two people that just wanted to be together, if only for that one memorable night. I never promised Valerie anything, nor did she demand anything. I saw her a couple of times in the next couple of weeks, and everything was very amicable. The job was drawing to a close and we would soon be off back to London. On the night before we left, I had a drink with her and we spent some time together, said goodnight and kissed at the end of the evening. When the realisation set in as to what had happened with Valerie, I knew that I had let Arlette down badly. I regarded it as just a brief romantic interlude that I wasn't strong enough to walk away from. I was made that way. I had always been involved with girls and women and tried to console myself that I did not love Arlette any less, but I think men love in a different way to women, as wrong as some people may think that is.

Two months later, when I returned home from work, I was confronted by Arlette with a letter in her hand. We always opened each other's letters, and she showed me a letter from Valerie: she was pregnant. I froze on the spot. Arlette was always a very composed sort of person but demanded to know what had transpired between Valerie and me. I explained but tried to play it down as much as possible. The letter went on to say that if I was married or with anybody else, she would never contact me again, but if I wasn't, she hoped to hear from me. Obviously, I ignored the letter and destroyed it. I later found out that she'd obtained my name and address from the company I worked for, which I don't think could happen today because of data protection. Arlette said we would never speak of this one-off incident ever again, which we never did.

CHAPTER 20

CANNING TOWN

Arlette worked for an estate agent in Whitechapel Road. She said a very nice property had come on the market for rental in Canning Town and she would have first choice, so we went and viewed the flat. It was enormous, on two floors above a shop. We liked it straight away and decided to take it. I had resorted to joining the firm again, and we had some nice business coming up. I also had ten grand that was safely put away in the bank account of a relation whom I trusted wholeheartedly and drew it out over a couple of weeks. Arlette and I visited The Daily Mail Ideal Home Exhibition that was on in Earl's Court every year. She was carrying about eight grand in her bag, and we came home with about £35. During the next couple of weeks, all the things we had bought were delivered. The flat looked like something out of *Homes and Gardens*. It was beautiful. We had the whole flat carpeted and painted, there were a new bathroom and kitchen, and when Arlett's mother, Isabel, visited us, her mouth dropped open in astonishment. She declared, "In all the years of being married, I have never had a home like this!"

I decided that I had had enough of travelling everywhere to building sites in the asphalt business and took a job driving for a company selling, repairing and supplying typewriters to many firms in London. The firm, Royal McBee, was situated in Worship Street, close to the city of London. I would deliver new typewriters to solicitors and barristers' offices in the Inner and Middle Temple, as well as banks and any other offices that were using typewriters, and collect some that had broken down and needed repairing. One of the drivers that also worked there was a Hoxton guy, Eddie, who was the funniest guy I have ever met and became a close friend. He came from a well-known family in Hoxton who were not averse to earning a few quid here and there.

Our foreman, Ted, was one of those people who had done just about everything bigger and better than anyone else. If somebody said they had found a wallet with fifty pounds in it, he would have found the same thing with a hundred pounds in it. He told us that in the war he had bailed out of an aircraft by parachute and the chute had failed to open; he was hurtling down to earth and certain death, but fortunately there was another Allied aircraft flying underneath and he landed on top of this aircraft. Falling at a rate of thirty-two feet per second in freefall, he would have crashed straight through the aircraft, if not swept off by the slipstream. He said all of this with a straight face, just plain lying, and must have thought we'd all been left on the doorstep that same morning with the milk. One morning, we were loading up the vans with the day's deliveries when Eddie turned to me and winked. I knew that there was something coming! He said, "Roy, you know that small grassy area outside my flats? I saw something this morning and couldn't believe my eyes. I saw a cat dig a hole in the grass, have a crap and then bury it." The big-mouth foreman then jumped in and said, "That's nothing new – all cats do that!" Eddie replied, "What, with a shovel?" The drivers, loaders and other workers all burst out laughing, and Big Mouth walked away with a scowl on his face, knowing he had been made a fool of.

Eddie was a lovely guy, a laugh a minute. We would walk together down to Shoreditch Church where Eddie would turn left to walk down to Hoxton Market where he lived with his wife Peggy and their two children, and I would wait for the bus to take me to Dalston. We would stand talking at the bus stop until I boarded the bus. On one occasion, I was sitting on the seat downstairs at the front, behind the driver, and as the bus started to pull away, Eddie jumped on the platform and shouted out my name down the length of the bus. I turned round and stood up, and everyone could see it was me. He shouted down the length of the bus, "See you later about eight at the launderette. Don't forget to bring all those shitty pants again, like last week!" I love a laugh and a wind-up, but I nearly died, and everyone on the bus was laughing. Another favourite stroke of his, when we were walking along Shoreditch High Street, was if he saw someone running to catch a bus, Eddie would throw a handful of pennies or ha'pennies after the running guy, he would stop when he heard money hitting the pavement and would miss the bus.

I once had to deliver an expensive machine to Bournemouth, which brought back some nice memories of working there asphalting, as well as memories of Valerie. I stopped for a meal at a café that the London guys would use and bumped into one of Valerie's old girl friends, who told me that Valerie had given birth to a daughter. In spite of various lines of enquiry, I have never been able to trace Valerie or any of her family and find it hard that I have a daughter maybe still in the Bournemouth area whom I have never seen and probably never will.

An interesting incident I found myself involved in was when a couple of faces I knew had carried out a bit of business that amounted to a couple of dozen rolls of suiting material. I did them a small favour by putting them in touch with a guy I had dealt with many times before in recent endeavours; he could be well vouched for and would not tuck them up regarding price. They were offered a good price for their wares, and both parties were happy with the deal. A week or so later, I was having a drink in our local pub with the two faces I had done the favour for, and as we were leaving, they transferred a roll of the same suiting material from the boot of their car into the boot of my car. I enquired, "What's that all about?" One of them replied, "That's a drink for putting us onto your man, who gave us a good price." I said, "I never expected more than a glass of beer," to which he replied, "There's no taste in nothing, Roy. Thanks again!" So, to turn the roll of suiting into Nelsons (Nelson Eddies readies), I went to the same tailor in Whitechapel Road, parked the van and carried the large roll of material across the pavement and into his shop. I got paid on, and then the tailor said, looking through the window, "Aare those two guys with you?" "They are Old Bill (police)," I said. "Is there another way out of here?" He showed me the back door that led into a block of old Victorian flats. Now I was holding a large roll of bank notes that the tailor had just paid me, and I needed to lose them somewhere. Up on the first landing was a large, old-fashioned, cast iron electrical distribution box that, with a stretch, I could just reach to open. I deposited the roll of notes inside and closed and locked the door, with the intention of going back that evening to retrieve the Gene Tunney (money). I walked round the block and back to the van, only to be accosted by the two Old Bill. "We wondered why you were taking a roll of material into that shop when your van clearly says your company sells and repairs typewriters." "What roll of material?" I asked. "We saw you carry a roll of material into that tailor's shop and want to know where you obtained it."

"You are mistaken, or there is something wrong with your eyes!"

One of them said, "Don't take the piss, we know what we saw." It was market day, and next to my van was a fruit and vegetable stall. The stall holder looked like one of the chaps and no fool, so I said to him, "Excuse me, pal, these are two police officers, and they are saying they saw me carrying a suspicious roll of material into that shop over there. Did you see me when I first parked here next to your stall?"

"Of course."

"Did you see me carry a roll of material across the pavement into that shop?"

"No, I never saw anything like that, and I have been here since early morning."

"Thanks, pal," I said and turned to the Old Bill. "I told you so. You must be getting me mixed up with someone else."

Then the swearing began and frustration set in. I said, "If there is nothing else, I have deliveries to make," and got in the van and drove off.

I returned to those old flats later in the day and found the loot still intact in the electric box. A nice day's work saw completion, all because I was not the type to be intimidated by these two tosspots, Starsky and Hutch wannabees.

A year after leaving the job, I met a friend of Eddie's who told me that Eddie had died. Eddie had a thumb and one of his fingers missing, which he told me he had lost in an accident in a saw mill when he had been a spindle turner. He had died at home, and it was said it could have been a blood clot from that accident that had taken a long time to work around his body and had finally hit his heart. I was greatly upset at hearing this terrible news and will always hold his memory in great reverence.

Arlette and I continued living in Canning Town in our lovely flat, and some weekends she would visit her mother and come home on Sunday evening. On one occasion, a friend of mine and a girl he was with came to see me as I was leaving to visit my mum and dad in Hoxton. I said if they would like to wait for me in the flat, I would be a couple of hours and on my return we could pop out for a meal, which we did. The following day, when Arlette returned home, she was pottering about in our bedroom and discovered some evidence of what had gone on with this pal of mine and the girl in our bedroom. I was confronted, and she obviously thought I had been involved. I told her the truth, that I had been at my parents' house and this so-called pal and his girl had taken a liberty in our bedroom while I was out of the flat. I could see she was in two minds as to whether to believe me or not. A week or so later, she declared that she was leaving and we were finished. This, coupled with the incident in Bournemouth, had decided her. I didn't hear from her for more than a week and rang her parents, who told me she had gone to Malvern in Worcestershire and was staying at a relation's place. I located this so-called pal and the girl and explained how I had been blamed for this incident and that I wanted her to accompany me to meet Arlette and convince her that I'd had no part in it. She apologised for what had happened and agreed to come with me. It was all explained to Arlette, who told me to ring her the following day, which I did, only to be told she did not accept the story and that she believed I had put this girl up to it and groomed her what to say; our five years together was over. In spite of the many phone calls to her that followed, we were never reunited, and I was left with the abandoned ruins of the dreams she left behind. Looking back now, I think, "How could I have been so blind, not to see the door closing on the world I now hunger for?" I continued living alone in our beautiful flat in Canning Town but never had much interest in it after Arlette had left. I stayed in it for almost six months, with no interest in anything and desperately wanting her back. I felt like a leaf upon the wind; I could find no place to land. She had touched my heart in places that I never really knew, I was words without a tune, I was a song still unsung, a poem with no rhyme, a dancer out of time. There have been many women in my life, at the last count more than two hundred, and not one ever measured up to Arlette. I think she set the bar and spoiled me for any real in-depth romance. She shaped my future life of drifting from one comparison to another, all because I was not strong enough to walk away from the incident in Bournemouth. I knew I would never love this way again and never have, right up to the time of writing this rather lengthy verbiage.

Roy Wild

CHAPTER 21

MELANIE

The pub we used to drink in was the Merry Monarch, and after leaving one day, I found my car refused to start. I'd opened the bonnet to see whether I could find the reason when a voice behind me said, "Are you in trouble?" I turned around to see a very nice-looking young girl standing there. We started to chat about this and that and she told me her name was Melanie and she lived opposite the pub. I invited her out for a meal in the near future and she accepted. She gave me her phone number and I promised to ring her. She must have been a good luck charm because the car decided to start. We began seeing each other over the next few weeks, and one day she suggested that we could make up a foursome with a friend of hers and a friend of mine.

On the arranged day, Bill and I picked the two girls up at the agreed spot. Melanie's friend was a rather large bird, at a guess about twelve stone, maybe more? Bill looked at me, and I said, "Nitto (say nothing)." We drove to a pub in Stoke Newington by the name of Robinson Crusoe, and Bill said to me, "I am not stopping. Have you seen the size of her?" I said, "Bill, we are only having a drink; this is not a precursor to your engagement to her. We'll drop them off in a couple of hours and that will be game shot." "No," he said, "I am not staying!" After a drink, Bill excused himself, went to the toilet, left the pub, walked over to the bus stop opposite and caught a bus home. When we realised he had left, she said, "I don't think he liked me, did he?" I felt so sorry for her, but what could I say? It was unforgivable; he had hurt her feelings and could have handled it better, but unfortunately, Bill did not quite grasp gentlemanly conduct.

I continued seeing Melanie until one day she dropped the bombshell that she was engaged to a policeman who worked out of the police station that was just round the corner from the Merry Monarch. She then asked me whether I wanted her to break off the engagement. “Why didn’t you tell me this before?” I asked. “I never thought I would become involved with you,” she said. I said, “You are forcing me into a corner to commit. I’m sorry, I can’t do that,” and I walked away. The chaps that used to drink in the Monarch started to drift away because the police started to make it their local, and if Melanie’s guy had found out that I was responsible for her blanking him and breaking off the engagement, he could have made it his business to have me fitted up. I could do without that – life was good! Plenty of birds, plenty of booze and plenty of Gene Tunney.

CHAPTER 22

JACK SIEGEL

I started working as a mini-cab driver in Stepney Green, based at a small office located within the borders of Bethnal Green and Mile End. I had a nice Ford Zephyr to work with, for which I paid x amount of rent, and although I was brand new at the game, it did not take long to settle in. There were about twenty drivers working at the cab office and always an abundance of work; I was earning a good wage, without any problems. I became friendly with a Jewish guy by the name of Jackie Siegel, who was a couple of years older than me. Jack was fast-talking and seemed to have a lot of contacts. He told me that he knew a lot of television stars and people who owned property in and around the West End, but as I say, Jack was a great talker. On the next corner to the cab office was a small pub where Jack and I would go in between jobs to have a sandwich and a glass of beer. On one occasion, he told me we would be going to the West End that coming Wednesday evening. Put on a suit he said. "We are going to meet some people." When I asked why, he said, "We are going to start our own car service." Jack was about to open up a new chapter in my life.

We started off in a club in Mayfair where Jack knew the owner, Cy (Cyril), who greeted Jack like a long-lost brother, as did some of the customers. Then onto another club, same thing. Then we had to meet someone in a club in Rupert Street, which runs off Shaftesbury Avenue. This guy was another good friend of his who owned property in the West End and had said that he would look after us. Nicky was waiting for us in the Rupert Club, and Jack introduced us and told him we were looking for a couple of offices to start a car service. Nicky said he had two empty offices in Wardour Street, right next door to the Latin Quarter nightclub. "How much do we owe you, Nick?" "Wait until you get established," he replied, and then we will speak again. I will send some work your way from the clubs

I own." He was a real nice guy.

Underneath us, on the first floor, was a clip joint where stupid men would be entertained by scantily dressed young women who would promise them all kinds of things of a sexual nature if they would buy the girl a drink. "Sure," said the punter, who invariably had a wallet bigger than his brain, and a bottle of cheap champagne would suddenly materialise. The girl would also ask, in essence, "Do you like me enough to buy me a teddy bear?" which were in abundance in a back room, probably bought as a job lot from a market stall. "Of course," said the punter. At the end of an hour or so, he would be given a bill for £200 or so, at which he would almost keel over and refuse to pay. The owner and one of his minders would confront him and try to persuade him to pay, with a veiled threat; if that did not work, he would be threatened with the police and charged with ordering goods and refusing to pay for them; if it went to court, what was his wife going to say, and the neighbours, when they found out all this happened in a clip joint and involved a young girl? He soon paid up! The joint was owned by a thirty-something Scots guy who would use our cars to take his girls home. I became quite pally with him, and he would come up to our office and sit chatting with me, regaling me with unbelievable tales of what some dirty old men got up to downstairs. There was no business acumen or business degree from Harvard needed for this kind of profession, the commerce was based entirely on separation and promises, separating the fools from their money and promises from the girls.

One day, when all the drivers were out on various jobs, a request came in for a car to take a couple of people from Hendon to another house in Mill Hill, so I took on the job. I arrived at the house of pickup and was told to wait a couple of minutes. Suddenly, there was a knock on the car window and there stood Maurice Gibb, of the Bee Gees, who said his partner would be out in a moment. Shortly after came Lulu, and I drove them both to Mill Hill and found myself the recipient of a large tip. Two very nice people.

I walked into the office one day, and sitting behind my desk was a face I had never seen before. He was a powerful-looking guy, wearing an expensive vicuna overcoat. He jumped up as I approached and was introduced to me by Ronnie, my controller, as Danny. He apologised for sitting at my desk and said he had also used the phone and offered to pay for the call. I said it wasn't necessary; if he was a friend of Ronnie's it was fine. He told me that he minded the door of various clubs in the area and he would be sending me a lot of work from the clubs, for punters who would need a car to take them home.

Almost immediately, calls started coming in concerning late-night revellers who were being turned out from the clubs and punters who had been gambling in the various clubs that Danny looked after. He was true to his word and asked nothing in return. He invited me out one day as his guest and took me to a very swish restaurant. He said, "If you encounter aggravation of any kind, you are to come to me, and no matter who it is or where, I will take care of it." I would later find out just what a force Danny was in the West End. I mentioned to Ronnie what had taken place at our meeting, and he told me there were some very powerful people in the area who were quick to exploit anybody new to the West End, but he had never met anybody willing to go up against Danny or anybody who was a friend of Danny. I questioned why he would do this for me, as well as sending all the work round to us. He confessed that he had told Danny about how I had given him a job as my controller just when he needed it. He'd also mentioned that sometimes, when the work had slackened off, we needed someone with influence to send us some orders for cars to take people home from the clubs. He and Danny had been pals since they were kids, and in the short time Danny and I had known each other, Danny had taken a liking to me. I started to make a few enquiries about Danny, and the answers came back one after the other: "The best you could ever have in your corner, but never make an enemy of this face," and "If you are a pal, you will never have a problem with this guy looking out for you." At about 2.00 one morning, I received a call from Danny: "Roy, can you send a car round to take me home? Could you come personally, if there is someone to cover the phone?" I picked him up outside Charlie Chester's Casino and we started the journey home to Holloway. I found out that he looked after a dozen clubs or so and that was where all the work was coming from. All the other minders who worked for him on the door of other clubs were under strict instructions to ring West Central Car Service when a car was needed. When we finally arrived at his house, he said, "Right, Roy, how much do I owe you?" I said, "Nothing, Dan, it's complimentary." He said, "Roy, I will ask you once again: what do I owe you?" I said, "How can I charge you when you send me more than half of the work we cover? All future cars for you are not to be charged for, and I have told all my drivers that I will cover their fare." He said, "Roy, there are two ways of doing this: you will take a fare off me or we will both have it out on the cobbles. Friendship is one thing, business is another." I could see his logic but still felt uncomfortable taking his money. I got him to agree that, by way of appreciation, I would take him for a nice meal sometime. It wasn't that I didn't want to fight him. I would have been quite willing if I'd had a regiment of the SAS backing me up, as well as a machine gun! We remained great friends, but he always insisted on paying any of my drivers who took him home in the early hours.

Another call I received during the early hours of the morning was for a car needed at the Raymond Revue Bar, which was a strip club, but quite up-market, not like some of the seedy joints that made up the West End. It was world-famous for the quality and beauty of its girls, who had to pass vigorous interviews before working for Paul Raymond. On this occasion, it was for a car to take someone to Edgware, so I told Ronnie I would do it and then carry on home. As I waited outside the club, a very beautiful girl materialised and said it was she who had rung for the cab. We started off and I learnt that her name was Marlene and she was not in admin, as I had thought, but was one of the strippers. She asked me my name and whether I was one of the regular drivers. I told her that I was the Edmundo Ross (boss) and I had come personally as we did not have a driver available. Laughingly, she said, "So you have given me special treatment!" "Of course," I replied. We arrived at her home about 3 am and she asked whether I'd like to come in for a coffee before driving home. I declined as I had a long drive home and had to be up fairly early to meet my partner, Jack, who was about to get us involved in another enterprise and wanted to run it by me. Marlene said she understood and paid me. I said, "Maybe we will meet again." She said, "I hope so."

She continued to use our services, and various drivers would collect her late at night and take her home to Edgware. Invariably, they would tell me she had asked about me and to pass on her regards. Finally, one evening, she called and asked whether she could book a car to take her home from a club at 1 am and could I come personally. I picked her up from a club in Charring Cross Road, and when we arrived at her home, she again invited me in for a coffee. I knew which way this was heading. She said she liked me very much and was always thinking about me, and she would very much like us to form a relationship. I said I was flattered, delighted and honoured, this coming from one so beautiful (and she really would turn any man's head, with a figure that would crack concrete at ten paces), but I was fresh out of a five-year relationship with Arlette and did not feel ready for another so soon. The look in Marlene's eyes was beseeching when she asked me to stay for the night, and this time I stayed and was so pleased I did, not for obvious reasons but because she was such a lovely person, although I was not very enthusiastic about what she did for a living. We stayed just friends to give me more time and breathing space.

Jack was friendly with the owner of the Merry Go Round, which was situated in the next street to the Windmill Club, famous for never closing its doors all through the Blitz of London. Jack had come to an agreement with the owner that we would take over the catering of the club; we'd pay a rent for the privilege and all the proceeds would come to us. We met the staff and chef and made them aware of what was about to happen, and Jack and I agreed that I would run the car service and he would look after our interests in the club. On some evenings, Jack and I would visit various clubs where he introduced me to various celebrities – the film star Harry Fowler, Alfie Bass, a popular East End actor, singer and actor Kenny Lynch, and actress Linda Baron, to name just a few. Many stars of film and television would be seen in West End clubs; it was the "in" thing to do. Working in the West End, I found that I was mixing with the wealthy, the louche and the creative who characterised sixties London.

One evening, Jack took me to a club in Beak Street and introduced me to one of my idols, none other than Jimmy Logie, the Arsenal and Scottish International, who had bought the club after his retirement from football. I was in my element talking football with this Arsenal legend. On another occasion, I took my brother Tony and a mutual friend, Ronnie Boyce, to the club. I turned the conversation round to football and the Arsenal club and said to Ronnie, "What about Jimmy Logie, who played for us at inside right?" Ronnie said, "He was one of my heroes!" I asked whether he'd ever met him, and he shook his head. I took Ronnie's arm, walked him over to Jimmy and introduced them. I left them talking, and later on Ronnie said,

"The people you know, Roy! Thank you very much. I will always treasure meeting Jimmy Logie." I remember when Jack had introduced me to Jimmy Logie, the thought crossed my mind: who's next – the Queen? Or my other idol, Frank Sinatra?

Sylvie, the lady who owned the Rupert Club, was an extrovert with many social graces who had lived most of her life in the West End and had seen it all! When Jack took me to her club, we hit it off straight away. She must have been in her sixties and would quite often give her rendition of "Second Hand Rose" that Barbra Streisand sang in the film *Funny Girl* in 1964, but on finishing the song, Sylvie would sing "from Shaftesbury Avenue" as opposed to "from Second Avenue" and would give a bow, acknowledging the clapping and appreciation from the regular clientele. I had, in the past, taken many girls and introduced them to Sylvie, who could immediately put anyone at ease; she would wait until the girl I was with went to the powder room and then she would say, "Another one! Where did you find this one?" and we would laugh. Sylvie was like an old-fashioned Victorian aunt, bless her wherever she is.

One evening, I was celebrating a friend's birthday in a club just off Charing Cross Road. One of the hostesses, Rhonda, called me over and asked whether I could arrange for a car to pick her up at 2 am and take her to Kilburn. Then she asked whether I could take her home, and said she would pay me. I assured her that was not necessary, considering all the work she sent us. I picked her up just after 2 am and at her invitation stayed the night with her. We had not been in bed more than a couple of minutes when I heard a noise. There was a baby in a cot on the other side of the room! That finished everything. I said, "Did you leave the baby alone all night?" "No, of course not. My friend is asleep in the other room," she said. The spell was broken, so I apologised and we just cuddled up and fell asleep till morning. Another one put down to experience.

Danny was still sending us more work than we could handle at the car service and would accept no payment other than letting me buy him a meal now and again, and he still insisted on paying our drivers for a car that would take him home. He was a twenty-two-carat guy. One evening there was a commotion at the clip joint downstairs that entailed a police presence. It transpired that a punter had been given a bill for £150 for a bottle of cheap, lukewarm wine and some old stuffed toy animal. He had nearly passed out when given the bill, had paid under pressure, then left the place and returned with two police officers to complain. The two police officers were from West Central Police Station and were well-versed regarding these goings-on in the numerous clip joints throughout the West End that were perfectly legal. I came down and was asked by one of the officers who I was. I explained that I had the car business on the floor above, and he told me there was nothing they could do as no law had been broken and more fool for this guy to part with his money! To crown it all, if this punter insisted on swearing and shouting he was likely to be arrested for disturbing the peace. I thought that was all he needed: lost all his money, arrested by the police, go home and tell the wife that!

A week or so later, Jack told me we had been invited for a meal at the Merry Go Round to meet some other people the owner had also invited. The club was quite full, and there was a friendly atmosphere, with entertainment supplied by a very good piano player. I was introduced to the manager and current hostess, a lovely girl by the name of Debbie, who looked remarkably like the English actress Francesca Annis. Debbie was a Geordie and had been brought up in Darlington. She promised to ring us every time a car was needed in the future for one of the customers of the club, which she did often. Next to the Merry Go Round was an old fire station that was no longer in use as a new one had been built in another part of the West End. This old fire station had been turned into a car park, and the stainless steel pole that most fire stations have, that fireman could slide down instead of using the staircase, had been left in place; when customers had parked their cars on the upper floor, they would slide down the pole as the firemen used to do. It was amusing to see men in smart suits sliding down one after the other, just for the hell of it, myself included.

Debbie asked whether she could make a regular booking for a car to take her home to East Finchley every night at 1 am. She lived alone just off Muswell Hill, Broadway, and a driver would take her home and receive a generous tip. Late one evening, I did not have a car to take her home, so I rang her and explained the problem. She asked whether I could possibly take her home, which I did. At her home, she took out her purse and asked how much she owed, but I said there was no charge in lieu of all the work she was sending us. During the day, she sometimes rang and asked for me. If I was not in attendance, she would speak to one of the drivers and ask what time I would be in? When this was relayed to me, there would be knowing winks and wind-ups from the drivers. One evening she asked me to come personally to fetch her, but an hour early as she wanted to take me and introduce me to someone special. I picked her up at midnight and we headed to Knightsbridge. We parked the car and entered a building just past the famous Harrods Store. We were shown upstairs to a lovely couple of rooms lavishly furnished. It was a very up-market club where a customer would be well-vetted before being allowed to become a regular visitor. The owner was a West Indian guy of advancing years, very friendly and smartly dressed, who was mingling with the clientele. When his eyes fell upon Debbie, he quickly came over, made a fuss of her and said, "Who is this, Debbie?" She said, "This is Roy I was telling you about." He smiled and said, "I have heard good things about you, Roy. You are always most welcome here." She introduced him as Len Calender, and I was drawn to him immediately, due to his friendly demeanour and sheer professionalism in the way he handled his customers. The name of the club was 37 Knightsbridge, although 37 was on the opposite side of the road; maybe it had originally been over there and he had moved across to a more prestigious position, being adjacent to Harrods.

After wallowing in the comfort and ambience of the club, as well as the company of this beautiful woman, it was hard to see how my life could be improved. In the early hours of the morning, we decided it was time to leave and we headed for Debbie's home in North London. She said it had been a lovely evening and was so pleased we had shared it together. Len had been quite taken with me and had promised to use our car service when any of his patrons needed to be driven home. Debbie, at this point, asked me to stay with her until the morning light, and I awoke as dawn unhurriedly came into the room. I watched her sleeping and pulled her up close; I heard her murmur in her sleep and felt an overwhelming feeling of closeness. From then on we were an item, and every time she would ring the cab office and ask for me, the drivers would break out into a song that was a big hit by The Four Tops, "Reach Out I'll be There". I would, with good humour, remind them who the guv'nor was and to watch their step.

The months rolled by and everything was going very well as far as the car service and the catering in the Merry Go Round were concerned. I was visiting many clubs with Jack and meeting people. Jack was always discussing new enterprises and schemes and one day said that we were going to be involved in a project that would dwarf anything we'd had so far. Bated breath time!

I called Len at his club during the day and asked whether it would be in order for me to pop up to the club that evening with two or three friends. "Of course!" came his reply, so later that evening we arrived at the club, did the introductions, with handshakes all round, and looked forward to a nice evening ahead. With me were Bobby, Oats (oats and barley, Charlie) and Cliff, who were all very impressed with the upmarket surroundings. I would later regret this evening for the reasons that follow: I was at the bar waiting my turn to order our drinks, with just two barmaids serving, when in between me and another guy, who was also waiting, there suddenly pushed in this Jack the Lad, Hooray Henry loudmouth who starting shouting, "How much longer have I got to wait for a drink?" I, with everyone else, had been waiting patiently as we could see the barmaids were run off their feet. Should we have been in an East End pub or club, things would have been different. Idiots like this never ever see the danger they are in; this only comes with an education of living on the streets. Oats sidled up to me, and I could see he was well wound up. He said, "Roy, walk away, I'm going to cut him." Oats always carried a cutter with him, and I had seen him go to work in a fight. A better person backing you up I couldn't imagine, except Danny, but I did not need backup this time. I pulled Oats over to a quiet corner and said, "Charlie, this is not the kind of place where there are fights. I was brought into this very nice club by a dear friend of mine and made most welcome by Len, whom you just met. He thinks an awful lot of me and has afforded me the privilege of bringing my friends, and you, Bobby and Cliff are the first friends I have brought here. If you cut this guy, there is going to be a lot of blood, women screaming, police involvement and I will have betrayed the confidence, trust and friendship of a very nice man. So as my pal, Charlie, I am asking you to give it a miss." He was still wound up, then looked at me with a smile and said, "Did you know that among all our pals, you are known as Roy the talker?" I gave him a hug and said, "Let's enjoy the evening." Len had seen us talking in the corner and me giving Charlie a hug, and he came over and said, "Everything alright, Roy?" I said, "Sure, Len, we were just reminiscing over some old memories, but that guy over there is a bit loud." "Yes," he said, "I have told some of his friends to pull him to order or they will have to leave," which they did soon after.

CHAPTER 23

THE ICE CREAM GAME

You have been putting in a lot of hours, Roy. How do you feel about having a break?" asked Jack. "What kind of break?" said I. Jack said, "Selling ice cream." I laughed. "Jack, what do I know about selling ice cream? You might as well ask me to sell seaweed!" He told me he used to be in the "cream game", and had an ice cream van parked up at a friend's house in the East End which was perfectly roadworthy. All it would cost me was the petrol for it and the cost of the ice cream itself that would be sold at a profit. He suggested I try it for a month. I ran this past my old friend Michael Isaacs and we decided to try it. It was not going to cost us anything, the van was taxed, and we needed to insure it and the contents; that was all. Jack took us to meet the supplier at the foot of Colney Hatch Lane, which ran off Muswell Hill Broadway, a stone's throw from where Debbie lived. The vehicle was to be returned at the end of each day because a long electric lead from the van had to be plugged in each night to keep the fridges cold, ready for the day's selling, and we would pick it up each morning.

Our first port of call was Exhibition Road in South Kensington, which is home to several museums and academic establishments including the Science Museum and the Natural History Museum, where there was always a large gathering of school children and foreign visitors. We would really clean up as far as custom was concerned. We learnt as we went along – an ice cream with a Cadbury flake stuck in the top, which used to be known as a 99, fizzy drinks, ice cream sandwich wafers – but this was unlicensed trading and we would occasionally be moved along by the police. If persistently caught, you would find yourself in the local magistrate's court and fined 10 shillings, but it was well worth the risk. If we were moved on by the same copper twice, we knew it was time to move to a new venue as a fine was imminent. Another favourite place was Admiralty Arch, which was at the start of the

Mall which ran up to Buckingham Palace. It was always alive with people visiting Trafalgar Square and the Queen Victoria Memorial, and the money we took there was unbelievable, but a long line of people waiting to be served soon attracted the attention of some lurking police officer, who sometimes would be sympathetic and tell us to pull round the block, so we would drive up the Mall in the hopes that the Queen would holler out of the window, "Two 99s please," but she never did. We would continue up to Hyde Park Corner and back into the Mall again, by which time the police officer would be patrolling somewhere else and before he returned we would have taken a nice few quid. It was all a game of cat and mouse.

After six weeks or so we gave up the "cream game". I was missing the West End and the people I knew and had not seen much of Debbie, so I returned to the cab office where we were doing really well. I called Debbie and told her I was back and was invited round that evening to the club. I had a few drinks with her and said I would be back at 1 am to take her home. Debbie was never a demanding girl, very laid back and easy to get along with, very touchy-feely and affectionate. She never ever told me she loved me, and in return, I never told her. We were just two people who enjoyed each other's company. I received a call from her one evening at about 8 pm, asking me to pop round to the club, and sitting at the bar was this vision of loveliness chatting to Debbie. "This is Roy I was telling you about," said Debbie, and she then turned to me and said, "This is my friend Janie." She was wearing a gold lamé dress, matching gold shoes and a gold wristwatch and had the most bewitching and beautiful face I had ever seen. When she spoke, an East Ender would say "diamonds came out of her mouth" She made the Queen sound like a cockney! And I suddenly started to believe in magic again. She was elegant and enticing, and so very friendly. We sat at the bar chatting the remainder of the night while Debbie was busy serving customers. The evening finally came to an end and customers left the club. While Janie was in the ladies, Debbie's next statement knocked me sideways: "Can you drop Janie home after you drop me home?" "But she only lives in Marylebone Road," I said. "Surely it makes sense to drop her home and then continue to North London as usual?" She looked at me and said with an air of impatience, "Roy, Janie likes you!"

I said in disbelief, "Don't you mind?" "Of course not. Janie is a good friend of mine."

So we dropped Debbie off at Muswell Hill and I headed for the East End, through Bethnal Green and then into Canning Town. "Roy!" Janie said. "Where are we going?" "We're going home to my place." She gave me a sideways smile. "Roy, you are so naughty!"

I was never one to have my romantic aspirations of paradise illuminated by the dashboard light. My lovely flat was far more inviting! At breakfast that I made for us the next morning, I caught her looking at me and I said, "Something wrong?" She said, "Of course not… Roy, you really are a superb person," but she pronounced it shuperb, which turned me right back on again. I later dropped her off where she lived and we both hoped we would meet again. Debbie and I met at her club the following night and she obviously knew what had happened. She had spoken with Janie and said that she had said I was a lovely guy. I never, ever saw her again, and Debbie and I carried on as we were, but that encounter with Janie, as brief as it was, will remain an indelible interlude in my life.

One afternoon, Jack announced that we would shortly be going to Israel. We would be investing in cold storage vans in Haifa and transporting cold meat and vegetables, which involved dealing with a friend of Jack's who was in that type of business. According to Jack, it could be a very lucrative venture. I asked whether we had the finance for the venture, and he assured me everything was in place. Jack was on the missing list for a couple of days, and then I received a call from a mutual friend that Jack had been arrested and, with three other guys I did not know, had been charged with the theft of two haulage vehicles containing Scotch whisky and mohair. I suddenly knew where the finance was coming from for the Haifa venture. Jack was remanded and bail refused; he was taken to Brixton Prison to await trial.

I had taken on a guy whom I had known for some years, Vicky, as another controller to help Ronnie out, as we were now very busy. One day with just Vicky, one other driver and me in the office, two guys walked up the stairs and into our office and certainly looked as if they meant business. One of them asked, "Are you Roy?" and I said yes.

"We were on that bit of business with Jack, and we have found out from a friendly Old Bill that the guys who got captured were grassed. The name concerned was Ray or Roy, so we have come to see you."

Vicky knew one of these guys and said emphatically, "No way would Roy do a thing like that. I would vouch for Roy all day long. I have known him many years and would trust him with my life."

"Just look at this logically," I said. "I had everything to gain had Jack been successful. We were going to Israel to start another business venture; why would I jeopardise that? Check with Jack if you are going to see him. You have given me a visit all on the strength of an Old Bill who got two similar names mixed up. If my name had been Gary or Mike, you would not be standing here now."

Finally, they said, "If you hear anything, contact us through Vicky, and this is what the scumbag who grassed can expect!" He then produced a sawn-off SG from under his coat and they left. When Jack's trial came up, he received a two-year sentence and all thoughts of Haifa were put in the waiting room for the time being.

At the club, Debbie introduced me to a young guy who was working for a large well-known insurance company as a claims assessor and had access to information concerning security for all their clients, such as whether there were any safes on the premises, alarms on the property, pressure plates fitted in secret rooms, etc. This guy was prepared to part with information concerning high-value clients. I told him that the people I knew were not into burglary and burglars were considered low life. I asked him which area he covered and was told it was Oxford and surrounding areas. I let him down gently by saying I would make a few inquiries and left it at that, so be careful, dear reader, whom you insure with – everyone is at it!

A very nice nightclub in the West End was the Rosendale in Shaftesbury Avenue, next door to the fire station. I became a regular visitor and friendly with the resident piano player, John, who was very much into Frank Sinatra and Tony Bennett. He would hear me singing along to the tunes he played and one day said, "You have a nice voice, Roy. Why don't you sing up here one evening?" which I did and it went down well with the clients. His call-up tune was a song called "Fine and Dandy" which he would always play when he first sat down. His wife was Linda Baron, the actress who later went on to star with David Jason and Ronnie Barker in *Open All Hours*. One night while I was in a pub in King's Cross, there was a shooting at the Rosendale and a large police presence, and I never went back to it. The clientele dropped rapidly and it closed.

Roy Wild

CHAPTER 24

PUBS, PARTIES AND PRISON

Debbie left the Merry Go Round and returned home to Darlington, and I terminated the car service and returned to the East End. I hooked up again with some old friends and the partying began. Booze was cheap, and all the guys would put a pound each in the "whip"; if you were bringing a bird with you, it was an extra 10 shillings. The booze was ordered with the guv'nor at the beginning of the evening and collected at "last orders", the cars were loaded up and off to the venue we'd go. The music was the Beatles, the Stones and all the groups that contributed to the Mersey sound. My brother and I used to drink in many pubs in the East End, but our two favourites were the Mildmay Tavern and the Marquise of Salisbury in Balls Pond Road, Dalston. The resident group at the Mildmay was fronted by a friend of mine, Robbie Leggett, who would sing Beach Boys songs as well as a couple of requests from me.

When people paid for a round of beer it was invariably with pound notes, and when the pub was heaving, the Jack & Jill (till) would overflow with paper money. The staff would put the excess in a heavy Toby Jug that sat on a shelf and looked very tempting. Three chaps that I knew started a fake fight between two of them, out rushed the manager and the staff to break them up and restore order, and lo and behold, the third member of the trio nipped behind the bar, grabbed the jug and its contents and then left the pub with the loot. When the crowd was asked whether they had seen anyone take the jug and money, no one had seen a thing.

A platonic friend of mine, Pauline, was a "hoister" (shoplifter) and was always skint, despite loading up in various West End shops, and would invariably get into me, asking for money and promising to pay it back. I always obliged by giving her £5 or so which she never paid back and I would have never accepted anyway. One evening, we were in the Salisbury when she said to me, "Do you see that guy over there? I am going to put a glass in his face in a minute! He is the father of my little boy and never comes to see him and never gives me a penny for him." I said, "Pauline, that is not the way to do it. If you cut him and you will, using a glass, the police will be called, you will be arrested and you could receive a prison sentence if he is badly cut and disfigured. That is wanton violence. Be shrewd; take him to court for maintenance. The court will make him pay. Hit him in his pocket." She listened and then said, "Roy, you always know what to do. Why hasn't a lovely fellah like you got a girlfriend?" I replied, "Pauline, I play the field. I have always been a roaming Romeo and my Juliets are many. I don't get involved and I don't get hurt. That is my philosophy." In the next breath, she said, "My parents are away for the weekend. Come home with me for tonight!" I said, "Pauline, I have known you for a long time, and you and I are like brother and sister. Please don't be offended, I think an awful lot of you, but it wouldn't work." Some time later, Pauline was tragically killed in a car accident driving home in the early hours of the morning after babysitting for a friend. I was very upset to hear this and attended her funeral. She was a rough diamond who could fight like a man but whose heart had a lustre that would put gold to shame.

Another incident that I witnessed began in the Mildmay. Three guys I know, who were into heavy stuff, were having a quiet drink when into the pub, amid loud shouting and laughter, breezed half a dozen guys whom I had never seen before. They became very loud and abusive to a couple of girls, and I thought, "Here we go! You are out of your depth, chaps; it will be off in a minute." Then they started staring at the three guys I knew, piss-taking and laughing, until one of the three walked over to them, grabbed the loudest one by the hair (by this time the band had stopped playing) and gave his hair a twist, forcing Big Mouth down to his knees. Out came a gun, which was put in his mouth, and he was told to close his mouth. When the mouth was closed, the gun was pulled out rapidly and the forward sight on the end of the gun pulled all Big Mouth's front teeth out with it. The rest of his firm, by this time, were terrified and with Big Mouth minus his teeth were dragged outside and made to point out the car they had arrived in. One of the three came back from their car carrying a car jack handle and told one of the six to open their car so he could be sure that it was their car and not one that belonged to somebody else. When that was established, the jack handle went to work: all the side windows, the windscreen and the rear window were smashed, then the two headlights and rear light assembly. The six were then thrown into the car that drove off rather rapidly, if not shakily. Suffice to say they never returned.

I made occasional visits back to the West End and had arranged to meet some friends at the City Club, which employed a pal of mine who minded the door as security. I arrived somewhat early and stood on my own, waiting for my pals to arrive. In walked a guy I had seen around in various pubs, and when he came over, I ordered a drink for him. He was not my kind of guy, had a bit too much to say for himself, or, as we say in the East End, "too much of what the cat licks its arse with". A short while later, four guys came into the club and were standing a short distance away when the guy standing next to me said, "Look at the state of these geezers coming up to the club dressed like that!" They were in casual clothes as opposed to me and mouthy. I said, "Don't worry about it," but his voice got louder and louder, and I said to him, "Have you come up here to have a drink or a fight?" The four faces had started to take an interest in what he was saying. Unfortunately, there was nowhere in the club to put your drink down, you had to stand with it in your hand, so I put my glass on top of a cigarette machine on the wall next to me. As I turned back, smack! one of the four guys slung me a shot that opened up a gash above my right eye that spewed out claret (blood) all over my white shirt and suit. Billy, my friend the minder, jumped in and pushed me into the women's toilet and stood with his back against the door, telling them they would have to go through him first. Meanwhile, the guy with all the mouth had shot down the stairs like a greyhound and disappeared. I told Billy what had happened and that I didn't know the guy at all, and he went outside to speak with them. Iris, one of the girls in the club offered to take me to her home and clean up my wounds, but I had to go to hospital as my eye needed stitches. Billy came back and said everything had been straightened out. They had apologised and said I was more than welcome to join them for a drink in the West End! I declined and drove myself to the German Hospital in Dalston where I had four stitches put in my eye. I waited for an encounter with the idiot responsible for the stitches but never had the pleasure of meeting him again and paying him what I owed him, if you get my meaning.

I was with a few pals in the Mildmay one Saturday evening when two girls approached me. I thought I was seeing double – they were twins! One of them asked me in a broad Scouse accent whether I was an agent, and I said, "An estate agent?" They laughed and said they meant a show business agent. They had seen me talking to the lead singer, Robbie, a couple of times and thought I might be his agent as well as the fact I was the only guy in the pub wearing a suit. They went on to tell me they were singers from a place called Hoylake, which is up on the Wirral in Liverpool. One was Pat and the other was Pam, and they had been to school with John Lennon's wife, Cynthia. They had a flat in the Finsbury Park area of North London. The following Saturday they were in the pub again and came over to say hello. There was not a party going for that night, so we decided to go to a club I knew in the West End and I invited them along. They nearly fell over as they had heard a lot about the clubs in the West End and couldn't wait. At about 2 am we headed for home, and I invited them to my flat for a drink to finish the night off. It was a case of just coffee and biscuits, as we'd had enough to drink, and at about 4 am I said, "If you are ready, I will take you home." Pat (I think it was) said, "Can't we stay here with you?" I explained there was only one bed and the settee and two of them wouldn't fit onto the settee, so one of you would have to share with me. After they finished in the bathroom (and borrowed my toothbrush), Pam shared my bed, and after a short while there was a knock on the bedroom door (I knew it wasn't the postman) and Pat joined us. Without going into too much detail, that was the start of every man's dream. I stayed with them many times in their flat, which was a bit awkward at times as they had a bunk bed, one on top of the other, and if I was with Pat, who had the top bunk, after a while she would whisper, "Why don't you drop down and see Pam?" Well, I was never one to argue in a situation like that, and that's what invariably happened unless they were staying with me. Many times when we were leaving the pub or a party, one of the chaps would say, "Put me in, Roy." I would always say, "Try giving one of them a pull!" but I always left with one on each arm. At that point, I really believed that magic existed.

An unusual incident happened to a couple of good friends of mine, Jimmy and Peter, who had just left a party and were waiting for a cab outside. A black limousine stopped, down went the window and Paul McCartney popped his head out and said, "Where are you going? Do you want to come to a party?" Oh yes! They were taken to a house in St John's Wood where a party was in full swing. Then one of the internal doors of the flat opened and in came John Lennon wearing nothing but a large hat and strumming a guitar, playing Norwegian Wood. Unforgettable.

I was with two pals, Patsie and Billy, in the Salisbury one night when Patsie introduced me to a guy named Jack, another Jack, but this one wore a hat and was known as Jack "The Hat" McVitie. The same guy who was killed by Reggie Kray at a mock party in Stoke Newington. A week later, I was standing in the same pub when Jack came over and started to chat. He suddenly said, "What do you think of this, Roy?" and produced a very nice-looking nickel-plated gun, rather small, the type you would expect to find in a woman's handbag. I said, "That's nice, Jack. Small, but it could get you out of trouble if needed," after which it was slipped back into his pocket. A week or so later, Jack was to become instrumental in the role of peacemaker in an incident involving me and three of my crew.

We pulled up one evening outside the Mildmay looking for a place to park and right outside the pub was a space in between two cars. Terry, who was driving, had pulled just past the space with the intention of reversing into the gap when behind us another car pulled into the empty space. Terry was all for jumping out and having a row, but the faces that were piling out of the car I had seen before and this crew were real heavy. I said, "Leave it, Terry," and we pulled the car round the corner and walked into the pub. This other crew were standing over the other side of the bar, and one of them was Jack, who winked at me. After a while, one of the guys made his way over towards us, and I thought, "Here it comes; there's going to be some altercation." He stopped in front of me and said, "I know you. Aren't you Rosie and Andy's son? I know your mum and dad. They live just along the balcony to me and my wife, and I always speak to your dad." Now the ice was broken, he called over the rest of his crew and introductions were done all round. Jack told the other three he knew me and we had enjoyed a drink together, so Harry, who had first approached us, ordered drinks all round. We finished up spending the night in their company and gaining some very influential friends.

I drifted back to the old firm I had worked with before, which resulted in a few nice bits of business. A friend of mine was Brian Scully, an accomplished thief. He would look for an empty shop next door to a jewellers and would take all night breaking through the wall with a club hammer and a cold chisel with an old sock or glove on top of the chisel to muffle the sound. He would beaver away until he finally got through and come away with a nice result.

Brian took a young girl out one evening, and on the second date an argument broke out in the car, so he stopped the car and told her to get out. A couple of weeks later, I was in the Merry Go Round with him and Lenny Hamilton when Ronnie and Reggie Kray made an entrance into the club with a couple of their firm. Brian needed to use the club toilet and Reggie followed him in. We suddenly heard cries of pain, the toilet door opened and Reggie emerged, bespattered with blood. He, Ronnie and the rest of the firm quickly left. I later found out that the girl that Brian had the argument with was a friend of the twins and had complained to Reggie, so he had given Brian an uncalled-for tune-up! We took Brian to the Metropolitan Hospital in Hackney, and when asked by the attending doctor what had occurred, I said that Brian had been involved in an altercation outside the club and we had found him on the pavement. He just shook his head and seemed to accept my explanation; we did not want any police involvement. This incident is recorded in Lenny's book *Getting Away With Murder*.

We were still having little earners now and again, and we rung a few cars. I was running about in a brand new Jaguar Sovereign that had been rung, and I needed to keep working if only to pay for the petrol to feed this beautiful beast. Then someone we knew stuck something up to us concerning a woman's tailoring factory. The owner of the factory had a son who told that "back-pocket" revenue was kept under the bed in the governor's house. The son wanted us to burgle the place and nick the money. I told him we did not deal with burglars; that was below us, and we gave it a miss. It also left a sour taste in the mouth that the son wanted to do that to his father.

A good friend of ours, Timmy Regan, who was in no way involved in any type of villainy, worked in his brother's betting shop. Mickey had a couple of betting shops in Portsmouth, as well as a large hotel on the seafront and a nightclub known as the Nelson. Timmy suggested we have a weekend away in Portsmouth and had cleared it with his brother that we would stay in the hotel, which was known as The Gay Hotel. (This was when "gay" meant happy.) We would stay in the hotel Friday and Saturday night and leave for London on Sunday after breakfast. This was all free, the accommodation, the food and the entrance fee into the Nelson, and it became a regular outing. One evening in the Nelson, I spotted a gorgeous girl with red hair and thought I would dance with her, but my friend Terry beat me to it. He stayed with her for the rest of the evening until we returned to the hotel. He asked me what I thought of her, and I said, "Words fail me." "Some you win, some you lose," he said with a smile. "Don't hold your breath," I thought. "We'll see about that."

We continued visiting Portsmouth every couple of weeks, and one weekend Terry could not make it for some reason. The Nelson was in full swing, and over came Bette, the redhead. She asked where Terry was, and then asked me to dance. The song that was playing was a romantic song called "It Must Be Him" by Vickie Carr. While we danced, we got to know each other she asked me what I did for a living. I soon swerved around that! She was absolutely gorgeous, and with her in my arms, I felt I was in nirvana. Eventually, she said, "When you and your friends first came to the club, why did you not ask me to dance?" I said, "Terry saw you first, maybe!" She said, "I wanted it to be you that I would dance with." In the early hours of the morning, I took her home and she invited me to stay the night, which I did. Back home, I called Terry and he enquired about the weekend and whether I'd seen Bette. "Yes," I replied, "and you have lost her. She is now with me." He laughed and said, "You slippery git!" to which I threw back at him, "Some you win, some you lose."

On another weekend, one of our crew, Bobby, hooked up with a girl by the name of Hazel, who told him that her previous boyfriend had assaulted her. Our guy and two mates went to see this geezer in a pub that Hazel had pointed out, dragged him outside and gave him a severe tune-up, so much so there was police involvement. Our three raced back to the Nelson and told us what had happened. We shot back to the hotel, collected all our bits and pieces, jumped in the cars and headed back to London. We never returned to Portsmouth because of that incident, and any romantic aspirations I had towards Bette disappeared quicker than a fist when you open your hand.

One of the absolute nicest places I have ever been to was Villa Dei Cesari, a restaurant on the Albert Embankment in Lambeth. Timmy Regan asked me, "Are you seeing anybody at the moment?" I said, "I have a book thicker than Mrs Dale's Diary – take your pick!" He said, "Sort one out and be my guest," so I took Chrissie, a girl I was seeing on and off. We met Timmy and his young lady in the East End and took a cab to the restaurant that was located in the mile between Westminster Bridge and Vauxhall Bridge, with the backdrop of the Thames. We were greeted by a commissionaire in full uniform and then entered an amazing room. There were live statues everywhere, dressed in full gladiator garb, as well as Roman soldiers with the short broadswords, plumed helmets and sandals. It felt as if we were in the middle of *Quo Vadis* or *Cleopatra*. When Timmy's girl took out a cigarette and put it in her mouth, a gladiator's arm came over her shoulder and lit it for her. We had a wonderful evening, and as we were leaving, a guy in Roman attire handed each of the girls a menu, rolled up like a scroll tied with a piece of red ribbon, as a keepsake, the final well-orchestrated touch. Chrissie and I went home on a cloud, with me toying with the idea of changing my name to Marcus Aurelius. Later, Chrissie said to me, "By the way, who is Marcus Aurelius?" I said, yawning, "Don't worry about it. Go back to sleep."

Somebody we knew worked for a women's clothing company, and to enable the delivery driver to get away early in the morning, the van was loaded up the previous night. It was arranged that we would pull the van out on the night before, with its full complement of women's coats, and take it up to our slaughter (lock-up). However, on the night it was going to happen, I had arranged to meet a lovely young girl for a drink, so I took her with me. I picked up the van about 10 pm and headed to the lock-up with Rita sitting beside me. Going through Hoxton, I was stopped by a police car and asked what I was doing in a large van that time of night. I told the police officer that I drove for the company that owned the van and was taking my girlfriend home. He demanded to look in the back and asked me for the delivery notes, which I obviously did not have. He became very suspicious and called for another unit. In no time, I was arrested and taken to Dalston Police Station and questioned. Three CID officers came into the cell and wanted to know the names of the people I was working with. I told them it was a one-off; I had been walking my girl home and found the van full of clothing and not locked, which they did not believe for a moment. They promised me a hiding if I did not stick up some names. I made them aware that I had taken a few hidings when I was training at school to get into the boxing team. They could see by the way I spoke to them I was well seasoned and no fool. I said, "If you are going to nick me, then get on with it." I appeared next morning at Old Street Magistrate's Court and was charged with grand larceny. The police opposed my bail application because they felt I might abscond.

I was taken to Brixton Prison and placed on remand until a case could be brought and built against me. By this time, the firm had heard that I had been nicked and the van in question was still in Old Street Police Station. The firm were going to try and nick it off the police, and with the van gone, there would be no evidence and the case would be thrown out of court. A daring plan! But on the night it was due to happen, for once the yard gates were closed and locked, so the plan was thwarted and I was banged up in Brixton Nick. It was filthy dirty and running alive with down-and-outs, and I thought, "I don't need too much of this!" I had a visit after a couple of days from one of the firm who told me they were going to apply to the Judge in Chambers for my release. On the second attempt, the firm's solicitor secured my release and out I came, ready to hook up with Rita again and enjoy the party on Saturday night. A nice few quid was collected and handed to me, and my status was elevated tremendously because I had kept shtum; I never violated the code and never stuck up any names. This is when you find out who you can trust on the firm you are working with; so many fold up after being promised lengthy sentences and hidings by the Old Bill. Life returned to normal for the time being while I waited for my committal at Southwark Crown Court.

A friend of mine, Bobby, said there was a vacancy for a driver in the firm he worked for, which was a safe installation company. The job entailed driving a new twelve-ton British Leyland vehicle delivering and installing safes to various establishments that wanted to protect their cash and expensive items. We worked in a gang of about four, one of whom was the foreman, who really knew the job. One of the first jobs we had was to deliver a twelve cwt safe to a jewellers in Dalston, Hackney, that had been broken into the night before. They had attempted to blow open the safe with an explosive and obviously did not know what they were getting into. They had used too much explosive and blown the safe up onto the next floor via a huge hole in the ceiling. The safe was still intact, and we had to get it out and install the new one, but the old one could still be opened and members of the staff were unloading various pieces of jewellery and cash and taking them downstairs until the new safe could be installed. It had to be done that day or they would have had no insurance. We managed to install the new safe and then had the problem of removing the damaged one. After removing the frame from the upstairs window, we put the head of the vehicle crane through the window, attached the safe and carefully lowered it onto our vehicle.

At this point, I would just touch briefly on the security of safe installation, or lack of it. One day, when one of the gang was acting as foreman as the regular guy was off sick, we delivered a one-ton Chatwood Milner safe to a wholesale jeweller in Hatton Garden. The job could only be done on a Sunday, at our request, due to the space our crane would take up and parking restrictions. The office where the safe had to be installed was on the second floor in the front of the building. We had been given the keys of the building and a plan of the office, and the safe was installed as requested. Some safes have a combination lock where numbers are used, some have a key as well as a combination lock and some have two keys and a combination lock. This safe had one key and a combination lock. The combination lock number for a new safe is set in the factory at manufacture, and the number and the key are handed to the customer in a large jiffy-type bag upon delivery. The recipient signs for them and can change the combination number if he wishes to, but very few clients do. But – there is always a weak link. The jiffy bag! The bag containing the key and combination number is not sealed with melted wax by the manufacturer; it is just stuck down like a regular letter. I see this immediately and think all it takes is to steam the bag open, take the combination number and take an impression of the key, not in the old-fashioned way you see in films, in a bar of soap, but in a cuttlefish, which is soft. Then forget about it for six months to a year and return to help yourself. The safe will show no sign of damage, as they usually do when someone tries to open them unofficially. Most people still believe the weakest part of a safe is the back and have to work all through the night taking the back off with a cold chisel and a club hammer, unless they use a thermic lance, which, if not handled properly, will burn up everything inside. The enquiry will possibly conclude that it is an inside job, but that would be of no interest to you while you are soaking up the good weather in sunny Portugal with a glass of champagne in your hand. Later, I will enlarge on how to pop a peter (safe) with a mattress and a condom. This is in no way encouraging the reader to get involved in a safe-breaking expedition, and certainly not by blowing it up, because for the novice or first-timer, the only Peter you will see is when you meet the real St Peter at those pearly gates.

An interesting job we had was to deliver a 10 cwt safe to the purser at Colney Hatch Lunatic Asylum in North London. We unloaded the safe, transferred it to a large sack barrow that was capable of handling the weight and were escorted by a guy in uniform to the purser's office where the safe was to stand. What we had not taken into account was that all the corridors were on an incline, and with a half-ton safe on a sack barrow, it took all our strength to hold it back. We were helped by a couple of guys who we thought were working there but were told later that they were inmates. They seemed quite normal and helpful, and when I mentioned this to one of the male nurses, he replied, "They have their days." It was a psychiatric hospital and closed its doors for the last time in 1993. It brought it all back to me recently when watching Jack Nicholson in *One Flew over the Cuckoo's Nest* and also that lovely film *Awakenings* starring Robin Williams and Robert De Niro.

Another job entailed delivering a one-ton safe to the Avon Tyre Co in Melksham, Wiltshire. We arrived there early afternoon and were told to site the safe in a very large office which was full of girls typing. A young lady came over and was asking us about various aspects of the safe, and as we had to spend the night in lodgings, I asked her what there was to do in the town. "Not a lot," came the reply. I said we were going to sort out somewhere to stay and asked whether I could meet her later for a meal and a drink. She agreed and we spent a pleasant evening together and then some time in the crew cab of our vehicle which was parked outside her house. Not the most romantic setting, but as they say, "It is not where you are, but who you are with." It's funny how a boring old journey can turn into a lovely evening. "Ships that pass in the night."

One morning, we had to take a small safe to a jewellers shop in Islington. When we wheeled it into the shop we saw jewellery and watches everywhere. The eyes of the other four lit up and everyone helped himself to an item or two. We obtained a signature for the safe and headed for an estate agent in Southend-On-Sea. As we drove away from the shop, one of the gang handed me a very nice watch and said, "This is for you!" I asked where it came from, and he explained from the last delivery where all that tom (tomfoolery, jewellery) was on show. I thought well, what is done is done, and put it in my pocket. We arrived in Southend and had just wheeled another small safe into the estate agents when one of the guys who worked there told us there were a couple of police officers outside, probably not happy about our parking on a roundabout. Before I could explain, one of the officers said, "We have had a complaint that there is a considerable amount of jewellery missing from a shop that you delivered to this morning." When I had confirmed the address, he said, "We would like you to accompany us to Southend Police Station where you will be searched, as well as your vehicle." This was bad news for me as I was still on bail and awaiting my committal date to appear in court. One police officer climbed in the cab of our vehicle with me, and the other officer climbed onto the back of the vehicle with the rest of the gang. The rear of our vehicle was full of ropes, heavy sacking and all sorts of equipment, so the perfect place to hide some of the missing items. We were travelling along a dual carriageway when the police officer sitting next to me told me to turn next right into the police station. Instead of turning on the indicator to turn right, I wound the window down and indicated the old way, by putting my arm out, and in my hand was the watch I had been given. I let go of the watch as we were turning so in the event of a spin (search), I would have nothing on me. An entirely different story on the back of our vehicle: they found all kinds of bits and pieces of jewellery that had been taken from the shop in Islington, so we were all banged up in a flowery (flowery dell, cell). Bobby was a good pal of mine, but the other two I was not very familiar with. The cell door opened and in came a CID officer to have a chat with us. He said, "Look, what we are prepared to do is this. There is no point in all four of you taking a nicking. Just give me one name to clear the book. In other words, only one of you needs to take the nicking. What do you think?" and he seemed to be directing this conversation to me. I asked if we could talk in the cell next door, and he agreed. I said, "Listen, pal, I am going to level with you. We are both men of the world, although on different sides of the fence. I am on bail and awaiting my committal date and I cannot afford to take another nicking while on bail. One of your officers searched me and found nothing whatsoever, so what am I to be charged with?" He pointed out that I was in charge of the vehicle so that made me responsible. He said, "The only chance you have is to convince one of the other three to hold their hand up," so we went back and I reiterated what he had said and asked each one of them to help me out. The guy with one eye folded up straight away and was about to burst into tears, Brian, the acting foreman for the day, was also totally gutless, and my pal Bobby steadfastly refused. I said, "I really need this help, Bobby. You can get me out of this. Look, you are going to be nicked anyway with all four of us and what is the point of that? You three have no past form and you, Bobby, are my pal. You have never even had a parking fine, and at most you will probably get a fine or a year's probation as it is your first offence. If it is a fine, I will pay it! And what is more, if this situation was reversed, I would do this for you." Try as I might, he would not do it for me and consequently all four of us were nicked. You find your true friends when your back is to the wall. I learnt a lesson here for sure: never work with part-time villains who revel in the notion but fold up when the going gets rough and are as nervous as a nun who has just found a man under her bed.

Dad came with me and waited in the court while I met with my solicitor and the barrister who was due to defend me. The barrister's advice was that if I pleaded not guilty and was found by the jury to be guilty, I would probably be looking at a four-year sentence, so it would be better to enter a guilty plea and receive an eighteen-month sentence. After the Judge had given me the customary pep talk about falling by the wayside after ten years or so and saying I should think about leading a more industrious life on my return to society, he weighed me off with the eighteen-month sentence I'd expected. I was never very impressed with the drip who was my defending brief. I think I would have been better represented by the Marx Brothers.

Roy Wild

CHAPTER 25

THEATRE OF THE ABSURD

After I was taken down to the cells, Dad came down to see me and we looked at each other through thick armoured glass. I could see the tears in his eyes, and I resolved never to see him cry again through my actions. I could only imagine when he returned home and Mum asked him how I got on, and how she must have cried, and Dad with his fine and exemplary Army Record, endorsed by his commanding officer.

It was late afternoon before I was put into a prison van and taken to the much-feared Wandsworth Prison, well-known for violence and strict discipline. I arrived there about 11 pm, changed into prison garb, which was an old blue/white shirt, shoes which were too big, an old pair of strides and a matching battle blouse, and taken to a cell. I was more than ready for a good sleep. The following morning at about 6.30am there was lots of noise, cell doors being unlocked and cons (convicts) doing what was known as slopping out. Unlike present day prisons which have a flushing toilet in their cell, there was no such thing then. In each cell there was a plastic pot that had to be used for urinating in. If you wanted to have a pony (crap) during the night you were supposed to ring the bell, and if the screw could be bothered he would let you out to use the recess – as it was called. If not you would be forced to use the pot and if you were banged up with three in a cell, you can imagine what it would be like for the other two guys who were subjected to these primitive conditions. I was assigned to the GPO shop again, dismantling old broken telephones. You could refuse labour if you wished, and quite a few refused to be subjected to this soul-destroying procedure, but it meant that you were banged up twenty-three hours a day in your cell.

Most of the screws were picked for their toughness and sadistic tendencies, but I got talking to one who was half friendly. He asked me what I did on the outside, and when I mentioned that at one time I had been a supervisor for a cleaning company in Hatton Garden, he said there was a position going for a cleaner and food orderly as one of the food orderlies had been transferred to another prison. If I wanted the job, it was mine! This was a godsend. The job entailed being unlocked at about 6 am and taken to the kitchens where all the food was cooked and brought to a very large stainless steel hot plate, ready for the cons who were about to line up for breakfast. There was a large pile of stainless steel trays with various compartments in them, one for dinner, one for porridge and one for pudding. The porridge was known as third-degree pig food, but you had to accept what was put on your tray. If a guy was hungry, he would do an Oliver Twist and ask for more. You could only oblige him if the screw was looking the other way.

This job was El Dorado compared to the GPO shop and the mailbag shop. I knew I had to work the system to get the best from it, keep a clean nose and get out as soon as possible, with no loss of remission or, better still, jam roll (parole). In between food times, we would sweep and mop the wing and generally skive. Our regular officer was known as Cookie (Mr Cook) and was quite a decent guy. He would tell us, "As long as you show willing to do a bit of work, you will not have me on your back! If you want to congregate in one of your cells for a smoke or cup of tea, you will get no problems from me." Sometimes he would walk into one of our cells where we had all gathered and have a chat about various topics. We all showed him respect, and in return he treated us like human beings, unlike most of the other screws who were always on a power trip. When Cookie was transferred to another prison, Mr Holdsworth took his place. He lined us all up around the hotplate and said, "Right you lot! Like it or not, I have been humped up with you, and there are going to be some changes made around here! Any man not doing his job will answer to me! I will in no way tolerate insubordination and anybody found to be flouting the rules will be put on a charge." And I was the first one to incur his wrath and be put on said charge. One day when hotshot Holdsworth was in another part of the nick, another very fair officer by the name of Mr Denton said my hair was a bit long and told me to get it trimmed by the barber on A Wing.

"Leave off Mr Denton, I have a visit this weekend from my parents."

He said, in a good-natured manner, "Go and get your hair cut."

I asked him if he was going over to A wing and if so could he escort me over there and then a I could get a blue band to bring me back (a blue or red band was a trustee prisoner and could wander around the prison unaided, also escorting other prisoners about the prison that would normally be out of bounds). He agreed to accompany me over to the other side of the prison and after, as stated, a blue band returned me to my wing.

When I returned, waiting for me was Holdsworth and his first words were: "Get your gear together, you're nicked!" That meant putting all your belongings into your empty pillowcase, rolling up your mattress (which was about as thick as a slice of bread), tying it up with a piece of string, hoisting it over your shoulder and being escorted down to C Wing. The officer in charge of the block asked Holdsworth what the charge was. He replied, "Being off of his place of employment without permission." No way was I going to tell this idiot what had happened. All would be revealed when I had an adjudication in front of the Governor the following morning. This is what took place! Two officers escorted me to his office and knocked on the door.

A gruff voice said, "Enter!"

"Right, Wild! Left right, left right, stand on the mat in front of the Governor and state your name and number."

There was an officer standing facing me and another one just behind, ready to grab me, as in the past many a governor had been pulled across his desk and assaulted by a violent con.

"Right, Wild, Mr Holdsworth has brought a charge against you for being off your place of employment without permission. What have you got to say with regard to that?"

"First of all, in answer to your question, Governor, and contrary to Mr Holdsworth's version of events, I had gained permission to be off my place of employment."

"You did? How so?"

"I was ordered by one of your officers to get my hair cut over on A Wing and was escorted over there by the same officer."

"Who was the officer who escorted you over to A Wing?"

"Mr Denton. And if I had refused him, I would have been facing another charge, one of disobeying an order."

"Did you make Mr Holdsworth aware of these facts?"

"No, Governor, he never asked me. He just told me to get my belongings together and said I was nicked. I find myself in front of you for obeying an order by Mr Denton."

By this time he was looking perplexed and pretending to read the charge sheet. Finally, he said, "OK, Wild, just consider this as a caution."

It was on my lips to say, "With respect, Governor, am I right in thinking a caution is only administered when one has done something wrong? At this moment, I cannot think of what that wrong could possibly be! I think that your findings should be omitted from my prison record," but I thought, "Leave it as it is. You have thus far beaten this piece of shit known as Holdsworth and he will probably have a strip torn off of him by the Governor." I was escorted back to H Wing by Holdsworth in stony silence. One up to the rebels! This kind of scenario would be repeated throughout the rest of the sentence and I never lost once! Considering the various altercations I had over ridiculous allegations by other prison officers, I think I missed my calling. I should have taken up the legal profession – who knows, in another life, I might have been a barrister.

The following morning after breakfast, our kitchen gang were called together by Holdsworth, and I soon realised that this was tail-between-the-legs time for him. He began by saying, "We got off to a bad start," and I said, "No, you got off to a bad start with your attitude on the first morning." He gave ground at that and said, "OK, let's work together," and in the coming months it was hard to believe it was the same man. Everything started to flow as sweet as a trickling stream.

One afternoon I was told there had been a request from the prison psychologist to see me in her office the following day at 2 pm. I was ushered to a chair and addressed as Roy, as opposed to Wild, and she asked me how I was adapting to prison life. Did I have any problems that I wanted to speak about pertaining to my incarceration or anything that extended to my private and home life outside? I told her that I had no problems of any kind except my loss of liberty. She said, "How do you feel about that?"

I replied, "You break the rules, you pay the price!"

"Would you break the rules again?"

"Of course not. This has been an awakening for me, and I feel total remorse." "Remorse for getting caught or remorse for the reason you are in here?"

"For the latter. I feel genuine remorse for the life I have been leading and for what I have done and I know this is not my true course. I am capable of better things!"

I knew where this was going and cute enough to know I was being assessed for future jam roll (parole) consideration, so I said all the things she was looking for and wanted to hear.

She was about thirty years of age and very attractive. Her office was on the Two's, and to get there she had to mount a spiral staircase wearing a rather short mini skirt, with a pair of legs that would have put Betty Grable to shame. If you think that was not torture to a load of cons down below watching her mount those stairs, you have another think coming. Guys would stop scrubbing floors, others would pause in their sweeping and lean on their brooms and even the screw on the wing would have an eyeful, then suddenly remember his position, and yell out, "OK, all back to work! She was fully aware of what she was doing!

On one occasion, I was escorted by a Red Band (a trusted prisoner who could wander about the prison unaccompanied) over to the main prison to pick up some cleaning supplies and had to pass through a workshop where the Category A men were working. Cat A men have yellow patches sewn onto the front of their trousers and coats and are classed as violent, as well as having a tendency to try and escape. Suddenly I heard "Roy" shouted out, and there standing up and waving at me was Danny, the same Danny who used to give me all the work from the nightclubs in the West End. He gestured towards the toilet, and I said to the Red Band that I needed to go to the toilet. If this had been a prison officer, no way would he have allowed me to even talk to a Cat A man, but he said, "Hurry up then, Roy." In the toilet, Danny and I embraced and he explained how he had got there. An up-market gambling club in Knightsbridge had a very select clientele, including some wealthy Arabs. Danny and his pal went in there in the early morning, each wearing a thermos flask (mask) and doved up (gloved up), and stuck up the gambling punters with a sawn-off SG. They cleared all the money off the tables and relieved the Arabs of all their expensive watches and gold chains. To show they meant business, Danny let one go into the ceiling, which brought down some of the plaster and a chandelier, then they scarpered with the loot. A couple of weeks later they got a capture, and because Danny had discharged a firearm, they got an extra three years; otherwise, they would have walked away with a neves (seven backwards). He asked me whether I had access to any sugar, tea or toothpaste, and I said I would try to get a Red Band to bring me over again as soon as I had what he needed. Just then the Red Band put his head in the door and said, "Time to go." He was worried that if I had been caught speaking with a Cat A man, he would be stripped of his Red Band. I secured for Danny what he had asked for and then found out he had been moved to a high-security prison up north somewhere. I never saw Danny again.

Another guy I hooked up with was Steve Delaney, an old-school safe blower, who would regale me with tales of some of the jobs he had done in different parts of the world. He had done time in McNeil Island Penitentiary in Washington, as well as Leavenworth Penitentiary in Kansas. He was the one who told me how to blow a safe with a condom and a mattress. The keyhole in the door of the safe would be fed with a condom pushed in until there was just the rubber ring showing. Steve would push plastic explosive into the condom until it dropped down inside the door with the ring still showing. Into that would be inserted a detonator, which was wired up to a light switch or hanging light. If there was a mattress on hand, or a thick carpet, that would be used to deaden the pop when it went, and a couple of buckets of water would be added. If the peterman (safe blower) knew his craft, he would throw the switch, there would be a small audible pop and the safe door would be open. It didn't always work as easy as that. Sometimes, the pop would damage the AED (anti-explosive device) inside the door and all the bolts in the door would be ejected into the main body of the safe, making it almost impossible to open. In the job in Hackney, when the jeweller's safe was blown up onto the floor above, we had to supply a safe technician to open it. It was very interesting watching him as he drilled a hole in the door, put thin metal feelers in and clicked it open.

Finally, I received the date to appear at King's Cross Magistrate's Court to face the other charge concerning the missing jewellery in Islington. I was escorted by two prison officers, and the CID officer from Southend was in attendance, as well as the uniformed P.C. who had ridden in the vehicle with me. The other three were also there: Brian, One Eye and Bobby, who was the only one represented legally. When the officers, Brian and One Eye had taken the stand, individually, the solicitor acting for Bobby spoke on his behalf, as he had been instructed. He swore my life away, said I was the mastermind and had suggested we steal a considerable amount of the jewellery and hide it on the back of my vehicle until we could have a divvy up. I listened to this incredulously; nothing was further from the truth. Bobby, the scumbag, had well and truly put me in it. The other two had pleaded not guilty and knew nothing about it. Finally, it was my time to take the stand. At this point, the magistrate is not supposed to be privy to the fact that I was already serving a sentence in Wandsworth and should not be biased or let it cloud his judgement. Who did he think the two prison officers were who had escorted me to the court – a couple of kissagrams?

He turned to me in the dock and said, "This is a very serious matter and I have studied it in some detail. There is no doubt in my mind that you were the ringleader and instigator of the venture in question. Have you anything to say?"

"All that has been said by the legal representative of Mr X (Bobby) is complete and utter fabrication. I was hoping you would have seen that, but by your recent remarks, obviously not."

"We do not need any more barrack-room lawyers in this court. I am awarding you a six-month sentence..." I thought, "I can handle that," when he dropped the bombshell: "which shall run consecutively." That meant he must have known I was already serving a sentence! It also meant it was in addition to the eighteen months I was still serving. There were gasps of amazement from some of my old pals who had attended and very detrimental remarks directed at the magistrate. Magistrates have a very limited knowledge of the law, and that's why they are often seen leaning over to confer with the Recorder or the Clerk of the Court to take instruction. At this point, Bobby would not look at me as I was taken downstairs to await the ride back to Wandsworth.

I arrived back with a few new internees, one of whom started a conversation with me. He told me his sentence was four years, as he and a couple of mates had some altercation with three police officers and in the fight one of the officers was kicked in the face and lost an eye. I was taken back to H Wing in time for tea and was glad to see the chaps had congregated around the hotplate to await my news. When I told them the six additional months were given consecutively as opposed to concurrently, they could not believe it. Even Holdsworth showed some surprise.

After a meal, the trays had to be collected and washed clean. Clean meant? A galvanised dustbin was filled up with hot water and the trays washed in what would become very dirty, greasy water after fifty or sixty trays containing all kinds of left-overs. No washing-up liquid in the nick to make things easier; that was not what we were in there for! I once heard a screw summing it up perfectly: "We do not ask you to come in here; you are here of your own volition. If you can't do the time, don't do the crime. You are in here for punishment for the crime you committed." I felt I had to put my whack in and said, "I agree with everything you have said so far except with regard to 'You are in here for punishment.' We are not here for punishment, we are in here 'as' punishment, the punishment being the loss of our liberty," and he agreed.

A week or so later, I was sitting alone in my peter with the door open when two big guys walked into the cell and said, "When you came through reception last week, you were talking to a new guy." I said, "Yes, I remember him." "What did he tell you he was in for?" they asked. When I told them, they said that was a load of crap. He was a nonce case and had been caught interfering with a young child. They had found this out from a pal who cleaned the Principal Officer's office and had access to records of new internees. A week later, the nonce case slipped on a bar of soap in the bathhouse and fell into a bath of scalding water. Well, that was the explanation given. After spending some time in hospital, he was put on Rule 43, which is when guys are isolated from other cons for their own safety, but they still get hurt when a screw deliberately looks the other way. After all, screws have children as well.

Another food orderly in our crew told me the following interesting story. His cousin was a bellman, which, in villain's parlance, is someone who can turn off an alarm in a building so that another person can make an easy entry. The bellman is shown the premises in question and erects a small red-and-white striped tent outside on the pavement, the type one usually sees when a telephone engineer is trying to locate a fault on the telephone wiring that is below ground. Access is gained through a cover that lies flat on the pavement, and because this is a usual sight, nobody ever takes any notice. The bell system alarm is turned off, and access is gained during the early hours of the morning.

The property of interest was a private flat in a very affluent area of London. Once the bellman had turned off the screamer (alarm), he left and the two faces proceeded to look for items of high value. They found a substantial amount of jewellery, which they deposited in a pillowcase from the bedroom, as well as a large bundle of letters secured by a red ribbon, which, out of curiosity, they also put into the pillowcase before leaving the premises. When they inspected the night's work, they found the bundle of letters were love letters from a female member of the royal family to the lady owner of the flat. The two chaps realised they had hit gold and considered selling these to a newspaper but were told no British paper would dare touch them. A German or American paper, however, would pay a fortune for the letters. Unfortunately, the bellman had left a thumbprint on the front door that was picked up by the police and run through the system. Because he had some past form, he was traced and arrested; he was promised a long spell of incarceration if he did not oblige with the names of the two guys who had the jewellery and letters. By this time, the Special Branch were involved, so more threats to the bellman who finally stuck up the names of the two faces in question. One of them was arrested a few days later, but the other had gone to ground and then absconded abroad. The officer told the face they had no interest in the jewellery that he'd taken but they had to have the letters back! The face said he was willing to do a deal, which was having his entire police record wiped clean. The officer reported his demands to his governor, and needless to say, those demands were met. He kept all the jewellery and cash, which was probably covered by the insurance company, and except for the police involvement, the whole escapade had turned into something quite rewarding.

The news of my return from the magistrate's court carrying an extra six months soon went around H Wing. A guy that I had spoken to a few times came into my peter and had a chat over a cup of tea, and I related what had happened and how Bobby had sworn my life away. He was a very powerful-looking guy known as Dave, who shared a cell with two other guys as he had suicidal tendencies and could not be in a cell by himself. I never had reason to believe he was anything other than normal; he always seemed very rational. He said to me one day, "I have just received my EDR (earliest date of release) so before I leave, give me the name and address of this guy Bobby, and when you get out, he will be in a wheelchair permanently. I had no reason to doubt his word. Most cons usually gave this guy a wide berth; he seemed strong on loyalty and would come down extra hard on anyone committing the cardinal sin of grassing on somebody in or out of the boob (prison). That doesn't apply to something like child or animal abuse; I would be the first one to inform any authority if I knew that was happening. I thanked Dave and said, "That's OK. It will be taken care of by the people I know."

I would, at this point, like to give thanks to the people who ran the nick magazine, *Better Times*. The editor was a friend of mine, Neville, who was a convicted bank manager, probably caught with his hand in the till. I was always amazed at the wealth of talent that was available in the boob. There were cartoonists and columnists who would collect interesting stories from around the nick, and the magazine would be published and distributed monthly throughout the prison. Somebody even had a poem published in the magazine. I would love to have the whole of that poem; it really struck a chord in me! I can only remember the first few lines: "Can you hear a vision, can you see a sound? Can a truth pertain to lying, can a square be round?" and the last line was, "If you find the answer, my friend, is in the affirmative, you have the greatest gift, the gift of peace of mind." There was so much in between that I have forgotten. I wish I had kept my copy of *Better Times* and had it put in my property for safekeeping.

One of our kitchen staff requested permission for his parents to send him his paints, paper and easel so he could work on his painting skills with a view to being employed as a landscape painter and cartoonist after his release. Our gang would occasionally pop into his cell and view his latest offering, which was quite good. One day while we were watching him work, an elderly guy, who had recently been weighed off by the court, joined us.

He said, "I occasionally paint," and the other painter said, "Would you like to paint something, if it doesn't take too long?" "Yes, I'll have a go," came the reply. A new sheet of paper was fixed to the easel, and in less than ten minutes, he created a forest glade with the sun shining down through deciduous trees. We watched all of this totally transfixed; this was food for the soul. "I'll have a go," indeed! Amid slaps on the back and handshakes, I said to him, "You could put this in a frame and put 'Constable' in the bottom corner and no one would know the difference!" Before anybody else got in, I asked whether I could have the painting, and he said, "Of course, take it!" When it had dried, he signed it and rolled it up, and I applied to have it put in my property. It went to Eastchurch with me and then home when I was released, and for many years it remained rolled up in the loft. I wish now I had put it in a frame because during the many house moves I have had, it was lost. It makes me sad to have stood in the face of greatness and then lost the painting.

I was called into the PO's office and told that the following week I would be transferred to Eastchurch Open Prison on the Isle of Sheppey. The PO was a decent man who had been transferred himself from Winchester Prison; he was a guy you could talk to and who would acknowledge you if passing by. He said to me, "You have been selected for Eastchurch, which is a privilege and nothing like a closed prison such as Wandsworth. Don't get involved in anything to jeopardize your stay there." I thanked him for his words of wisdom and knew I would abide by them.

CHAPTER 26

BUTLINS AGAIN

Early one morning, I left Wandsworth accompanied by two prison officers. They were quite chatty and amicable, and we stopped for a cup of tea in a roadside cafe. When we arrived at Eastchurch, the red-and-white striped barrier was lifted, the two officers introduced themselves and in we went. There were cons strolling about everywhere, much the same as I had seen it on my last visit ten years or so before, and I thought, "I like the look of this!" The two escorting officers shook my hand as they left and said, "Don't forget to behave yourself."

I was taken to reception, kitted out in prison clothing and taken to hut eighteen. Eastchurch had been an airfield in the last war, and the huts had been used by the young airmen who piloted the Spitfires and Hurricanes in the Battle of Britain, to whom we all owe so much. Each hut housed eighteen cons, nine down each side, with a large wood-burning pot-bellied stove in the middle. After the usual introductions and chat, I soon settled in. The following morning, I was assigned to the Farm party again, picking potatoes, spring onions, carrots and other vegetables, collecting the swill from the kitchens for the piggery and clearing out the deep litter from the chicken houses with a shovel and wheelbarrow. This would not be allowed today as there is some evidence that the dust that accumulates from chicken droppings is related to bronchial trouble in humans. Health and Safety would have a fit if they witnessed what we had to do in that very dusty environment.

Here is an incident that took us all by surprise. One sunny day, one of the guys in our party, also named Roy, told us on our smoke break in the middle of a large field that he held a pilot's licence. You hear so much bull s**t from some of the cons, what they have got outside and what they are going to do when they get out, and at the end of their sentence, they leave wearing an old donkey jacket with WIMPEY on the back. So much for high flyers! Anyway, Roy told us that at 3 pm, which was our next smoke break, his fiancée was going to fly over the prison in his plane and tip the wings to say hello. We all looked at each other, enough to say, Yeah, right… but at 3 pm, as we settled down to have our smoke break, there came the drone of an aircraft. We all looked up, including Roy, and started to wave, and sure enough, I'm damned if the wings didn't tip up and down. Time to apologise, methinks! Roy never spoke about what he did for a living, but in a quiet moment when our hut was empty, he told me he was also a bellman, will wonders ever cease. And solely for the uninitiated, the name of the construction firm WIMPEY, I am told, stands for "We Intend Making Profit Each Year" or "We Import More Paddies Each Year".

After a couple of months on the Farm party, I had had enough and put in for a change of labour. I was assigned to the Garden party. There were about twenty of us in the group, and the officer in charge was a Mr Lomas, a young ginger-headed screw, who was a nice guy and put up with a lot from the piss-takers in our crew. When we were marching down the avenue to do some digging or weeding, we would march in formation, two abreast in a long line, with Mr Lomas at the head. Someone from the back would shout out, "Mr Lomas!" Lomas would say, "Garden Party, Garden Party, Garden Party, 'Shun! (Attention)." It would have been easier to just say Halt! Then he would walk down the line and ask, "OK, who called out?" Somebody would say, "What do you mean, Mr Lomas?" "What do I mean?" said Lomas. "Somebody called my name." One of the cons would turn to his mate and say, "Did you hear anybody call out Mr Lomas's name?" "Not me," came the reply, blank faces all around, every one a piss taker. We would carry on marching and it would all start again, with Lomas about to tear his ginger hair out. Finally, he just ignored it when his name was called, all good fun.

Every morning after breakfast, we had to make our beds and tidy our lockers. At 8 am, the hut officer did his inspection and the hut gained points that were reckoned up at the end of the week. The best and tidiest hut won some tobacco provided by the prison. One morning, Mr Lomas came to inspect our hut and stopped at my bed. He said, "That all looks very nice, Wild." Then he put his hand in his pocket and pulled out a shilling piece. "I am going to flip this up in the air, and when it lands on the blanket, I expect it to bounce high enough for me to catch it. That tells me that you have really pulled the sheets and blankets tight."

"Leave off, Mr Lomas," I said. "It all looks very nice."

"That is how a soldier has to do it!"

"If I want to be a soldier, I'll join the Army," said I.

He flipped the coin and it didn't bounce high enough for him to catch it. "Come now, Wild," he said with a smirk on his face, "you can do better than that," and strolled out.

I just mentioned tobacco a moment ago, which brings me to an interesting observation. Each con was responsible for sweeping and cleaning the space to the left of his bed, and on the floor between every bed was a coconut mat. I have seen these mats, over time, get smaller and smaller as they were pulled apart and the threads rolled up in a cigarette paper and smoked by those who could not do without a cigarette.

I teamed up with Dennis, a guy from Ilford, and both being Londoners, we intended to stick together in our work and attended the films that were put on in the camp every weekend. Dennis and I were approached one morning by Mr Lomas, who asked us whether we would be interested in looking after the church gardens for the vicar. I said we would pop over and see him and find out exactly what was involved. Lomas said it would be better if we attended the service on Sunday morning as he was always dashing about here and there, but on Sunday he was always in attendance. The church was C of E and one of the modern types of churches, so on Sunday morning we sought out the vicar, who was a very young guy by the name of Bryan Dobbs. We introduced ourselves and arranged to speak to him after the service. After the congregation had all left, he took us into the vicarage and told us what he wanted done. It amounted to keeping the church grounds clear of fallen leaves, planting some flowers that the vicar would buy and bring into the church and generally keeping the place looking decent. We agreed straight away, and on Monday morning Mr Lomas dropped us off on his way to the other side of the camp. We couldn't believe we had fallen into this blinding job. We'd started to clean up the grounds when the vicar made an appearance and invited us to go into the church for a cup of tea when the smoke break siren went off, which we did. In a small side room, he made the tea and passed round a biscuit tin, and we all sat down. He asked us about ourselves and our family life, and then he told us why he'd joined the church and trained to be a vicar. He asked us whether we would like to attend the church service every Sunday morning, and we thought it might be folly to blank him and spoil a good thing. I said we would attend and jokingly said, "With a proviso!" "What is that?" he asked and I replied, "That now and again we sing my two favourite hymns, 'There's an Old Rugged Cross' and 'Nearer My God To Thee'." He looked at me, astonished. "You are familiar with these two? One of them is my favourite! Maybe you could read the sermon sometimes on a Sunday morning!" I thought, "Steady, Vicar," but I did just that a couple of weeks later. After finishing our work on our first day, I remarked, "You know, Dennis, I think there really is a God above." On another day, when we were making a cup of tea and helping ourselves to the biscuits, I opened a small cupboard and there stood beside a silver chalice a half bottle of sacramental wine that was used during Holy Communion. I said to Dennis, "Why don't we drink a toast to our luck in being given this job?" So we poured out a decent measure each and toasted our good fortune. They say God moves in mysterious circles! But there were dark clouds gathering on the horizon about to descend on us in the shape of a certain P.O. May.

One morning at smoke break, we entered the church, put the kettle on and settled down to enjoy a cup of tea and biscuits. Suddenly we heard heavy footsteps coming our way. Into our small room stepped Principal Officer May, who was a bit of a tyrant. He took one look at the two of us and roared, "What the bloody hell do you two think you are doing?" Before we could explain, we were told, "Get your gear together. You're nicked." Like Holdsworth, he believed in shoot first and asked questions afterwards. We looked at each other as if this idiot had lost his mind. We headed back to our hut, collected our personal items and made our way up to the "block" where he was waiting for us. He banged us up in one of the cells and told us we would be on Governor's Adjudication in the morning to explain ourselves. We were due to appear in front of the Governor at 10 am, and just after 9.30 am I looked out of the small window and saw one of the guys we worked with hoeing some flower beds adjacent to the cells. I asked him to run down to the church and tell the vicar that we had been nicked and were waiting to see the Governor at 10 am. Within minutes, we saw the vicar hoisting up his cassock as he made his way, at a run, up to where we were. I said to Dennis, "Let me do the talking when we get in the Governor's office!" It was the same procedure as before, except we were joined by the vicar.

"May I ask what the charge is against these two people?" asked the Governor. "They were off their place of work," piped up May," and were helping themselves to various unauthorised refreshments and biscuits that belonged to the church!"

"It may interest you to know," said Brian the Vicar, "that I gave my full permission for these gentlemen to make themselves a cup of tea, and I put a tin of biscuits at their disposal, but only at smoke break, 10 am and 3 pm. This I did due to the excellent work they have been carrying out. They have totally transformed the facade of the church, which is a credit to both of them." We listened totally enthralled. The Governor directed his questions at us and said, "Did either of you make P.O. May aware of this?"

I replied, "In all truth and with respect, Governor, Mr May was not at all cogent in his approach. He never gave us the time or chance. If he had, we would have been only too pleased to, but it was a case of 'you're nicked – get yourselves up to the block.' And if we could have explained to Mr May, it would have saved us having to spend the night in the cells awaiting your good judgement." Did I know how to shovel the bullshit to him or what?

Now comes the summation and the verdict. The Governor, scratching his head: "There appear to be cross purposes and words, and I am awarding you both a caution and would advise you to accept it at that!"

A caution again! What did we do wrong? Everything we did was with permission. He would never show up one of his officers in front of us; hopefully he had a word with Mr May, when we were out of earshot, regarding his over-zealous attitude. I had seen the Governor out and about in the camp and he didn't seem a bad guy; he would always acknowledge us. He was ex-Military and had been a tank commander, and his face was quite disfigured from some conflict abroad. He was known as "Bread and Water Brown" and had probably been in charge of a closed nick, maybe high-security, and used to giving prisoners who came before him bread and water as punishment, which, at one time, was quite prevalent in closed prisons.

Dennis said to me on our way back, "You were terrific! You should have been a brief." I replied, "That P.O. should have had a word first with a certain Mr Holdsworth of Wandsworth Nick before he took me on."

There were various classes one could attend if one wanted to further one's education or just for something to do. One of the classes taught the playing of musical instruments, and a friend of mine in the camp who attended the music class told me of an incident that occurred early one evening. It makes you wonder what could possibly go wrong in music lessons. A guy in the throes of learning the guitar was just sitting there strumming, and another guy who was learning the trumpet came up behind him and blew the trumpet loudly in his ear. He turned round in a terrible rage and with the flat of his hand struck the bottom of the trumpet mouthpiece, which was still in the guy's mouth, knocked out two front teeth and split one of his lips. He was taken straight to the camp hospital where the lip was stitched, and the following day he was taken to a dentist in Sheerness to have his mouth inspected for damage and no doubt two false teeth. On a lighter note, still outside the hut where music was taught, I saw one of the officers shout out to a group of guys tending some flowers, "Anybody know anything about music?" Three or four hands shot up in the air. "Right," said the officer, "you three! Help me move this piano!" Boom, boom! They didn't obey the cardinal rule: never volunteer for anything in the nick.

There were two sports officers on the camp who were like nut and bolt. Mr Payne you could talk to, a good family man who would tell me about his children and other aspects of family life, a tall rangy type of guy, as opposed to his colleague, Mr Able, short and squat, who accosted me one day to enquire where I was off to.

"To the church," said I. "Is there anything else?"

"Haven't you forgotten something?"

"Not that I can think of!"

"You should address me as Sir."

I was close to exploding. "If you can tell me where you were knighted and for what reason, I will be only too pleased to do as you ask!"

"It is common courtesy to address me as Sir."

"Doesn't courtesy work both ways then?" I shot back. "You address me by my surname, as you do, and I, with respect, will address you as Mr Able." Game shot!

He toddled off muttering to himself. A far cry from the likes of Mr Lomas, who never stood on ceremony and just did his job, tempered with tact and common sense.

A funny incident occurred concerning Mr Lomas. He had strolled into our hut for no particular reason, with the guys just lounging about smoking and chatting, when the conversation turned to football. As various teams were being discussed, a difference of opinion broke out between one of us and Mr Lomas, who was from the West Country and had the lilt, too. He suggested that the guy he was talking to did not know much about football.

The guy said, "If I called you a brainless idiot who knows fuck all about football, you would nick me for insubordination, wouldn't you?"

"Yes, I would."

"But if I only thought you were a brainless idiot who knows fuck all about football, you couldn't, could you? If I only thought it?"

"No, I couldn't if you only thought it!"

"Well, I think you're a brainless idiot who knows fuck all about football!"

We all rolled up, as did Mr Lomas, who took it all in good part.

Mr Payne made me aware that there would be a job available in a couple of weeks' time in the sports hut, which would entail looking after and cleaning football boots after an inter-prison football match, as well as other duties such as marking out the white lines on the football pitch and tennis courts, which were out of bounds for anyone except the prison officers and their wives and families, and putting dubbin on the football, which, in those days, was leather with an inner tube that had to be pumped up. One weekend, the two PT officers arranged an inter-hut sports day, including an obstacle race. One of the obstacles was a large tarpaulin, secured to the ground at each corner with a peg that the participants had to crawl under. Dennis and I, the day before the race, thought it would liven things up if we got a load of sawdust, ashes from the stoves in each hut and some black oil from the metal recovery shop, mixed it all up and spread it on the ground and then secured the tarpaulin over the top. The games finally started, with all the cons cheering on the competitors from their own hut. When it came to the obstacle race, about ten of the runners were crawling under the tarpaulin and we could hear muffled swearing and hooting. When they emerged from the other end, they looked like something from the Black & White Minstrel Show. The stragglers following up had no idea what was going on, and they also crawled under the sheet, only to emerge to shrieks of laughter from the watching crowd that included many officers' wives and their children.

One lovely sunny day, I was on the football field marking out the white lines when I needed to go to the toilet, which was a considerable walk away. I decided to use the ditch that ran along the far side of the pitch, so kneeling down, I did a hit & miss (and you know what rhymes with that!). Suddenly a loud shout I heard: "What do you think you are doing?" and running towards me was one of the prison officers. I never knew the name of this officer, but his sobriquet was Mickey Mouse. He was a little weasel of a guy who looked like Herr Flick in the TV programme *'Allo 'Allo!*

All out of breath, he said, "Get your gear, you're nicked!" I asked him what the charge was, and he said, "I believe you were in that ditch to collect some contraband that has been left there." I looked at him as if he was mad and told him as much. The following morning, left right, left right, stand in front of the governor, give your name and number, and I thought, "This is becoming a bit monotonous." In the funereal atmosphere of the adjudication room, Mickey Mouse gave his evidence.

"Well, Wild," opened the Governor, "you have a charge levelled against you that you were on the far side of the football field about to retrieve some contraband that had been left there. What have you got to say in evidence against this charge?"

"Well, Governor, this is a totally unjust charge levelled against me and has created a schism between myself and your officer, who is trying to put me in an inimical position. I have too much respect for your officer to call him a liar, but at this point, I would remind him, as well as your good self, of the phrase 'terminological inexactitude'." Two blank stares! "The charge against me is totally unsupported by any evidence. As you are probably aware, my duties consist of being in charge of the sports hut and working alongside the Sports Officer, Mr Payne. At his instruction, I was marking out the white lines on the football pitch in readiness for the upcoming inter-prison football match this weekend, and I was taken short and needed to pass water. Bearing in mind it is a long walk to the nearest ablutions, I thought if I knelt down so as to not offend any of the officers' wives and families, whose houses are quite close to the camp, it would be alright, and that is what I did. I had no intention other than to relieve myself at a critical moment. And may I ask, at this point, whether any unauthorised items of contraband were found in the ditch?"

The Governor, looking at the weasel and raising one eyebrow: "Did you search and discover any contraband in the ditch?"

"Err, no."

"OK, Wild, take this as a caution and get back to work."

"Thank you, Governor, for a very professional investigation."

They both knew I was taking the piss. At that moment, the score stood at Roy 3 Screws 0 and parole report still intact!

Snow and cold winds came bursting in, heralding that winter was upon us, but it was lovely and warm in the sports hut, with the big pot-bellied stove roaring away and jacket potatoes cooking with some butter pats I was given by a pal who worked in the kitchens. In one corner of the sports hut was a small room with a lock for which only Mr Payne and Mr Able had the key. We all, at some time, want to know what is behind a locked door, don't we? So, with a small, thin piece of plastic inserted into the lock was, I loided the door open. Inside was a lot of sports equipment: new football boots in boxes and quite a few leather pump-up footballs which, when deflated, lie flat. Years ago, a door could be opened using a thin piece of celluloid as in a credit card, inserting it in between the striker plate and the brass tongue and giving it a slight push, so that's where the term "loid" comes from. I knew as soon as I looked at the lock I could have opened it with an ice cream cone.

One morning, while I was sitting in the sports hut toasting two pieces of bread, with the snow falling thick and fast outside, the door suddenly opened and in came an officer covered in snow, about two inches thick on his hat. I had seen this guy about the camp but had never had any occasion to speak to him. First words from me: "Cold out there, isn't it, Guv?"

"Freezing," he said. "What are you up to?"

"I'm just about to start dubbining some football boots and making a cup of tea," which I was really not allowed to do between smoke breaks. My reasoning was along the lines of, if those that work in the kitchens can have a cup of tea any time of the day, so can I, so I say to him, "It's no time to be outside in this weather. Would you like a cup of tea?"

"If there is one available, sure."

So he and I sat round the hot stove and started chatting.

"Who do you support in football?" he asked.

"I'm a Londoner and have supported Arsenal, like my father, all my life."

He told me he managed a children's team in a nearby town in Kent. A short while later, he stood up to leave and thanked me for the tea. I said, "Anytime you're passing, pop in. I'm always here." Lying in bed that night, I thought of what had transpired and the germ of an idea came to mind.

The following week, he turned up nearly every morning, cold and covered in snow. By now, it was a cup of tea and a piece of toast. I turned the conversation around to the team he coached.

"Are you funded by the local authority for the strip the boys wear and the boots and balls?"

"No, of course not. We rely on the parents helping out, fundraising and raffles."

"Must be hard at times," I said, and he smiled ruefully and agreed.

"Well, I had better make a move."

"No peace for the wicked," I remarked.

"That's about right," he said, pulling on his greatcoat.

And now it was shit or bust time! Make or break! I pulled out of a bag three brand new deflated leather footballs and said, "These are for you and the boys of the team." He looked at them and said, "Where did you get these?"

I replied, "It doesn't matter. Put them under your coat."

He looked at me and I thought he could have reported me, put me on a charge, trying to bribe a prison officer, and I would have lost the job and possibly returned to another closed prison, but I thought I had groomed him well and over a period I knew who I was dealing with. He looked at me and smiled and said, "Thank you very much. I owe you!"

I said, "Not at all. Your company is enough," but I knew what I wanted.

The following morning he turned up and said over a cup of tea, "What can I do for you? Do you want some tobacco or something?"

"No, of course not. I got those items for you and the team. There is no payment expected, but I am being considered for jam roll..."

"What is that?"

I laughed and said, "It is slang for parole, and if you could give me a decent report, that would be more than payment. I need three good reports to be in with a chance." "Consider it done," and we shook hands.

I had one from the bird in Wandsworth, the psychologist in the mini skirt, one from Brian Dobbs, the sky pilot (vicar), and now a good report from this officer, making three, and in the fullness of time, with a fair wind and a little luck, I would be heading for pastures new.

Christmas was approaching and a show was being arranged in the large dining hall. The prison authorities paid for a professional show business couple to take part, a guy and his wife with a few songs and a bit of magic, and the word was put out for any of the cons who had any talent in singing or anything else that would entertain. A few of the cons were kept busy knocking up a makeshift stage with long hanging curtains by kind courtesy of some of the officers' wives. They also asked whether anybody knew the words of "There's No Business like Show Business" to sing in the grand finale. Out of six hundred cons in the camp, only one knew the words: me! It was a fitting song made famous by the American show business legend Ethel Merman. I had to write the words on a piece of paper and one of the officers' wives typed them out to be given to the stage performers for the end of the show. My job, with another guy, was standing behind the long curtains and opening and closing them in between each act. Finally the show came to an end and all the performers sang that famous song to loud clapping and cheers. It was such a lovely feel-good experience on that cold Christmas night and made you forget just where you were. The following day we all had our Christmas dinner that was traditionally served by the prison officers.

Dennis had now been released, and I had hooked up again with Lenny Hamilton, as well as my old pal from Hoxton, Brian Sculley. Lenny, Brian and I were always together and were sitting outside my hut one day when an officer approached us and told Lenny he had a police visit. Should you have a police visit, it is your right to refuse the visit as the police have no jurisdiction inside a prison, but if they want to see you for something like an extra charge, you can still refuse but it is pointless because when you receive your EDR, the police will be waiting for you outside the prison and you will be the recipient of what is known as gate arrest. It is better to see them on a visit, and if they tell you will be arrested on release, it gives you time to prepare. Lenny left us to go on the visit, and when he returned a couple of hours later, he told us he had been asked to be a witness against the Krays, in particular Ronnie Kray, who had burned Lenny with a red-hot poker. It was actually a butcher's sharpening steel, hotted up on a gas ring in a club known as Esmeralda's Barn in Wilton Place, Knightsbridge. Lenny described this in his book *Branded By Ronnie Kray* that he went on to write with some help from me and was kind enough to give me a nice dedication in the book. If he agreed, they would pick him up at Eastchurch at a later date and photograph his injuries with an infra-red camera. They wanted as many charges as they could get against the Krays. Lenny asked Brian and me what he should do. He did not want to break the villains' code of "No matter what, you never grass," much the same as the Mafia code of omerta, the code of silence. We told him that only he could decide. I think the anonymous letter he found lying on his bed in Wandsworth Prison before he came to Eastchurch may have decided him. It threatened his children if he went witness against them, so he agreed to stand as witness for the police.

I, meanwhile, was starting to get quite a bit of aggravation from the other sports officer, Mr Able, while Mr Payne was on leave, so I decided to give up that very good job and put in for a change of labour. I applied for a position in the tailor's shop, but was assigned to the worst job in the nick that all the cons tried to avoid, the Met Rec (metal recovery), amid cheers and clapping from all the cons on the parade ground. It was dirty, repetitious and boring. You sat at a bench dismantling large transformers that had been used on the London Underground. We worked from a large shed, and the transformers were delivered by a mobile crane with a regular driver who was also called Roy (which is derived from the French "roi", meaning a king and a leader of men!). We became quite pally, and after a month or so, Roy said to me, "I get on very well with the officer in charge here. Do you want me to have a word with him to see whether you could work on the crane with me as a banksman?" I told him that I was very familiar with cranes and had worked a 19RB as well as a 22RB when I had worked for Mears Bros. I thought to myself that I probably knew more about cranes than he did. He discussed it with Mr Morton, a no-nonsense, sometimes gruff but fair guy, who seemed impressed with my experience and gave the OK for us two to work together. That got me out of the works shed. As well as transformers being delivered, there were large rolls of copper wire encased in rubber sleeving, and the best way to separate the rubber from the copper wire was to burn it off. The banksman's job was to make different signals to the crane driver to lift or lower and to hook and unhook the chains. One didn't need the brains of Einstein to do this job, but it was interesting. When the rolls of copper wire were due to have the rubber burnt off, they would be loaded onto a trailer and driven by a con known as "Large" to a distant field. They were thrown onto a fire that was always smouldering, and large columns of black smoke would rise into the air. The following morning, they would be brought back to the prison and sold on. About a month into the job, Roy mentioned that Large had just received his EDR and would be released in a couple of weeks. He suggested I have a word with Mr Morton and apply for the tractor driver's job, which I did. I needed to produce my full driver's licence, which had to be sent from home. A week later, he called me into his office to say my licence had arrived and if I still wanted the job, it was mine. Still want the job? I nearly fell over myself! I thanked him profusely and started to leave his office, but he said, "Not so fast. There are two forward gears on the tractor, fast and slow, and if I catch you zooming about in the fast gear, you will lose the job. Is that clear?" "Crystal, Mr Morton," I replied.

One morning Roy and I were instructed to deliver bags of chopped wood to various officers' houses outside the prison. There we were, back in Civvy Street! We did a couple of deliveries, and I noticed that one of the addresses was that of Mr Lomas. When we rang the bell, his wife opened the door and asked us to take the bags round to the back of the house. Then she invited us in to have a cup of tea. What a lovely woman! She said we were welcome to smoke, so out came our tobacco boxes and we started to roll a cigarette, but she offered us each a Players cigarette and pushed a nice Ronson lighter over to us. We were used to having a flint inserted into a piece of wood, and a razor blade would set off a spark into a tinder box, causing it to glow sufficiently to light a roll-up. We thanked her profusely for her kindness, and she said we were always welcome to a cup of tea.

On our many journeys to the fire that burnt off the rubber, as soon as we were out of earshot, I put the tractor into high gear and we flew along just for the thrill of it, but we couldn't keep it up as we were driving through fields and Roy was hanging on for grim life. Often, when we arrived at the fire, we would stretch out in the sun and have a smoke, and all was well with the world. Another interesting thing that dropped into our lap, so to speak, was when one of the officers was transferred to another prison, all his possessions were loaded up in the van and he moved out. We were driving past the back of the empty property and I noticed there was a downstairs window open. We stopped and went into the property, and lo and behold, the phone was still switched on. I rang home and spoke to Mum, and then Roy spoke to his people. What a result! If we had been caught in the property, we would have said that we had seen the window open and had come into the house to make sure there were no children playing in there who could get up to mischief or possibly hurt themselves. Or it could have been a burglar – the place was running alive with them!

After being the tractor driver for a month or more, Mr Morton asked me to step into his office for a moment. He told me that Rickard (one of the cons) had been making his morning and afternoon tea and had had the privilege of making a cup for himself too. Unfortunately, Mr Morton had caught him thieving his tea, sugar and coffee and wondered whether I would like to take his place. At this point, I thought, "This calls for some buttering up!" I said, "Yes, of course! The way that Rickard has repaid your kindness is deplorable. I will never forget the opportunity that you have afforded me. You entrusted me with driving the tractor, which far exceeded my expectations and has been my best job in this camp, and for which I thank you! Do the same conditions apply with regard to making myself a cup of tea at smoke break?" "Yes, exactly the same!" he replied, and I started the next day. This was a no-nonsense guy who, in his career, had seen it all, but he certainly liked what I had to say, and after a week or so of my extra little job, a packet of biscuits mysteriously appeared in which I was invited to partake.

One morning we were surprised to find our regular hut officer had gone on leave and a new officer had been assigned. He lined us up and asked for name and number all the way down the line. When he heard my name, he paused, looked at me rather intently and said, "Wild, hmm!" Then, from his tunic pocket, he took out a little black book, leafed through the pages and said, "Oh yes, I've heard all about you, Wild."

"And what would that be, Guv?"

"You have got the worst name in the camp for skiving. "What have you got to say about that?"

"I think you have been sadly misinformed, Guv. That accusation levelled at my good self is totally without foundation, and I have been hurt and deeply wounded by your callous observations." He said with a smile, "I will be keeping my eyes open!"

"That is always a good idea, Guv, otherwise you won't be able to see!"

"I'll be watching you, Wild," he said before moving on down the line. Other officers had obviously marked his card about me as I'd always managed to stay one step ahead of them.

Another one of our pals, Ivor Bloom, was in charge of the indoor swimming pool in the camp and he, Lenny and I used to get about together. One day I was driving by the pool and decided to pop in and see Ivor. I found Lenny had popped in as well, and after having a smoke and cup of tea at the poolside, Lenny said to Ivor, "Did you get the pool temperature right?"

"I'm not sure. Feel it and see what you think."

Lenny knelt down and put his hand in the water. "I think it feels alright. What do you think, Roy?"

I knelt down and had just put my hand in the water when Lenny came up behind me and gave me a push and I nose-dived into the pool with all my clothes on. This had been a "get-up" planned by the two of them, the kind of thing I would have been involved in. I did love a wind-up, but now I was soaking wet with the tractor parked outside, and I had to drive to the reception to get some dry clothing. As I came out of the pool entrance, one of the farm officers saw me soaking wet and asked what I had been up to. I said I had stopped to help Mr Bloom move some heavy equipment and had slipped on the wet poolside and had fallen in. That seemed to satisfy him, and he carried on with a piss-taking grin on his face.

Lenny was released just ahead of me and said he was going straight onto the Witness Protection Scheme. When I got out, he added, we would have a word with Nipper Reid of the RCS (Regional Crime Squad). Leonard Reid was leading the investigation against the Kray brothers and was instrumental in their capture and conviction. "So that you can come and live in the safe house, I have your mum's phone number and will contact you there. When you have your EDR, let your mum know and she can let me know." We touched hands on the night and Lenny was released early next morning.

One afternoon, a blue band (privileged con) turned up at the Met Rec and told Mr Morton that a con by the name of Wild was wanted at the governor's office right away. For what? Had they had enough of me and were transferring me to a closed nick? All kinds of wild ruminations were running through my mind. I had, on three occasions, beaten all the charges levelled against me at Governor's Adjudication in Wandsworth and in Eastchurch and had three good reports. Maybe they thought I was too much in command of the language and would invariably tie up an officer verbally. Was I just a bit of a thorn in the establishment's side? I didn't know what to think. The blue band took me to the block and I was admitted to the Governor's office. "Ah, Wild," said his nibs. "I have a duty to inform you that you have been granted parole and your release date is March 16th." That was just a couple of weeks away, thereby saving me three months; my original date was my brother Tony's birthday, May 16th. I thanked the Governor for the good news and walked out of his office with a renewed sense of euphoric optimism. Back at Met Rec, all the chaps asked what had happened and I told them rather emotionally that I'd got the jam roll. There were well wishes and handshaking all round. I had done it – worked the system, beaten all the charges levelled at me and gained my freedom much earlier than expected – and for the next week, I was walking on cloud lucky seven. I wrote to Mum and Dad and told them the good news. The only two officers I told were Mr Lomas, who wished me well, and I thanked him for his professionalism and putting up with me winding him up occasionally, and Mr Morton, who said rather gruffly, "Well done, Wild." I thanked him for his kind consideration with regard to the tractor job and the tea-making job.

On the day of release, I was awoken by the night screw at 5 am. Most of the guys had said, "If I am asleep, Roy, wake me up." Some were already awake, and it was emotional saying goodbye and shaking the hands of these guys with whom I had shared my life and who were all in the same position as me. We had all risked our loss of liberty, and when we knew we had made the wrong choice, we just got on with it.

The night screw took me to the dining hall for an early breakfast, then onto Reception where it was an absolute pleasure to degarb the prison-issue clothing and put on my own. I was then given £47-50 discharge money, as well as a rail ticket to take me from the nearest station, Queenborough, to Victoria Station in London where my Dad was waiting for me. I fell into his arms, tears all round, and I said, "Dad let's go into the bar. I am dying for a Mackeson," which is what I used to drink. We stood there and had a couple of drinks and then headed home to Mum, who opened the door and started crying. I gave her a big cuddle and was adamant that I would stand by my decision that villainy was over for me. I would go to graft and never upset my parents again.

I met up again with the firm that I had formerly worked with. They were all pleased to see me and told me they had a few nice things lined up. I said, "Thanks for the offer, but this last bit of bird (bird lime, time) is game, shot and match for me. I am going to graft," which they all accepted, so we went our separate ways. I later knew I had made the right decision as a couple of them received eight years for bank robbery and came out after five years and four months. They weren't out very long, went back for the same offence and drew a twelve-year sentence. That could have been me! Many times I lay in my prison cell thinking about the primitive conditions, the terrible food, the paedophiles marching by the hotplate that I used to attend, and I would think, "This is not your true course, Roy. You are better than this and capable of better things. If you were that good at this business, you wouldn't be in here now." I missed having a nice car, a nice home (I lost my lovely home in Canning town) and all the lovely suits and the compliments I'd be given; I missed going over to Arsenal, eating in fine restaurants and always having a lovely girl on my arm, small things that at the time I took so much for granted. I missed wearing a wristwatch and a pair of cufflinks, that I have always worn, raising my hand to stop a cab, and being measured for a new current suit, but mostly I missed Mum and Dad.

No, it was not my game, but I am pleased that I was incarcerated a few times in Brixton Nick, Wormwood Scrubs, Wandsworth Prison and finally Eastchurch, twice. Oh, I nearly forgot! I was in Alcatraz once, but that was for a day visit when I was on holiday in San Francisco. If ever I was rehabilitated, it was not through the efforts of the prison regime, it was because of my own common sense. Imprisonment did me a big favour and gave me a chance to pit myself against the establishment. They won the big one by taking away my liberty, but I view that as being of my own volition. In the book *Oscar Wilde: The Aftermath*, which described his incarceration in Reading Prison, he is quoted as saying, "As if written in words of fire on the walls of my cell, nothing, but nothing, can be worth this!" When I read that, I realised there was nothing more precious than freedom.

My brother Tony came to see me on Mum and Dad's last visit to the camp and said he and three of his pals had booked a holiday in Italy, at a seaside town called Alassio. One of the pals had dropped out and it would be nice if I would agree to take his place. I immediately agreed, thinking it would be the perfect opportunity to shed the prison memories and system from my psyche. Little did I know the lasting impression it would have on me. Nothing was ever straightforward when yours truly was involved.

Once released, I took a couple of driving jobs until the holiday in Italy came around. I made contact with Lenny, who was on the witness protection scheme and lodged in a safe house in Boreham Wood in Hertfordshire. I made contact with a former girlfriend and took her with me to visit him. The door was opened by a plainclothes police officer who had been told to expect me. There were hugs and handshakes, and he invited us to stay the night to do some catching up. Lenny told me that the police moved him around a lot to keep one step in front of the Kray firm because word was coming through the grapevine that he would find a whole lot of grief should he take the stand and be a witness for the prosecution.

After a couple of weeks, Lenny was moved to a large luxury flat in Etchingham Court in North Finchley and had given my name to a senior officer, Mr Bert Trevette, who ran a rule over me; with assurances from Lenny that I was a good pal, I was approved and moved in. We made friends with a few people living there, and our neighbour was Simon Dee, the famous disc jockey. It must have been very expensive, but that never affected us because our rent was paid by the RCS (Regional Crime Squad).

CHAPTER 27

ALASSIO & MONTE CARLO

We flew from Stansted Airport and landed in Nice in the south of France. From there we travelled by coach to Alassio, a beautiful town and beach. Our flat was above a small restaurant and ice cream parlour. It was so hot you could not walk on the beach without some kind of footwear. We had been there a couple of days, soaking up the sun and enjoying the sights, when it was suggested we hire a car and drive to Monte Carlo, which was roughly forty-two miles away, via the towns of Menton and Sanremo.

The car was a Fiat 500, so small you would have to step outside to change your mind. Only two of us were drivers, and Danny did not feel comfortable driving on the opposite side of the road, so it was down to me to handle the driving. We started off early one morning, and about ten miles into the journey, we came upon two very tanned beauties in shorts thumbing a lift. I stopped the car and we asked them where they were heading. As they were going to Monte Carlo, we told them to jump in. One of the girls managed to squeeze in between our two pals in the back, and the other one sat on the lap of my brother on the front seat. We had travelled no more than a couple of miles when we were flagged down by two motorbike police in white helmets, white gun holsters and white boots. I stopped and exited the vehicle and asked what the problem was. The officer looked at me blankly and then rattled off in French. We couldn't understand each other, but with a lot of gesticulating on his part, we finally understood he was telling us we were overloaded in the car and two of us had to exit the vehicle before we would be allowed to carry on. Claire and Julie got out of the car, but we knew they would have no problem getting a lift into Monte Carlo. Any car following with a couple of young guys in it would burn the breaks out stopping for these two. We agreed to look out for them in Monte Carlo.

We soon came across them, and they had hooked up with a couple of American guys from their home state of Seattle. Handshaking all round, after which the girls told us that they would be continuing to Athens and then to London before flying back home, so if I could give them my number, they would give me a call to let me know they were on their way.

Our holiday came to an end and I returned to Lenny's flat. Julie finally called one Saturday and said they had just landed in London from Greece. Lenny and I had already made plans to go to a party that night, so I arranged to leave our flat key with an elderly man downstairs. I also mentioned to Julie that my bedroom was down the corridor on the left if they wanted to place all their suitcases and bits and pieces there as Lenny might not be too pleased to come home in the early hours and find two strangers and his bedroom full of their luggage. We arrived home from the party at about 3 am to find Claire fast asleep on the settee and Julie spark out in my bed. She awoke after hearing me in the bathroom cleaning my teeth, and when I walked in, she looked up all sleepy-eyed and said, "Hi Roy! Do you want me to get up?" I said, "Of course not, just move over." She stayed with me for a week, doing the sights of London with Claire by day and returning to the flat at night. Julie and I exchanged addresses and promised to stay in touch, but sadly we never did. Nevertheless, it was a lovely interlude in my life that frequently surfaces in quiet moments, and of all the romantic liaisons I have had, this one compares with the best, as brief as it was.

CHAPTER 28

THE SAFE HOUSE

Whilst living in the safe house with Lenny, I decided to drive back to Hoxton to visit Mum and Dad. When I stopped at the lights in Archway Road, the car engine cut out and would not start, so I pushed the car, a Ford Zephyr, into the kerb and phoned the AA, of which I was a paid-up member, to come and give me some assistance. I gave the car registration and make to the girl on the other end of the phone, who said an AA patrolman would be with me within the hour.

I said to her, "That sounds like a London accent you have?"

"Yes," she said, "I live not far from where you have broken down."

We chatted for a couple of minutes and I asked her her name, which was Denise. I said, "Why don't you let me take you out for a nice meal?"

She laughed and said, "I'm not sure – I don't know you."

"I'm a nice guy, and I don't take liberties. Come out with me!"

"I have no idea what you look like."

"I feel sure you will like what you see." She was still a bit hesitant, but I knew I now had her interest.

I said, "To give you some idea what I look like, did you see Steve McQueen in *The Magnificent Seven*?"

"Yes!"

"Well, I look like his horse." She burst out laughing and agreed to meet me, so we arranged a time and place for the following evening. I arrived and sat in the car and was suddenly startled by a vision of loveliness tapping on the window. "Are you Roy?" she asked, and I knew it was Denise. We drove to a very nice restaurant just up the road in Highbury and she was delightful company. Afterwards, we went for a drink, and then I invited her back to our flat in Etchingham Court. She said, "It must be very expensive to live here." I said, "It is paid for by the police." Just like a woman, she was very inquisitive, but obviously I never told her too much. I gave her a tour of the flat, which was completed by showing her my bedroom. We stood facing each other and I felt sure she wanted me to kiss her, which I did. After about an hour, I heard the front door of the flat open and told her it was Lenny. I left her in the bedroom tidying herself up and fixing her makeup. She finally came into the front room and I introduced her to Lenny and the other guy, who I was not familiar with. She suddenly said, "Roy, I can't find my bracelet!" She had left her handbag and a large gold charm bracelet on the table in the front room while I was showing her the flat. We all looked for the bracelet, but nowhere could it be found. Denise started to cry and said it had been a present from her father. I was ready to bash the shit out of someone, so I took Lenny into my bedroom and said, "Len, I am going to bring this girl back into this bedroom to try and console her, and then I am going to take her down to sit in my car. When I return to this flat, if that bracelet is not on the table, I will show you two a war you never thought was fucking possible." I returned to the flat five minutes later, and lo and behold, the bracelet had been found behind the settee. How could it have jumped off the table and come to rest behind the settee when there were just the two of us in the flat? I drove her near her house and dropped her off on the corner. She said, "I will not be seeing you anymore, Roy. I think you are a lovely guy, but the company you keep frightens me." I was very upset and had strong words with Lenny for allowing this to happen to a guest in our home and bringing in the vermin who tried to nick a young girl's bracelet.

Witness protection officers were usually changed around every week to avoid corruption and witness intimidation by the Kray firm. If we were going out for the night, an officer had to tag along. He stood out like a sore thumb and the company we were with was never very happy, so invariably I would convince him that Lenny would be OK with all our friends and persuade him to have the night off. Officers were usually a bit reticent about doing that because if anything went wrong, their job would be on the line. To allay their fears, I would tell them where the party was and I would call them at their home and tell them everything was fine.

Danny was a witness protection officer who was living with Lenny and me. One evening, we took him with us to meet some friends in Hoxton for a drink and picked up Jeanie on the way. Everyone knew that Danny was a police officer and watched their Ps and Qs. We then went on to a party, and Danny had never been to an East End party before. He'd had a few drinks that loosened him up a bit and became quite taken with Jeanie, who would turn any man's head when she was dancing. "OK if I dance with Jeanie?" he said to me. "Sure, go ahead," I said. Off came his coat, thrown over the back of an armchair, and then onto the floor with Jeanie.

A short time after, one of my pals, Freddie, motioned for me to meet him outside for a breath of fresh air and said, "Have a look at this." In his hand was Danny's warrant card, known in criminal parlance as a "W". When Danny's coat had been thrown over the armchair, Freddy had hoisted his dummy (wallet) out of the inside pocket and taken out the W, which, in the hands of a villain, was gold dust.

Freddie said, "We can go to work with this, Roy." I replied, "Fred, villainy, as I have told you, is game shot for me. I go to graft now." The following morning in our flat, Jeanie and I got up and heard strained voices coming from the living room. Lenny and Danny were talking, and Danny told me he had lost his warrant card, which his boss would consider sacrilege, and he could lose his job or be demoted, especially if his boss found out he had been at an all-night party and had failed to protect Lenny adequately. Danny by this time was close to tears. I told him I had to drop Jeanie off and would go round to where the party was and ask whether it had been found. When I got to Freddie's, I said, "Look, Fred, I know more than you do the advantages that card can bring, but it means Danny could be sacked and lose his pension, and he is married with two small children. I know he is on the opposite side of the fence to us, but he is not a bad guy, and I have just left him close to tears. Let me have it – I will tell him a story! – and up in Heaven, you will have a tick put against your name."

When I arrived back at the flat, the look of expectation on Danny's face dropped when I said, "Well, we have looked everywhere, and what I need you to do now is tell me, who is the best boy in the girls' class? I held up the warrant card and said, "Have a look at that, pal!" "Where was it?" he said, his eyes filling up. I said, "When you put your jacket over the armchair, it must have fallen out, and it was at the back on the floor." How could it possibly have fallen out of the wallet? The mistake that Freddie made was putting the wallet back in the coat, but whether Danny picked up on that point he never said; he was only too pleased to get it back.

Here's another quick story involving the "gold dust" that I mentioned. Two villains had copied a police warrant card and rushed into a jewellers shop, showing the warrant card. They said, "We have received information that this shop is about to be raided by armed robbers. We have our officers outside and do not want you to be put in any danger, so lock yourselves in the back room and we will let you know when it is safe to come out." The owner and a young female assistant hurried into another room, and when they finally emerged, the place was devoid of all the jewellery on show. As soon as that warrant card is shown, people assume it is a police officer standing behind it. Not always so! Beware.

A much nicer incident ensued after Lenny came in at about 7.00 one morning and sitting down to breakfast told me he had spent the night with a girl he knew. "Do you know what amyl nitrite is?" he asked me.

"It sounds like some kind of explosive to me!"

He laughed. "No, it's a medically prescribed drug for people with heart trouble."

"What's the connection?"

"If two people are making love and the man uses amyl nitrite, it enhances his performance and he can keep going all night."

"I've never heard of it. How do you know this?"

"The girl I stayed with last night introduced me to it, and you wouldn't believe what it does to you."

"I don't think I need anything in that department."

"Try it when the time is right – you ain't seen anything yet!" He carefully unwrapped a clean handkerchief that was lying on the table and inside were six small glass phials. "What you do is break one into a soft cloth and inhale deeply just before doing the business. You will be amazed." He wrapped three of them in a piece of tissue and passed them to me.

At the time, I was seeing a girl who had recently off-loaded her boyfriend, and one night I took her home with me and she stayed the night, as she usually did. At the end of the evening, just after cleaning my teeth, I broke one of the phials open in the bathroom and inhaled. I didn't feel anything at all when the party began, so to speak, and I thought, "Well, this is either going to turn me into Kid Dynamite or I am going to finish up in the back of an ambulance." Hotdog! It really worked! I did some research on this drug after the forklift had helped me out of the bed and found that if people who suffered from angina experienced chest pains or a tightness in the chest area, they could just inhale deeply a few times and it would regulate the heart again. Welcome to the world of amyl nitrite! I won't begin to elaborate on what happened to the remaining two phials. I will leave it to the reader's imagination. Suffice to say I needed a good holiday!

I stayed friends with a guy named Robert whom I had met in Eastchurch, and we met up in a pub one Sunday lunchtime. We were swapping stories of some of the things we had got up to in Eastchurch, and I started to tell him the story of how I had come across Danny in Wandsworth and how I had come to meet Danny in the West End. Listening to our conversation was a guy nearby who had two enormous scars on the sides of his face from temple to mouth; he turned out to be Robert's cousin. "What do you think of Danny?" he asked me. I have always been very astute when it comes to assessing a situation that could rapidly go wrong and immediately realised this was a time to exercise caution. "I only met Danny through a guy who worked for me," I replied, "and never mixed with him socially. Danny put a lot of work my way, and in return I supplied a car to take him home every night. Other than that, I never really knew him." Pointing to his scars, he said, "This is what that bastard did to me." I made a few sympathetic noises and left it at that. I was pleased that I had turned up on my own and not taken a couple of faces I knew. They would have probably replied, "What do you want, sympathy? Look in the dictionary. It's in between shit and syphilis," and then it would really have been off. I neatly side-stepped a situation that could have quite easily got out of hand and I still have the firm belief that diplomacy usually wins.

My old pal Billy Scola, who trained with me to be a cab driver, told me a very strange story. Late one night, a friend of his, another cab driver, dropped off his last fare, turned off the "For Hire" light and headed for home. Standing on the kerb in Bayswater Road was a young girl who waved him down. He stopped and told her he was not working but if she was going in his direction he would drop her off. She said she needed to get to the end of Oxford Street, which was on his way. On reaching her destination, she asked how much she owed him, and he said as it was on his way home, there was nothing to pay. She offered him a cup of coffee as a thank you, so he parked the cab outside and followed her into a very nice and well-furnished flat. After the coffee, he felt unwell, and that was the last he remembered. He woke up in a strange bed, the flat was empty and the girl was gone. He drove home and during the day his condition worsened. The following day, he went to see his doctor and relayed exactly what had taken place. The doctor examined him, finally asking to look at his deaf and dumb (bum). In the doctor's own words: "You have been got at." Someone had sexually assaulted him while he was drugged. The very next day, he went to the police station nearest to the incident and reported what he had been subjected to. All the details were taken and he was told the police would investigate this very serious allegation. After two weeks of hearing nothing from the police, he called the investigating officer and was told inquiries were still ongoing; should they hear anything, they would let him know. A further two weeks passed and he received a letter asking him to attend a meeting at the police station. He was ushered into the office of a high-ranking officer who told him that the flat owner was a prominent MP in the current Government and the Home Office had told this officer to terminate the investigation into the assault. On hearing this, the victim of the assault had to be physically removed from the office, amid shouting and distress and the thought that he would have to live with this very unsavoury incident the rest of his life.

I was out with my old friend Frankie Shea, who, as I previously mentioned, was the brother-in-law of the Kray twins. We got around to the subject of Frankie writing his autobiography, so I contacted my cousin who was in the upper echelons of the newspaper world in Fleet Street and was very interested in what Frankie would have to say. He invited Frankie and me to meet him in the Strand Palace Hotel where he had reserved a table for lunch. Waiting in the restaurant were my cousin David, a colleague he had brought with him, and the British agent of Stephen King, the horror writer who has sold more than three hundred million copies of his books worldwide, many of which were turned into Hollywood films. They interviewed Frankie, who knew possibly more about the internal workings of the "Brothers Grimm" and the "Firm" than anyone else! The conversation finally turned to villainy in general, and they were astounded at some of the things Frankie and I had been involved in. The agent said he would mention all we had said to Stephen King and this could be the beginning of making it into a film.

I received a phone call a couple of days later from a guy who introduced himself as Marcus from Meridian TV. He wanted to make a programme about crime and asked whether we could meet. I told him if we met it would be just with him and I would want expenses. He readily agreed and asked how much. I told him £100, and he agreed immediately. I asked him to meet me in the graveyard behind Shoreditch Church. On time, he turned up and out came the customary notebook. I told him there would be no names other than mine and no locations or dates. He agreed and passed over the £100 expenses. We talked and talked, while he took notes, and Frankie Shea's name came into the conversation. Marcus said, "Do you know Frankie?" and I told him Frankie and I had been pals since we were about sixteen. He said, "Do you think we could meet Frank at some time?" I said I would have a word with him and see what I could do, but if we met, he would have to come up with expenses again. "Of course," he said. I ran this past Frankie and he agreed to meet Marcus, so we arranged a meet in a small cafe in Grays Inn Road, Holborn. We stayed about an hour and then left, with Marcus telling us he would be in touch.

Frankie and I would meet in Harlow in Essex as Frankie was living in the Bishop Stortford area of Hertfordshire and Harlow was pretty central for both of us. On one of our meets, he told me he was not going ahead with the proposed film as his mum was very worried about it and was still very afraid of the Krays. He had told her that there was no problem now as they had both passed away, but she was still frightened of the people they knew. I said, "Frank, this could come to an awful lot of money, especially if there is the chance of a film being made," but no, he would not upset his mum, and I respected that. Maybe I would have taken the same decision if it had been my dear old mum.

An old friend of mine, Nicky, and his family ran their own pub in Hoxton and I would occasionally pop in to have a drink and spend an hour or so with him. I told him about Lenny and I living on the witness protection scheme, and he suggested we come down one weekend. After our first trip there, we became quite regular, and one evening Lenny mentioned that he would have loved to have had a pub; even now he would like to try serving behind the bar. Nicky said, "Get behind the bar now, Len, and see how you get on," so Lenny started to serve the customers and became quite adept at it. It became a regular thing; he loved the serving and the banter with the customers and would never accept any payment except a glass of beer now and again. When Lenny and I were at home and I went out for the night in the East End, Lenny would drink in Hampstead at The Spaniard's Inn and The Bull & Bush, two world-famous pubs. Hampstead is a very affluent area that encompasses The Bishops Avenue, better known as Millionaire's Row, and Queens Road that I will have occasion to mention later.

Lenny was mixing with some very wealthy people, who became quite awestruck by some of the tales he would regale them with. These wealthy people had never met anyone from the East End, let alone someone who was familiar with the infamous Kray twins. Drawing on my own experiences, all birds love a villain; whether it is the excitement of bucking law and order and the establishment, I'm not sure, but it seems to act as some kind of aphrodisiac to young ladies, who now say they love a "bad boy". What does that mean? Possibly someone who plays Knocking Down Ginger or nicks something out of a supermarket. These "bad boys" could never do the things we got up to in our time. Most of the old-time villains I knew have now been laid to rest. There are security cameras everywhere. All staff wages are paid into their accounts electronically, there are no large stashes of cash anymore, no more wage snatches, bank robberies or violence. If you want to nick large amounts of money, you do it on paper, as it is done in the City; alternatively, you become an MP at the Palace of Varieties, aka the House of Commons. Anyway! Getting back to Hampstead and Lenny…

Lenny and I were due to spend the evening at Nick's pub and arrived there about 7 pm. At the time, I was working as supervisor for a cleaning company in Hatton Garden and had a van with the name of the company on both sides. The rear of the van was full of mops, buckets, brooms and various cleaning products. Lenny was soon behind the bar serving and after a while told me that he had promised a young girl, one of the Hampstead set, that he would take her down to an East End pub and let her meet some East End people, which she was really looking forward to. He asked whether I could run back to Hampstead to pick her up and bring her back to the pub. I arrived at her address, which was quite near the famous Leg of Mutton Pond where local people skated when it was frozen. I knocked on the door, which was opened by a very pretty girl who said, "Are you Roy? Come in. Cordelia won't be long." I said, "So it isn't you I have come to meet?" "No!" she said, laughing, in an American accent. "I am her flatmate." I was sitting waiting when descending the stairs came one of the most beautiful women I had ever seen, dressed straight out of Vogue, culminating in a vision that ambushed my senses. She introduced herself as Cordelia, we said goodbye to her flatmate, and I thought, "No way can I ask this beauty to get into my work van!" She asked where my car was, and I said I'd had to park a couple of streets away to find a parking spot. "Shall we go in my car, then?" she said. "Where is your car?" I asked, and she pointed to a brand new Triumph sports car. "Would you like to drive?" so I took the keys from her hand, opened the door for her and we set off. She was asking me all sorts of questions about the East End and the pubs, and I thought, "No way am I going to take you back to where Lenny is and sit you down all night looking a million dollars," so I took her to The Green Gate, a very popular pub in Bethnal Green Road. We parked opposite, I walked round and opened the door, and Cordelia had a problem trying to get out but managed it in a ladylike way. By this time, all the chaps drinking out on the pavement were clocking over. We had to cross a very busy road, and I took her hand. It was then that old adage came to mind: "She was enough to stop the traffic," and that is what actually happened. Whether it was politeness or merely to catch a glimpse of Cordelia, who knows? We entered the pub amid admiring glances from most of the punters and had a job getting to the bar. I asked her what she would like to drink, and naively she said, "I don't know! I'll have the same as you!" I said, "Cordelia, you will not look the part with a pint of Mackeson in your hand," so I ordered her a double Bacardi and Coke. From there I took her to another pub in Roman Road – more attention – then on to a pub in Hoxton, then to the pub where Lenny was waiting. I said to her in the car, "I hope we meet again. Now I am going to be in trouble with Lenny as I was supposed to bring you back here, but you looked so lovely I wanted you selfishly for myself." She leant across and kissed me passionately and said, "I'm glad we had the evening together. Let's go and face the music." This was about ten-thirty! We walked into the pub amid some saucy remarks from Nicky and his family, and Lenny, exasperated, asked "What happened to you two?" Cordelia said, "I asked Roy to show me some of the East End and we stopped for a couple of drinks." She bailed me out – shrewd girl! Later Lenny said with good humour, "I must have been mad asking you to pick her up, knowing what you're like around women." I said, "Len, I am what I am. Have you heard the expression 'Act in haste, repent at leisure?'" He had no idea what I meant! We later dropped her off at her home, she kissed Lenny and me and squeezed my hand. We then picked up my van and on the way home, he told me she was being kept by an oil sheik who paid the rent on the house in Hampstead and had bought her the new sports car. A week or so later, he told me that Cordelia was quite taken with me. She probably saw me as a diamond in the rough, I thought, as opposed to the Hooray Henrys whose circles she mixed in. I replied, "When I am cotchelled up with a couple of million in the bank, maybe I'll look her up again."

Whilst we were living in the safe house, Lenny secured a job driving around the very wealthy owner of the Ronson lighter company in his rather grand Rolls Royce. A couple of months into the job, Lenny became somewhat disillusioned with it. He would report for work at the owner's estate in Hampstead and drive him to work somewhere in the West End as part of his daily duties, but on some days the owner would stay at home and Lenny would be given a list of things to do within the estate. The car would be washed and vacuumed, and on this particular day, Lenny was told to clean and wash the car that belonged to the daughter as well, and then to clean and wash the car of the son. He considered this to be not part of his duties. The following day while he was driving, Lenny voiced his objections; the owner became quite irate and said, "You will do what you are told. And when we return to the house, there are some rods in the garage you will use to clean some of the drains that appear to be blocked around the house." "I am not your lackey," said Lenny. "You want them cleaned, do it yourself." This was said in the middle of heavy traffic on the way to the West End. He said, "I have quit," then opened the driver's door and walked away, leaving the owner stranded. He could not drive the car himself due to a medical condition, and all the vehicles behind were blowing their hooters, impatient to continue moving on. When Lenny returned to our flat and regaled me with the day's happenings, I said, "Good for you, Len. That is exactly what I would have done. This is how the landed gentry view the likes of us, below their level. Imagine that guy being banged up in Wandsworth. He would not last the week."

When the Krays' trial came up, they were sentenced to thirty years each. Lenny was never called as a witness as the police had so many charges against these two latter-day Robin Hoods, as some people viewed and indeed remembered them. The police continued to pay the rent on our flat but informed Lenny it would only continue another five weeks and then he would be on his own. I took a flat of my own in Victoria Chambers, which was in EC1 near Old Street Tube Station. By this time I wanted to be on my own, no coming and going of the random people Lenny would bring home, not forgetting the scumbag who nicked Denise's gold bracelet. It's true I was always taking home people that Lenny didn't know, but the only guy I took home was my brother, once. All the rest were lovely girls that improved the ambience of the place and always made Lenny's eyes light up in approval.

CHAPTER 29

OB-LA-DI, OB-LA-DA

Another story I am about to relate reminds me of something from the Charlie Chaplin and Max Sennet era. I was driving home from work one afternoon and was caught up in some heavy traffic when I saw at a bus stop a girl who was obviously waiting for a bus. She looked into the car a couple of times and I motioned for her to come over. I found out she was going to Islington and lived quite close to me, so I offered to drop her off. On the way home, she told me she worked for a company that imported menswear and cufflinks. Just to make conversation, I said I had always worn cufflinks and had quite a few pairs. I asked her whether her company had a catalogue, and she replied that she would get one for me. "Does that mean we are going to meet again?" I said. She smiled and said, "If you would like to." She was a typical South American, quite dark-skinned, long jet black hair and a lovely face. I asked her about her family background, and she replied that her father's family came from Uruguay and she also had a Uruguayan name that was never used. She went by the name of Jenny. On parting, I gave her my phone number and she called me a week later to say she had some samples of cufflinks in boxes; she asked whether I would like to meet her and have look at them. I met her from work and on the way home she showed me about a dozen samples. I picked out five and asked how much I owed her. "Nothing," she said. "I got them for you!" I took her that night for a meal by way of a thank you, and we saw each other for the next couple of weeks, during which time she really loaded me up with cufflinks and tie pins. On her day off, we had a nice meal in a restaurant, and then she invited me back to her place for a coffee. Without wishing to go into further detail, we finished up in her bedroom, where she started to show me some photographs of where her parents came from back in Uruguay. Her house backed onto two pubs, The Rosemary Branch and The Southgate

Arms, and Jenny's bedroom looked down onto the latter's yard, which was full of used beer barrels and crates behind a locked gate. This is the part where Charlie Chaplin and Max Sennet come in! Things were starting to get interesting between us when suddenly she froze. She had heard a key turn in the front door and said, "It is my Dad. He will kill me!" I'm no coward, but I had visions of Pablo Escobar putting his head round the door, so, discretion being the better part of valour, the bed was vacated rather rapidly, up went the window and I had to drop down into the pub yard, wind my way through the barrels, and climb over the gate. I walked round the corner into Southgate Road, stepped into my car and drove away. Phew. Narrow squeaks, I've had a few, but managed to sidestep most of them.

I was invited to a party in Chelsea by a guy I met in Eastchurch. Barry came from Fulham, and it was the typical crowd of Sloane Rangers. I asked Barry how much the whip was, and he said he had taken care of it. Parties with the Chelsea Set were somewhat different to East End parties. The parties I was used to always had lots of beer and spirits, sometimes a bowl of jellied eels and sandwiches. At this party, it was bottles of various wines, and it didn't take long for the Hooray Henrys to get turped up and start acting stupid. The girls were typical Chelsea, long blond hair and high boots. Barry came over with a beautiful girl who looked remarkably like the British film star Julie Christie. I was not sure whether she was one of the gang, but all the guys were congregating around her like flies around the jam pot. Barry drifted away to say hello to someone else and left me speaking with her. She told me her name was Kathy Bennett and asked me where I came from.

"The other side of the river," I said.

"I thought you weren't from around here."

"Why?"

"You speak and dress differently."

"Is that good or bad?"

"It's nice to see a man in a suit, like yourself."

We stood drinking and talking most of the night, and finally people started to drift away. Before I left, I said to Kathy, "Are we going to meet again?" "I would like that," she said. She scribbled her phone number on a piece of paper with an eyebrow pencil and kissed me on the cheek, and I baled out.

I called her two weeks later. You mustn't show too much enthusiasm. I have never been one for all that eager beaver business; it can work against you! No promises; let's keep it simple. We made a meet outside the Odeon Marble Arch, strolled romantically through Hyde Park with her arm linked in mine and had a nice lunch in a restaurant by the Serpentine. This was our first date, and you try to create a good impression. All was going very well until Kathy, reaching across the table for something, knocked over a full cup of tea. The waiter rushed over, cleared the table, cleaned it and replaced everything, amid profuse apologies from Kathy. She was so embarrassed. I said to her, "Is this your way of creating a good impression?" and smiled so she could see I was just winding her up. By this time her lovely face had resumed its natural hue. I reached across the table, squeezed her hand and said, "Don't worry about it."

We carried on seeing each other, and I stayed with her in her flat that was in a square off King's Road in Chelsea and she came to the East End and stayed with me on numerous occasions. I used to drink in a pub just off King's Road, and a guy I was on nodding terms with wandered over one day and introduced himself as Duncan. He was quite a nice-looking man in his early forties, at a guess, and over the next couple of weeks we became quite pally. He was the head of a department in a large financial company. Out of the blue, he said, "Roy! I have seen some of the girls you have brought into this pub, and everyone has been a beauty, especially that Jewish girl. What is the secret?" I said, "Be a nice guy first, then 50% romantic and affectionate, and 50% indifferent. Obviously, looks help as well, and I have my mum and dad to thank for that. In my case, I am from the East End, and the girls from this part of the world very rarely come into contact with people like me; because I am always suited, they often ask whether I'm a gangster! Why they ask that I have no idea. Maybe it's just the persona I give out!" He said, "I will have to try that." He went on to tell me he had taken on a new girl in his department who was due to start on the following Tuesday. We were both in the pub the next Monday, and Duncan asked whether I would be there at lunchtime the following day as he would be bringing the new girl with him and buying her lunch. "As I have said, I have seen you with many lovely girls, but this one is right up there with them all!" "Really?" I said. "I can't wait!" Kathy had previously told me she was starting with Duncan's company and he would be taking her to lunch. I suggested that we have a drink that evening before heading off home and he agreed to meet me later. I picked Kathy up and we headed for the pub, where Duncan was standing at the bar. He turned round when he heard my voice, spied Kathy holding my arm and nearly had a fit. "This is the girl I am due to bring here tomorrow! I should have known better with you!" he said, all in good humour. I said to him, "Well, where is this lovely girl who is up there on par with my Kathy?" No answer except a rueful smile.

A relation of mine, Dick, who was married at one time to my Dad's sister, invited Kathy and me to a party at his flat. While people were turning up at Dick's place in anticipation of the party, his brother Ronnie said to me, "Roy, I have seen you with so many gorgeous women, but this time I think I have topped you. I have pulled a nurse who works in the Whittington Hospital, and you have got to see her! I have to pick her up in twenty minutes." Dick said, "I think you are biting off more than you can chew, Ronnie. I have seen many of the girls that Roy has been with." "No," said Ron, "I'll have a tenner bet on it, Roy!" "Ok Ron, if that's what you want!" I went to meet Kathy at the King's Cross Station and did she look a picture! Thigh-length boots and shorts, all topped by her beautiful face. When we arrived back at Dick's for the party, I could see Ronnie's car outside and knew he must have returned with his nurse. Kathy and I walked into the party room, and everyone looked at her, she was so stunning. After introducing her to some of the company, I said to Ronnie, "What do you think?" He was gracious in defeat, pulled out his wallet and passed me a ten-pound note. I later said to Kathy, "Put this in your purse. It is down to you that I won the bet."

Kathy started a new job in Victoria Street, Westminster, at the BP Building and had been there about a week when we arranged that I would pick her up and we would have some lunch. I entered the building and inside the concourse was a uniformed security guy sitting at his desk. I told him I was there to pick up Kathy, and he looked on the computer for her department. He said, "I will give her a call to let her know you are waiting. I remember who she is – she started here recently?" I said, "That's the one." Then he said, "There are a couple of hundred girls working in this building, and she is the loveliest of them all. You are a lucky guy!" To which I replied, "I wouldn't have it any other way." After a couple of minutes, Kathy stepped out of the lift, walked over to me smiling, kissed me on the cheek and took my arm. We walked towards the entrance with me looking back giving the security guy a wink and him giving me a wave and looking on wistfully.

Kathy later moved from Chelsea to Redcliffe Gardens, Kensington, and we lost touch for a while and then met up about six months later. She told me she had married someone she'd met and he had turned out far less than her expectations of him. Disappointed, she had called a halt to the marriage and moved out.

Despite having a pocket full of good intentions, we never resumed our prior relationship. The years rolled by, I got married and had two children and one day we decided to have a nice day out at Southend-on-Sea. Late in the afternoon, we called into a MacDonald's and had just sat down to eat when the door opened and in came two women with three children. One of the women kept looking over at me and then leaning over to say something to her friend. Suddenly, I realised it was Kathy, but not the Kathy I remembered. This woman had gained considerable weight, but I found it hard to avert my gaze. We finished our food and left the restaurant, and when we reached our car, I felt like putting my family in the car and nipping back on some pretence that I had left something behind. I wanted to let her know I had recognized her and ask how she was, but I decided it was better to leave the past in the past. The image of Kathy on that day haunted me for some time afterwards, and my thoughts kept returning to the past, how beautiful she was, how embarrassed she became when knocking over the cup of tea in the restaurant in Kensington Gardens, how I won the tenner at the party because of her beauty and how alike she was to Julie Christie. Many are the times I have scoured Facebook looking for her, just to say hello and how are you, so far to no avail. I'm just glad we had some time to spend together, and I hope wherever she is she has found happiness and is safe. If ever she reads this book, I'd like her to know that she touched my heart in places that I never really knew. You were special. *Hora e sempre*: now and always.

I would often meet up with my old pals from Camden LMS Railway Depot, Billy Davis and Patsie Murphy, who were also committed Arsenal supporters. One day, Arsenal played Wolverhampton Wanderers, who went on to beat us by two goals to one. At a party that night, there were some northern guys who had come down to support the "Wolves" and the discussion soon got out of hand, with them making derisory comments about Arsenal and how they had beaten us. Patsie and Billy became incensed. Patsie ran down to his car parked outside and returned with a shotgun, threatening to shoot someone if any more remarks were made about Arsenal. I couldn't believe it – all over a game of football? This was just one of the incidents I was to witness while a pal of these latter-day Butch Cassidy and the Sundance Kid.

One Saturday, Billy told me that they had a football match the following morning over at London Fields in Hackney and they were two players short. Would I take the job of goalkeeper? I agreed without thinking it over. It meant getting home about four in the morning from that night's party, being on parade at the match by 10 am for the kick-off at 11, and then another party until the early hours. At the field, there was a small brick changing room for us to don the strip, and I had to borrow a pair of boots. The team we were pitched against were all black guys. We kicked off, and in less than fifteen minutes, the other team was awarded a penalty against us for a foul. The ball was placed on the spot, and before I could blink, the ball was in the back of the net. We were well out of our depth against this team. In less than twenty minutes, another four found their way into the back of our net. Just before the half-time whistle, we were looking at six nil. Billy and Patsie were getting well wound up and I knew something had to give. The plan of action decided upon was that we would change goalkeepers. Thank God for that! For us, the game got worse and the final whistle saw us trailing at 11-0. Deadly silence from us in the changing rooms, with the black guys celebrating their enormous win; if looks could kill, they would have all been ironed out on the floor. On the way back to our cars, Billy and Patsie were almost inconsolable, with Billy threatening to go back and cut a couple of the other team. It wasn't quite the right time to say "I wonder if the Arsenal had a couple of their scouts watching the match and wanted to sign a couple of our team."

The following Saturday, we went on from a party in Islington to the flat of a woman named Margie and continued the party there. All of a sudden, there was a great eruption, and a guy came raging into the kitchen. From what I could make of it, his girl had had too much to drink and had gone up into one of the bedrooms to lie down. A short time after, she had wobbled down the stairs to tell him someone had interfered with her while she was inebriated. He was rucking and ranting and threatened to kill whoever was responsible. My pal Mickey said, "Are you sure this happened? Maybe she imagined it due to the amount of booze she had drunk." The guy then accused Mickey of being the perpetrator and Mickey told him to fuck off. The other guy grabbed a knife and tried to attack Mickey, but Margie and his sister grabbed him and took the knife from him. I told him Mickey and I had been in the kitchen since we first arrived, and his sister and Margie vouched for us. He carried on ranting, so I said to him, "Look, Mickey is a married man and would never do something like that. If this happened to your girl, it makes me sad to hear it, but if you continue to accuse Mickey, it will get out of hand. He's likely to fetch something from his car and shoot the shit out of you." "Yeah," was his response, "I will stick it down his throat!" I said, "Listen, pal, that is the talk of a silly man. You don't know who you are dealing with. Let it go." He walked back to his girl, who was sitting on the settee, and sat at her feet to comfort her. Eventually, Mickey secured one of the girls at the party for a dance, and as they passed the guy, who was still sitting on the floor with one of his hands flat on the carpet, Mickey trod on his hand. He gave out a shout and it all started up again. Intentional? I never found out. Mickey apologised, but I knew his heart wasn't in it. I said to him, "Let's get out of here," and I took him to a nice club I knew in the West End. "Never a dull moment."

A rather sad story I was involved in started with a coach trip to Margate. About thirty of us set off at 8 am in lovely sunshine for a day at the seaside. When we arrived, we made our way to the famous Dreamland amusement park and went from one attraction to another. At the Big Wheel, Jackie and Billy decided they would have a ride. The rest of us were at the barrier watching our two guys getting higher and higher until finally they were right at the top. We could see the car swinging backwards and forwards dangerously, when suddenly Billy was ejected outwards and came crashing down right at our feet. It was terrible to behold, and we were all in a state of shock. An ambulance and the police were called, but I think we all knew that Billy had sustained serious injuries.

Billy was taken to Margate Hospital and we all waited outside. Finally, a white-coated doctor emerged from the building and informed me, very sadly, that our friend had died. When Jimmy heard the news, he went into hysterics and we did our best to console him. We then had to try and locate our coach driver, and after scouring a couple of pubs, we found him and told him about the tragedy. We left Margate soon after and that evening watched coverage of the accident on the early television news. A couple of weeks later, we all attended Billy's funeral with his family.

I would sometimes drink in a pub in Islington with Dick and his brother Ronnie, who introduced me to a butcher, Stan, whose shop was next door to the pub. We soon became quite pally and he bought my car, which at the time was a Mini. He said, "Always pop into the shop, Roy; there'll be a nice piece of steak for you." In those days, I was a meat-eater, although I am ashamed to admit it today. Next door to his shop was a ladies' hairdressers, and whenever I visited the pub, the same girl would come outside, say hello and engage me in conversation. After a while, Stan commented on this and warned me she was a Greek girl. She had three brothers who would not take kindly to my striking up a relationship with her, as they liked to court and marry within the Greek community, and it would not be worth the agg I could find myself in. After that, I stayed away from the pub completely in case I fell by the wayside and threw caution to the wind. On passing Stan's shop a couple of weeks later, I popped in to see him. As we were speaking, a car pulled up outside and Stan said it was his governor. I thought he owned the shop, but he said no, he just managed it. When the guy came into the shop, I was introduced to him and we exchanged which part of London we each came from. He told me his surname and the street in the West End where he lived, and I said, "I used to know a girl from that street who I was once involved with." "What was her name?" he said. "I might know her." I gave her full name and the name of the flats she lived in, and he said, "That is my wife." I said, "Sorry, I had no way of knowing! I'm sorry if I have embarrassed you." He said "That's OK," but not very convincingly, and behind his back, Stan gave me a wink. I am willing to bet when he got home, he said to his wife, "I met an old friend of yours today," and then the quizzing began. I also realised how Stan was able to keep loading me up with steak on every visit. He never had to pay for it.

I was having a drink in Fulham with a pal of mine who was expecting his girlfriend to pop in and join us during her lunch hour. She arrived with another girl who worked in her department. She was a very beautiful Jewish girl named Judy, who looked remarkably like Elizabeth Taylor. My pal and his girl went to sit at a table, leaving Judy and me chatting at the bar. She was vivacious and friendly and laughed easily. She mentioned her parents lived in Bournemouth, but she much preferred London. Before they left, she gave me her office and home number and a week later, we spent the day together. This soon developed into a regular thing. She told me she was moving out of the flat she shared as there was not much privacy and was taking a lovely little cottage in Boston Place, which was just off of Baker Street NW1. We met one lunchtime and I could see she was stressed over an incident at work. She sat close to an office window whilst typing and had put a paper cup full of coffee on the open window sill. The wind had blown it off and down onto a foreign visiting couple three floors below, and they had come into the building to complain and seek some compensation. The security guy for the building had gone from floor to floor, with the couple in tow, trying to find the culprit. They finally arrived on Judy's floor and she admitted she was to blame. I said to her "Why did you say you were responsible? There are five floors, with a couple of hundred windows that the cup could have blown out of. Why did you own up to that? You should have said you knew nothing about it. None of us is responsible for the way the wind is blowing." The couple in question had demanded £50 compensation to pay for dry cleaning of the garments, and Judy gave them a cheque. I said to her, "As lovely as you are, I think I have to take you in hand and give you an education in the ways of the world."

One day over lunch, she told me an ex-boyfriend, a Jewish guy by the name of Lawrence, was pestering her to resume their former relationship and was becoming a nuisance. I offered to have a word with him and called him later. When he picked up the phone, I said, "I am calling on behalf of Judy. She has asked me to tell you she has no desire to have anything more to do with you, and what's more, she is now with me." "Who are you?" he asked. "I am just the guy in the middle, the guy who is giving you a friendly warning that as from now it stops! I have your phone number and Judy has your address! I don't have any agg with you and you certainly don't want to have any agg with me by a visit to your address. Do you understand me?" I put the phone down, and suffice to say, there were no further calls.

We continued seeing each other for some time, but I was also seeing Kathy and two or three other girls. For a week or so, I could not reach Judy on the phone at her work or home, and one day I came face to face with a friend of hers, Eileen. I told her the problem, and she said, "Have you not heard? She is in St Mary's Hospital in Paddington, recovering from an overdose, trying to commit suicide over you, you bastard." I said, "Hold up a minute. I never ever made any commitments or promises to her. As far as I am concerned, we both enjoyed each other's company and I never put her in the promised land. I am so sorry for what she has gone through and the thoughts she must have been wrestling with, of which I had no idea, but I feel I cannot be held responsible for what has happened. I feel a visit from me to the hospital would not be a good idea, but please let her know that we have spoken." She said she would let Judy know, and she walked away. I mentioned in a previous chapter that I think men love in a different way to women. I sincerely believe that a woman cannot be in a continuous romantic and sexual relationship without becoming emotionally involved.

Just prior to starting my last and final incarceration at Wandsworth and Eastchurch, where I eventually received parole, I was walking through Hoxton and saw a very pretty young girl sitting on the wall outside the block of flats she lived in. I thought I'd file that for future reference. I saw her again the following week and we spoke and she said her name was Yvonne. We met a few times after that, but she suddenly told me she was engaged. I said that I was not the kind of guy to waste her time or mine; neither was I the kind of guy to impede another man's happiness. However, if she was not very happy with her arrangement, I would be happy to continue with our relationship, if that is what she wanted. We continued to see each other, and she would let me know when she was out for the evening with the other guy and what time she would be home. I would be waiting in my car outside her flat, and he would walk her up to her mum's flat, and say goodnight. After a couple of minutes, I would hear the lift door open and he would emerge and run across the road to catch the bus home. Two minutes later, she would also take the lift and come running over to my car, and we would spend the night in my flat. Sometime later he developed mental problems and became violent and she was forced to break off the engagement. I console myself with my former statement, "I would not impede another man's happiness" because he never ever knew that Yvonne and I were seeing each other. After a while, I had things to do and Yvonne had her life and we didn't see as much of each other as we used to. We remain good friends right up to the time of writing, and I feel sure that Yvonne would join me in remembering those lovely times when she and I were together.

On one particular weekend, when I was with a few of the chaps having a drink in the Mildmay Tavern, in walked Yvonne, whom I had not seen for quite some time, with another very pretty girl who she introduced as her sister Chrissie. They stayed most of the evening in our company and as there was no party scheduled for that night, I suggested we finish the night off at the Merry Go Round in the West End. At that point, Billy, one of my friends who had been making up this foursome, said to me whilst we were at the bar ordering a drink, "Which one are you with?" I replied, "Which one do you like?" He said, "Yvonne." I said, "That's fine with me." We headed for Billy's car that was just outside, and he put Yvonne in the front seat next to him and I was in the back with Chrissie. She said just after we'd left, "I have heard all about you, Roy." "How do you mean?" I asked. She replied, "How you like the girls and you are always with a girl." I said, "You have heard right in both instances. I am with a girl now and I very much like you!" We finally arrived and entered the club. I introduced Chrissie to various friends and we had a very nice evening. We carried on seeing each other over the following months, and Chrissie obtained a flat for herself in Newington Green, North London. I would stay with her at times, and sometimes she would stay with me at my flat.

When things were going well, I bought a boat that was in less than good condition from a private seller in Caversham, Berks, and had it delivered to a marina on the River Lea where I worked on it all through the summer. The boat was a 27ft Norman cabin cruiser which slept three in the forward cabin, two in the main cabin and one in the wheelhouse. The beautiful wooden interior had been totally neglected, but I brought it back to its former glory. The inside of the vessel looked beautiful but it took a lot of hard work. Then I started on the exterior and took advice from a couple of old Jack Tars (ex-naval guys) who had their own boats in the yard. They told me what paint to use and how many coats; it had to be marine yacht paint, which is waterproof and has anti-fouling properties built in. Finally, at the end of summer, the restoration was complete and she looked a picture.

Chrissie and I were friendly with a lock keeper on the river at Harlow Mill, a certain Frank Carr who was employed by British Waterways, and at times we would take the boat upriver to visit him for the weekend. My cousin Joanie and her husband Arthur would come and see us in the marina and they caught the bug and purchased their own small craft. It was something nice to look forward to on a weekend when the four of us got together.

After a while, I gave up my flat and, at the invitation of Chrissie, moved into her flat, as by this time we had become an item. I decorated the whole flat and built a fireplace with an aquarium below it, level with the floor. It had a light behind it, and when the room light was out and just the aquarium light on, it really looked lovely as it lit up the carpet.

CHAPTER 30

REPUBLIC CÔTE D'IVOIRE

This is a series of vignettes of my experience working for the Embassy of Ivory Coast, a former French colony in West Africa.

In 1969, after my release from prison, I received a call from Jeanie, who was working for a recruitment agency in the West End. She told me a request had come in from an embassy in Belgravia for a driver, and it appeared to be a very good job. She made an appointment for me to attend an interview the following week.

I arrived at the Embassy in Upper Belgrave Street and was shown into the office of Mr Mobio, who was the Financial Attaché. He explained to me, in English with a French accent, the intricacies of the job and what was expected. It was Monday to Friday, two hours for lunch, wages paid weekly and various duties, which included visits to other African Embassies, the Foreign Office, the Aliens Office, and Buckingham Palace. Two drivers were employed, and we would look after the Embassy cars. The First Car, the Daimler Limousine, was used only by the Ambassador himself and sported the flag of Ivory Coast on the front. The number plate read RCI (Republic Côte d'Ivoire) or read backwards ICR (Ivory Coast Republic). The other cars were a very big Buick Electra 225, seven litre, two Ford Executives and a Jaguar, all of which had CD (Corps Diplomatique) on the number plates and on the windscreen, as well as a Mercedes that was used only by the Ambassador's wife, who was known as Madame Ambassador. She was taken shopping and to visit other Embassy wives by her own driver, who was an Ivorian. My first job was delivering a letter from the Ambassador to the Foreign Office. This was handed to me by his secretary, Leah, a very nice, friendly black girl who shared an office with his second secretary, Nicole. I had to find my way around these vast British establishments, but I had some help from the other driver, Paul.

My first visit to Downing Street was about a year before the big wrought iron gates were fitted because of the IRA threat. At the time, there was just one police officer on duty. He saw a diplomatic car, waved me in and then asked me my business. I then drove through the arch opposite Number 10 into the Foreign Office quadrangle, parked the car and entered the building. Facing me was the most beautiful staircase I had ever seen, sweeping to the left and the right. I expected any moment to see Errol Flynn and Basil Rathbone in that epic sword fight in the film *Robin Hood*. Someone pointed me to the office I needed and the letter was delivered. I made frequent journeys to the Foreign Office and the police officers got to know the car and me, but now they would ask me to open the boot and after a cursory glance inside would wave me through. Then one day, I saw that big gates had been fitted and there were many police officers inside, most of them carrying machine guns. I now had to show ID as well as open the boot, although they knew me and the car was diplomatic. I suppose they had to be seen doing their job. We were fortunate not to have to wear a chauffeur's uniform and hat with the usual cockade on the front; we wore our own suits. This Embassy never stood on tradition, which I much preferred.

Leah, the Ambassador's secretary, asked me to pop into her office and asked me a favour. She was living in Baker Street, Marylebone, and wanted to live closer to the Embassy. Would I be kind enough to help her move? She did not get on too well with the other driver, Paul, who was a bit doddery and set in his ways. She and I loaded up an Embassy car with her bags and small items and took them to Belgravia. All the while, Leah asked me questions about myself and the UK, although it was sometimes hard to understand her with her French accent and limited grasp of English. Suddenly on the car radio came a song that she loved: "Chirpy Chirpy Cheep Cheep" by the group Middle of the Road. She said, "Oh, Monsieur Roy, please make it louder!" and sang along with the song, word perfect. After that, Leah and I went on many excursions on behalf of the Ambassador or his wife.

One day, Leah asked me to come to her office as the Ambassador wished to speak with me. His enormous office was adjacent to Leah's and looked out onto Belgrave Square. She said, "He is waiting for you!"

I looked at her with a quizzical look. Pourquoi?

She smiled and said, "Don't worry."

So I knocked at the door, and a voice said, "Oui."

I pushed the two doors open and the Ambassador said, "Good morning, Monsieur Roy."

"Good morning, Excellency. You wish to speak with me?

"Yes, I would like you to take my two children out for the day tomorrow!"

"Where would you like me to take them?"

"You know London very well. I will leave it to you," and with that, he pushed an envelope across his desk and said, "Here are some expenses for the day. If you can bring the car round to the front of the residence in the morning at ten o'clock, I will make sure they are ready to meet you."

The following morning, the two children were waiting on the front steps of the residence, I settled them in the back of the Buick and we headed for Madame Tussauds. These two children were amazed at all the wax statues, if not a little nervous, they looked so real. After a couple of hours, I took them to lunch at Wendy's in Regent Street, which they loved. For the afternoon, I took them to Regent's Park, bought them an ice cream, and finished the day off by taking them to Hyde Park before returning them to their residence. When I checked the balance of the money their father had given me, which was a hundred pounds, I found I still had forty pounds. The following morning, I was again called to his office, and he thanked me and said his children really had a lovely time. I said it was a pleasure and offered him the envelope with the balance of forty pounds. He waved it away and pointed to me. "Pour moi?" I said.

"Oui," said he, and I thanked him profusely. All in all, a very nice day.

Mr Mobio and I had become very friendly. He did like a pint of beer, and next to our Embassy was a lovely old pub, The Horse & Groom. One lunchtime, he was passing the large garage where the cars were kept at the back of the Embassy and invited me for a drink. The small room that Paul and I shared whilst waiting for a job was below ground, with a window that looked out into the mews about five feet high. When Mobio was passing by at one o'clock, he would knock on the window, and that was my cue to join him every day for a drink. I introduced him to the small group of guys

I usually drank with, and he became one of the crowd. One day, he told me his birthday was approaching, and one of the gang suggested we buy him a cut glass vase and have it engraved. It was presented to him on the day, and it was so good to see his infinite pleasure.

The people I drank with were from all walks of life; there was Joe the milkman, who delivered the milk around Belgravia, my good pal George Webb, the Director of Chrysler Military Sales, a couple of estate agents, Alan, who drove for Camelot Car Hire in Belgravia, and a couple of his fellow drivers, and Rufus, a guy from Camberwell, South London, someone from my walk of life. He and I would sometimes speak in cockney slang and the rest of the gang would have no idea what we were talking about. Another guy who became a close friend was Steve, who was attached to the Diplomatic Corps and drove for the Embassy of Zaire, which was formerly the Democratic Republic of the Congo. Steve was a Welshman and looked very much like the singer Tom Jones. He also looked like the kind of guy you would think twice before upsetting. He drove the Ambassador around, much like I did, with one difference: on top of his Daimler Limousine was a blue light, the same as the police and emergency services have, which later featured in a very funny incident.

Steve also had a little black book that was full of the names and phone numbers of many good time girls in and around the West End who were always ready to oblige the many diplomats that were visiting from Africa. I was never sure whether Steve was paid in kind or some remuneration was offered by the girls, or whether it was all done as a favour. In many instances, Steve would turn up to meet me in an open-top Ford Mustang that belonged to a young lady who was friendly with a diplomat in Steve's embassy, and Steve would fill up with petrol kind courtesy of the embassy who were not aware as all embassies have petrol accounts with local filling stations and there is never a fine check. There is nothing to stop a person taking a diplomat's personal car to be filled and giving the plate number of an embassy car; it all depends who is working on the pumps and how friendly you are with them. In our embassy, a diplomat had to pay for his own petrol and only the engine oil would be paid for by the Government of that embassy, and that also applied to repairs; they had to be paid for by the owner of the car.

Steve was very friendly with one of the girls in his little black book and would send work her way by putting her in touch with one of the visiting diplomats. One day, we had arranged to meet in our local pub after work, and as the evening wore on, I told Steve I was going to leave as I had to catch a train home as there was not an embassy car available. He said, "Take my car. I can walk home." He lived in a lovely flat just the other side of Belgrave Square in Eaton Mews North, which was paid for by his embassy. We left the pub and I asked which one was his. He pointed to a beautiful red E-Type Jaguar. I thought he was at the wind-up, but he said it belonged to one of the friendly girls in his black book who did not need it for the week and had left it in his care. These cars were much sought after and always drew admiring glances. It was the hardtop version and the one I preferred over the convertible. I thanked him and said I would return it the following morning to his flat. Driving home, I was astonished at the power of this car. I loved the long, sloping bonnet in front of me and the amazing overall shape. I parked it outside our flat and could not help glancing back as I mounted the steps to our front door. The following morning, I delivered the car back to Steve and we sat in his flat with his wife Bernie. He told me he was about to give a guy a pull; it was someone who lived in the mews and was pestering Bernie as she arrived home from work each evening. When I asked who the guy was, Steve said it was the actor, Peter Sellers. I think Steve finally caught up with him and marked his card. One look at Steve and I know he would have backed off a bit rapid, and he never spoke to Bernie again.

That Saturday morning, we agreed to have a lunchtime drink in The Horse & Groom before I continued home. I was heading across Belgrave Square and walking towards me was a lovely mature-looking woman who said good morning! I replied the same, and a few steps past her I suddenly remembered who she was: she was in one of the Bond films and played the part of Pussy Galore. It was Honor Blackman! I turned around to look at her, and she had stopped and must have been looking at me after I had passed her. She gave me a wave and I waved back and continued to the pub to wait for Steve. I relayed this back to him when he arrived, and he said, "She must have been interested to have stopped when you passed and clocked you from behind, as well as giving you a wave. I am surprised, knowing you, that you did not speak to her and make a meet. You could have brought her in here for lunch – that would have made a few of the gang sit up, to see you with Honor Blackman on your arm!" I said, "Yes, I must be losing my grip. Anyway, she would have had to get in line."

Some diplomats could be very generous, depending which embassy you worked for. A pal of mine, Ted, drove for the Kuwait Embassy, and one of the diplomats had asked Ted to teach his young daughter to drive. Ted agreed and the Father bought his young daughter a brand new Mini, which used to be parked in the underground car park in Park Lane as there were no parking facilities at the Kuwait Embassy. After some time, the daughter lost interest in the lessons then gave up completely, and the car just gathered dust in the underground car park. Her father was finally recalled to Kuwait and Ted had the task of driving them to Heathrow. When they said goodbye, the father presented Ted with a solid gold Longines watch. Just before they boarded the plane, Ted remembered the Mini in the car park and asked the diplomat what he wanted him to do about it. "Where are the keys?" the father asked. "Hanging up in the Embassy," said Ted. "Keep the car for yourself," the father said, which was a lovely generous gesture. In the pub, Ted showed me the watch but said rather disappointedly, "Look at the back!" It said "Property of the Kuwait Government". I said, "So what, Ted? It doesn't detract from the watch. It is beautiful as well as very expensive, and when it's on your wrist, who knows?"

After I'd been a year or two with the Embassy, Mr Mobio asked me to pop up to his office as he had received a letter from Inland Revenue who wanted to know what British subjects were working for the embassy. This enquiry was sent to all foreign embassies, who could totally ignore it and were under no obligation to respond because of diplomatic privilege. He marked my card as to what to say should we be the recipients of a visit, which did not worry us at all as no one is allowed to enter an embassy except by invitation, not the police, Inland Revenue or anyone else as that would contravene the diplomatic immunity that all diplomats, as well as our own abroad, are afforded. One morning about ten o'clock, Paul and I were in the chauffeurs' room having a cup of tea when a head popped round our door and said, "Excuse me, are you working for the Embassy?"

"Who are you?" I said.

"I am from the Revenue Services," he said, showing an ID card. "We are trying to ascertain which British subjects are working for foreign embassies."

"For a start, you are trespassing and should not be on embassy ground unless you have written to the embassy outlining your inquiry and in turn been invited."

"My apologies. I was not aware."

"I suggest, then, you go away and brush up on your protocol concerning future visits you might have to foreign embassies."

Not to be put off, he then said, "Are you two British subjects?"

"Yes, I was born in the UK."

"Well then, you are obliged to pay income tax."

"Not true!" said I.

"I think, with respect, I know a bit more about taxation than you do!"

"I would not for a minute dispute that, but on this occasion you are wrong."

"How so?"

"When you receive your weekly or monthly pay, do you pay tax?"

"Of course I do."

"How many times on one wage packet do you pay tax?"

"Once, like most people."

"So do I. My tax is stopped at source."

"By whom?"

"The Ivory Coast Republic Revenue Services, West Africa, and no one pays twice on one wage packet. What you are asking me to do is pay your revenue services as well, and that would be illegal, morally illegal!"

"And how are you paid?" he asked, this time thinking he has got me.

"I am paid in French francs."

"And how do you spend them?"

"I take them down to the French Crédit Lyonnais Bank in Piccadilly and have them converted into pounds sterling." Got him! Silence all round!

Finally, he said, "Well, it would be in your interest to pay tax to the

British Government."

"How could it possibly be in my interest to pay twice? Perhaps you would let me know when you yourself have decided to pay twice and I might consider it."

He thanked me for my time and then it was tail between the legs and a rapid withdrawal. This all thanks to Mr Mobio marking my card.

I usually had an embassy car to take home each night, but on this occasion, there was none available and Leah suggested I borrow her car to take me home. The following morning on the way to work, I was halfway up the Mall when I became aware of a police motorbike on my tail. He drew level and waved me down.

"Do you know what the speed limit is here in the Mall?" he asked.

"Fifteen miles an hour, isn't it, officer?"

"You were doing thirty miles an hour, twice the speed limit. What's the excuse?"

"I am running late. I have to pick up His Excellency at our Embassy as he has a very important meeting at the Foreign Office."

"Which embassy are you from?"

I told him and he said, "In future, leave a bit earlier and allow for traffic. Meanwhile, you had better get on your way and watch your speed."

"Thank you, officer," I replied. That was a bit of quick thinking on my part.

In complete contrast to that incident, and also involving the police, Mobio called me and told me we had to go to Oxford Street to buy some new clothes for Roberto, who was the butler in the Embassy, as well as a couple of maids, who would all be accompanying us. So Mobio and I, with Roberto and the two maids in the back, reached the shop and I parked right outside the store, facing the traffic in rush hour. The others left the car and walked into the shop and I sat in the car waiting. A police car stopped behind me, and then there was a loud knocking on my window. I lowered the window and a police officer said, "Move it," in a very aggressive manner.

"I am waiting for the Financial Attaché," I said.

"I don't care who you are waiting for. Move it, or I will move it!"

"This is a diplomatic car and is covered by diplomatic privilege. It might interest you to know that a matter of weeks ago, one of your officers put his hand on one of our vehicles. My Ambassador sent a strong letter of complaint to the Foreign Office, which was passed to the Home Office, your governing body. The police officer in question was taken to task and could have lost his job, so go ahead and do what you have just threatened me with."

"You effing diplomatic mob are all the same," he muttered, got back in his car, pulled round me and sped away. I was never one for exploiting diplomatic privilege, but he was the one with the attitude problem. If he had said, "I can see you are in a diplomatic car, but can you pull round the corner and wait?" I would have said, "Certainly officer." My contention is "it is the approach every time" and it is good to see that there are some things that are beyond police control.

When our Ambassador received an invitation to attend a party in another embassy, usually on an evening, and if for some reason the Ambassador wished to decline, he would pass it down to the next one below him, and in this case it was the Chargé D'Affaires, who also declined and passed it down to the Commercial Attaché, who passed it down to the Financial Attaché, who was my boss and the last in line. He could not say no as it might be construed as snubbing the invitation, so Mobio asked me to drive him to the party, which was attended by various ministers from the UK Government and other dignitaries from various embassies. Mobio's command of the English language was still fledgling and he sometimes struggled to keep up and felt out of place, so he always asked me to accompany him. I was always attired in a suit and usually outshone those present, and no one knew who I was. After consuming a couple of drinks and sandwiches, I spied a young lady in a ball gown making her way towards us.

"Hello, there," she said in a rather plummy voice, "and who are you?"

Mobio remained silent and I said, "This is Mr Mobio, the Financial Attaché of the Republic Côte d'Ivoire in West Africa, and I am his assistant in the embassy."

"How lovely!" she said.

"And what do you do?" I asked.

"My father is with the Colonial Office, and I work with him."

"How lovely," I said, giving her the same treatment but without the plummy voice. Various people came over to say hello, and after a couple of hours, we left, with plummy voice waving us goodbye. I thought as we baled out I should have given her a pull. I felt sure she was up for it the way she kept glancing over, with an additional wave now and again. These society birds always did turn me on. Memories of "Shuperb".

Another of my duties was to drive His Excellency to Buckingham Palace for the annual Garden Party, where members of the British Government and show business stars rubbed shoulders with other members of the landed gentry and society. After I dropped him off, he would walk across the road and enter the palace through the Queen's Gallery, and I would park the Daimler on the parade ground of the Duke of Wellington Barracks with all the other diplomatic cars. Late in the afternoon, as guests were starting to drift away, over the loudspeaker system in the barracks the car for the Ivory Coast Ambassador would be called and I would pick him up outside the Queen's Gallery and take him back to our embassy. It was considered an enormous privilege to be invited by the Lord Chamberlain's Office. Finding the invitation card drop through the letterbox would send the recipient into untold raptures and cause one-upmanship on friends and neighbours. Personally, I would sooner spend an afternoon over the Arsenal.

My pal Steve and I were invited by some of the girls who worked in a nearby car hire company to their annual Christmas party. While I was dancing with one of the girls, she asked me why Steve was carrying a gun. I assured her he wasn't, but she said she had just finished dancing with him and insisted it was. "What would he be doing with a gun at a Christmas party? I said. "It is probably his wallet," and she seemed to accept my explanation. I got hold of him and said, "Have you got that gun on again?" He carried, now and again, a replica in a holster (whatever for, beats me!). I said, "Steve, if you get caught with that by the police, your feet will not touch the floor. You are not on the diplomatic list and are asking for trouble."

Steve's Daimler Limousine he drove for Zaire had, as previously mentioned, a blue light on top that flashed when a switch was flicked on the dashboard. My colleague Paul worked at the embassy all the week, then went home to his house in the country, which was situated in the wilds of Suffolk. He invited Steve, his wife Bernie, Chrissie and me to join him, and we had a lovely weekend in a very rural environment. We started back for London on Sunday afternoon with the two girls in the rear of the Daimler, sipping drinks from the built-in cocktail cabinet. There was an adjustable glass partition between the driver and the rear seating to allow the Ambassador to make a confidential phone call. He could also speak to the driver through an intercom that could be turned off or on from the dashboard. Suddenly, Steve and I heard the glass being raised behind us, as the girls probably wanted to speak about something private, not realising their conversation could be heard by us just by the flick of a switch, but it was only girl talk. In front of us was a traffic holdup, and Steve said, "We are not having this!" He pulled out of the queue and sped up the outside, flicking on the previously mentioned blue light that sat on top of the Daimler. Suddenly a police officer jumped in front of us, waved us down.

"Why do you have the blue light flashing?" he asked.

"I'm rushing the Ambassador back to London for an emergency meeting."

"Is the Ambassador in the back of the car?"

"Of course, that is what I have just told you!"

"And who are you?" he asked me.

"I'm the Ambassador's chief security officer and we are in a hurry!"

This idiot of a police officer then demanded to speak to His Excellency, and Steve said it was not possible. The police officer was trying to squint through the blacked-out windows. "Why is that not possible?"

"Because I assume you do not speak Swahili," replied Steve, and with that, he lowered the glass division and spoke some made-up gobbledygook to the non-existent Ambassador. "You will be reported to the Home Office for delaying His Excellency at a most important time!"

The officer backed off immediately and waved us on. You can slide a long way on soft soap and an equal amount of bullshit.

One of my friends whom I drank with at The Horse & Groom was George Webb, who was the Director for Chrysler Military Sales and had an office just off Belgrave Square. He looked slightly like the film actor Michael Caine and wore similar black horn-rimmed spectacles. Mobio became part of the gang, and we would spend our two-hour lunch break in the pub. One day, George asked us whether we were busy at the Embassy. Mobio said, "Comme ci comme ça," which I had to explain meant so-so. "Ok!" George said. "When we finish here, come back to my office and we will have a drink there." Mobio was all for it, and George gave me a twenty-pound note to pop into Binnelli's Delicatessen and purchase a bottle of Scotch to take with us. He also invited Joe the milkman to join us, and just after three o'clock, the four of us clambered onto Joe's Express Dairies milk float. With the empty milk bottles rattling around in the back, he drove us to George's office where we held a very convivial symposium, chewing the fat and drinking. Now I remember, with great nostalgia, the Director of Chrysler Military Sales and a diplomat riding on a milk float to spend some time having a sherbet with Joe the Milk and me. Priceless!

For some reason, His Excellency was called back to Ivory Coast and the Chargé d'Affaires became acting Ambassador. Mr Viera was not the easiest of people to get on with. I was called to his office and instructed to meet two visiting diplomats at Heathrow Airport the following morning. I pulled the car into the VIP enclosure and waited for them to surface in the VIP lounge. I immediately picked them out as they were the only two African people there. I identified myself and delivered them to Mr Viera's office. I was needed the following morning to take him and these two diplomats to a couple of addresses in South London, namely Lewisham and Crystal Palace. On the way there, one of the diplomats in the back complimented me on my driving, as well as my knowledge of London, for which I thanked him, and continued driving with one hand resting on the automatic gear stick and the other hand on the steering wheel.

A couple of minutes later, Mr Viera said to me, "Do you always drive with one hand?" "I drive how I feel comfortable, Mr Viera!"

"Isn't that a bit dangerous?" he said.

"I have driven this way since I passed my test way back in 1959 and have never had an accident. I have driven articulated vehicles, tank transporters and forklift trucks, as well as just about any make of car you can mention, and in addition, driving His Excellency about in the Daimler, and he has always been satisfied. He even trusts me to let me drive his two children about! But if you feel your person is compromised or in any danger, I will willingly take you back to the embassy where you can request another driver for the day."

That shut him up; not another word from him. He was a little, jumped-up prat who thought he would exercise his newfound powers as acting Ambassador, but this never cut any ice with me. This would not be the last encounter I had with him. There was one that really put the cat among the pigeons.

The embassy had by this time engaged the services of another driver, a young Irish guy by the name of Ray Flannery, who was a very amiable guy and easy to get on with. One day, all three of us were standing outside the garage where the cars were kept when up drove a lovely brand new Jaguar Sovereign, and who stepped out of it? None other than Mr Viera.

"Is that your new car, Mr Viera?" I enquired.

"Yes," he said and started to hand me the keys.

"What are those for?"

"It needs a wash!"

"What are you telling me for?"

"I want you to wash it!"

"I don't wash cars for you. I am employed by the embassy, not you, and washing your private car is not part of my duties. I and the other two drivers look after the embassy cars."

"You will wash it," he said.

"Is that right? There's the hose and car washing equipment; you want it washed, you wash it."

"I will see His Excellency about you," he said.

"I suggest that is exactly what you should do, Mr Viera."

He then left to go to his office, and I went to see the Ambassador. I explained what had taken place between Mr Viera and myself; he listened intently and then signalled that it would be dealt with. I thought he would come down on my side as Leah had told me that there was no love lost between Mr Viera and the Ambassador. She also told me the following day that Mr Viera had been summoned to the Ambassador's office and it had been made clear that his car was a personal possession and he was responsible for its maintenance and upkeep. To me, in boxing parlance, a knockout in the first round!

But it didn't end there. A couple of months later, while the Ambassador was away on a trip, the president of Ivory Coast sent his two daughters to the UK to learn English and learn about the English way of life. I had to pick them up at London Airport and take them to Guildford in Surrey. They were about thirteen or fourteen years of age, and one was black and the other was white. The white girl had been adopted by the president as a child. I delivered them to the given address where the door was opened by a man and a woman who welcomed them in and said they would see me in a month's time. When I returned to pick them up and take them back to London Airport, the traffic was heavy and I started to worry about them missing their flight, so I put my foot down. Coming through Godalming, I was stopped by a police car and asked whether I knew the speed limit.

"Thirty," I replied.

"You were doing fifty."

"I know that, but these two young ladies are the daughters of the president of the Ivory Coast Republic and they have to catch a flight at London Airport."

"Sorry about that. I can see you are in a diplomatic car, but I have to give you a ticket."

"This further delay could cause them to miss their flight, and these two girls are equivalent to our royal family. Would you have taken the same stance if it was Prince Charles and Princess Anne in the car?"

No comment! I had to wait while he wrote out the ticket and I was reported for speeding. About a month later, I was summoned to appear at Godalming Magistrate's Court and explained it all to the magistrate who said it was a rather unusual incident and asked whether I was claiming diplomatic immunity. I explained that I couldn't as I was not on the diplomatic list at the Foreign Office. He said, "While I can commiserate with you, you have broken the law and the very minimum sentence I can offer you is a five-pound fine, with no points on your licence because of these unusual circumstances. Should you be able to produce a letter from your embassy, the five pounds will be reimbursed." I thanked him for his considerations and asked whether I could have time to pay. He looked at me incredulously and said, "You can't afford five pounds?" I said, "I do not carry cash with me, but I will send the court a cheque." I had no intention of paying the fine on principle. On returning to the embassy, I explained to Viera what had happened and that if he could give me a letter for the court, they would waive the fine. He flatly refused, with no explanation – tosspot! So no letter ever found its way to the court, and I never heard another word. I think it was Viera's way of getting back at me for refusing to wash his car. But karma was waiting in the wings. A week later, he was arrested coming out of a West End club in the early hours of the morning very much the worse for wear. He had no identity on him but claimed diplomatic immunity. He was thrown into the back of the hurry-up wagon and spent the night banged up in a cell while the police continued their inquiries. He could hardly issue a complaint to the Foreign Office about how he had been treated by the police as his conduct was totally unbecoming for a diplomat. What goes around comes around.

One of the guys who used to drink with us seemed to know what was going on in Belgravia as far as jobs were concerned and told me that Rex Harrison, the film star, was looking for a chauffeur. I had seen Rex Harrison on a number of occasions when he had popped into The Horse & Groom with his wife at the time, Rachel Roberts, and they always arrived in their coffee-and-cream coloured Rolls Royce. "If you fancy a change," he said, "I can arrange an interview for you." I had been with the embassy three years and thought I'd give it a spin, so an appointment was made for me. I arrived at Rex Harrison's home in lovely Grosvenor Crescent and was ushered by his secretary into a large, beautifully furnished room. He came into the room, strode over to me, shook my hand and offered me a seat. He was exactly as you see him on film and beautifully spoken. His secretary served tea on a silver tray, and he said, "Tell me about yourself, Roy." He was impressed by what I told him about my work at the embassy, then said, "I hope I have not got you around here on a wild goose chase. At the moment, I am appearing in a stage show at the Haymarket Theatre and we are not sure how long it is going to run. I really just need someone to drop me at the theatre every night and pick me up afterwards." "So it isn't full-time employment then?" "Unfortunately not, and my apologies if I have taken up your time on a fool's errand." I thanked him, we shook hands and I left, thinking I had come a little closer to my idol because he was a friend of Frank Sinatra.

The embassy cars were serviced and maintained by a company in the West End, and I was stepping out for a while with the receptionist who worked there, a certain Theresa. I was one day introduced to two guys who had their own car repair and servicing business in Battersea, South London, and after chatting with them I could see there was an opportunity that could be beneficial to both of us. The following evening in the pub with Mobio, I mentioned these two guys and how they would be much cheaper than the West End company. If we switched to them, it would save the embassy some money, so he told me to go ahead. I popped over to see them and said I had secured the contract for them to look after our vehicles. Furthermore, I told them every time they worked on one of our cars, they were to put a score (£20) on top for myself when they submitted their invoice, to which they readily agreed. One lunchtime, Mobio told me glumly that he had big trouble (his words) with his BMW and he thought that the gearbox was finished. I said that could be very expensive, and he nodded. After we returned to the embassy, I gave it some thought and felt sure I could solve the problem. I rang the guys over in Battersea and asked if they could put a new gearbox in a BMW or repair it, whatever was necessary, and they assured me they could. I arranged with Mobio to take his car to the garage the following morning, and he asked me how much it would cost. I said, "Blaise, it will cost you nothing." (Blaise was his first name, which I only used socially.) "Don't worry about it," I said. "This is just between you and me; it will take about two days. I will take you home tomorrow night and pick you up the following morning, and during the day I will collect your car and bring it back to the embassy." In a couple of days, I picked up his BMW, which was now running as sweet as a nut, and delivered it back to him. I said, "Why don't you drive it round the square and see how she runs?" He did and returned with a big smile on his face. "Trés bon!" he said, beaming.

When I gave him the invoice for payment (which was for many hundreds of pounds), I told him to look at the number plate on the invoice. It was the number plate of the Embassy's Ford Executive, and suddenly the realisation hit him. He clapped his hand on his forehead and exclaimed, "Mon Dieu!" He stood up from behind his desk and shook my hand and thanked me. I said, "That's OK, Blaise. You owe me a beer," and we both laughed. I did that favour for him for two reasons: one he was a friend and a very nice guy, and two, I was getting a nice few quid here and there and that favour gave me an element of protection because he was the one with the embassy purse strings; in the grand scale of things, his political career was in my hands. I still received my score on top, as arranged with the two guys, so a nice little tiggle was had all round.

Another reason I gave him that consideration was that as a diplomat, he could order any amount of alcohol, as well as cigarettes, from a company that was owned by the brewery giant Courage and would get it at the diplomatic price, which was unbelievably cheap. He could put in an order all through the year, whereas I, as an English subject working for a foreign embassy, was allowed only one order per year at Christmas time. Every time Blaise was about to put in an order, he would ask me whether I wanted anything, and I would order a case of whisky, which would cost me £12, as well as gin, Bacardi and Advocaat for Mum. When mixed with lemonade, it made a popular drink for women known as a Snowball. I also ordered cigarettes for Dad and me, but in 1970 there was a cancer scare and I decided to stop smoking. On my birthday, when I was driving around Hyde Park, down went the window and out went an almost-full packet of Dunhill, and I have never smoked since. I feel somewhat guilty for providing my Dad with all those cigarettes, as he died some years later, in 1983, of a lung-related disease, but he had been a smoker all his life.

The Ambassador Steve drove for lived in Bishops Avenue, Hampstead, which was also known as Millionaire's Row. Houses at the time started at two million, and the singer Gracie Fields, who was famous for her rendition of "Sally", had a house there. The Ambassador and his house were looked after by a friend of Steve's who was known as Ghana John, and he became a friend of mine, too. One evening, when the three of us were enjoying a drink in a local pub, he asked me whether I did any house maintenance –

electrical, plumbing, anything in general. I said I had a friend who was a qualified electrician, meaning Mike, whose best man I had been. John said he could put some work our way for a consideration, as there were things that needed doing back in Hampstead.

Mike was all for it, and I received a call from John, who invited me to view the residence. I was amazed at the size of the house; it was palatial, with a full-size swimming pool and tennis court in a very large garden. Hanging from the ceiling in the entrance hall was a lovely cut-glass chandelier that lit up a beautiful carved wooden staircase. John asked us to come on the Saturday morning as there was something wrong with the wiring of the chandelier. Mike and I traced the fault, and he wrote out a bill, which John sent to the Commercial Offices of the embassy. I picked up the cash from John, who deducted his agreed whack, and we all had a nice little bunsen burner.

The next episode was a leak up in the main bathroom. John had loosened a nut under the sink, and that had caused a leak while the Ambassador was in the shower. John was instructed to call in the plumbers, who arrived shortly after in the shape of you know who! Mike made out the invoice, same procedure, same whack all round.

Then His Excellency said that winter was on the way and the pool should be drained and cleaned, so John called in the pool maintenance people, and I'll let you guess who they were. We knew as much about swimming pools as we did about the flight deck of Concord, but John at least knew how to drain it. All kinds of things were added to the invoice (flush all pipework with anti-virus liquid; check all nuts, bolts and unions). We used to kill ourselves laughing and never once did we ever see the Ambassador, thank God. He might have recognised us as the plumbers, and if he had seen us cleaning and draining the pool, I suppose we could have said, well it's all to do with the water Guv!

Ghana John called me one day to ask whether I could drop off a bottle of very expensive champagne to an address in Park Lane. It would be delivered to me at my Embassy, and I would drop it off on my way home. I made my way to the block of flats, pressed the bell and the intercom said, "Come up to flat four." I rang the bell and was confronted by a vision of loveliness who looked to be in her early twenties. She said she was expecting me and invited me in. She offered me a coffee, and while she was busy in the kitchen, I had a look at the many photographs on the walls. I had paused at one when she entered and said, "Do you know who that is?" I had seen the face somewhere before and was trying to recollect who the elderly gentleman was. "That is Harry Raelbrook," she said. "Have you heard of him?" "Of course," I said. "I have worn his shirts for years. They are on par with Cecil Gee shirts." Some time afterwards, Harry Raelbrook went into liquidation but surfaced a year or so later and started another range called Mr Harry Shirts – same guy, same quality. My final thoughts before reaching home were, "I wonder who is financing that flat in Park Lane?" As if I didn't know.

In Piccadilly was another office of the embassy that handled sales of coffee from Ivory Coast and was run by Mr N'dere and his wife. I received a call one day from Leah to pick up Mrs N'dere and take her shopping at Brixton Market. Also working at this office was a tall, very lovely and friendly Haitian girl by the name of Micky Piere, who rolled her eyes when I asked for Mrs N'dere. On the way to Brixton Market, she sat in the back of one of the Ford Executives I was using and seemed to have an attitude problem. She never said a word, and when we arrived, I opened the rear door for her to alight. She stepped out and strolled off with a rather regal gait, beckoning me to follow. My job was to sit in the car and wait, which is what I should have done. She went from one stall to another, purchasing groceries and vegetables, then turned to me and said in a superior voice, "Take these back to the car!" No please or thank you! I said, "What did you say?" She repeated her last statement. I said, "I am not your servant; do not treat or speak to me like one. I am a commercial chauffeur, and I work for the embassy, not for you. You want your shopping taken to the car, take it yourself." And on that note, I strolled back to the car. She was furious and had one of the stallholders carry it for her. Not a word was spoken on the way back to her office. She alighted from the car and her parting shot was, "I will speak to the Ambassador about you." "As you like," I replied. A guy from her office unloaded all the shopping and carried it inside. Now I knew why Micky Piere rolled her eyes when I first asked for Mrs N'dere, who thought she was the Queen of Sheba. I knew I was on safe ground as Leah had told me often that the Ambassador did not like his staff or cars being used for anything other than diplomatic business.

Leah mentioned to me one day that she had bought a new car from a Triumph agent over in West London and it would be delivered brand new in three weeks' time. However, she would not be there to take delivery of the car as she had completed her three years in the UK and was allowed to travel back to her home in Ivory Coast for a three-month holiday. She asked me whether I would take delivery and sign for the vehicle, which I agreed to do. I asked her what she wanted me to do with it, and she said I could keep it and use it until she returned. Leah departed for Ivory Coast, and two weeks later, her car was delivered. It was gorgeous, a bright yellow convertible Stag sports car, and Chrissie and I used it for three months. In the three years that Leah and I had known each other, I had never found out that she was married and her husband was back in Ivory Coast taking care of his timber business. We would go out shopping for the Ambassador's wife, buying clothes in Selfridge's for his children, and Leah always referred to me as her English husband. We had a nice, friendly relationship. Finally, her holiday came to an end and I picked her up at Heathrow. She was so pleased to see me and was looking forward to seeing her new car, which I had washed and polished and locked up in the embassy garage. She was ecstatic when she saw it and hugged me and thanked me for taking care of it. Then she told me her husband Serge would be arriving in a couple of weeks and she would introduce us. She called me to her office one day and there he stood. We shook hands and he gave me the once over. "Leah has told me all about you," he said with his French accent, which I detected was not too friendly a statement, but it passed. I often saw him running about in the Stag, and one day he pulled round to our garage, jumped out and said to me, "Monsieur Roy, wash the car."

"Are you talking to me?"

"Yes.",

"Here is the hose and bucket. Your car, you wash it!"

"You know who my wife is; she is His Excellency's personal secretary."

"For what it is worth, I don't care if she is the corn beef inspector's wife! That is not an embassy car and does not warrant my having to wash it."

"I will see Leah about you," he said.

"Do that," I said.

Five minutes later, Leah came into our chauffeurs' room all flustered and said, "Oh Roy, I am so sorry! My husband was very wrong to ask you to wash the car and I have told him he must not speak to you like this!"

"Leah, you and I have been great friends for more than three years, and I would do anything to help you, but I will not be spoken to by your husband as if he is a diplomat. Mr Aggosie and Mr Mobio have never asked me to wash their cars, and if they did, I would be pleased to do so as they are both gentlemen, but your husband has no standing in our Embassy whatsoever. If I had complained to His Excellency about your husband's attitude, it would have made it awkward for you." More apologies from Leah, but I assured her that her husband's attitude had in no way affected our friendship. The relief was plain to see. I assumed it was a case from her to him, "Wait till I get you home."

Three weeks after this incident, he strolled round and apologised, shook my hand and invited me into The Horse & Groom to buy me a drink. He told me he owned a logging business or some kind of wood company and offered me a job as an overseer, with a house back in Ivory Coast. I declined the offer, telling him I knew nothing about timber or logging and it was too large a leap to make. After that, we became firm friends. He just needed a bit of straightening out, for which I think I marked his card admirably.

Gretchen and myself reminiscing at the Lock cottage in Sawbridgeworth

My two lovely boys, Smokey and Gizzy

My daughter, Sandra and myself

Myself, my lovely mum and my brother Tony in 2001

With my cousin Joanie and her husband, Arthur

Gretchen and I on the rim of the Grand Canyon in Arizona, in 2012

Myself with a monster locomotive in Kingman, Arizona 2012

Gretchen and I on a tour of the Arsenal stadium

In the cowboy town of Oatman, Arizona, in August 2012

A lovely lunch on a river boat with world champion, Ricky Hatton

With my good pal John Conteh at an evening of boxing

My two good pals, John H. Stracey and Charlie Magri. Two great world champions

A great night of Boxing with friends, John H Stracey on my right and Colin McMillan front row

My son-in-law Steve and my brother Tony attending an evening of Boxing

With Frank Bruno at a Boxing evening

A lovely evening at the 'London Hilton' with Kym Marsh, who starred in Coronation Street

Myself and my daughter Gretchen, with son-in-law Steve

My Daughter, Gretchen and myself

Just taken delivery of my new Ford Kuga.
I received more compliments on my two-tone shoes!

My daughter Sandra and I, dancing at a family get together

CHAPTER 31

MARIO

Within sight of the embassy was another pub that went by the name of The Pig & Whistle. It was there I met an American guy, Mario, who was rather loud and brash, and three of his friends. After buying my friends and me a drink, he said to me in a heavy Bronx accent, "I have seen you in here a couple of times. I have made a few enquiries about you and you seem a regular stand up guy." He was straight out of *The Sopranos*, Mafiosa written all over him. He was heavily built, with hands like a bunch of bananas, and in the coming months I saw him take on many guys in arm wrestling contests on the bar and never once lose. One day, he invited me to a dinner party at his flat in Grosvenor Crescent Mews, which was behind St George's Hospital on Hyde Park Corner. On the following Sunday night, Chrissie and I went to his flat and found quite a crowd there. Mario, wearing a full chef's whites, including the tall chef's hat, served up tagliatelle with a bolognese sauce that tasted like food from the gods. Apparently he had been a commis chef in his younger days. Six of us sat round the table, and when we had finished, we retired to the sitting room and the next six sat down to be served. All this was accompanied by an abundance of red wine. It was a lovely way to spend an evening and meet some very nice people. Mario asked me what I had on for the following morning, and invited me to breakfast. The next morning, I pulled into the mews with the Embassy's Buick Electra, which was almost as long as a bus and, I thought, being an American car, might remind him of home. Breakfast consisted of some left-over bolognese sauce on two slices of toast and endless cups of coffee. We then retired to the front room where he regaled me with the following narrative.

He had been involved in some fraud back home in the States pertaining to bearer bonds to the tune of six million dollars. He was operating with another guy from the States and two English guys, one a well-known producer who worked for one of the UK's television networks and whose name I had seen many times when the credits started to roll. It was their intention to cash these bearer bonds in the UK, but the American FBI had made the UK authorities aware they were on their way, and Mario and the other American guy were arrested as they landed at Heathrow and their passports impounded. The UK arm of the scam were also arrested, and all four were bailed at the magistrate's court while the British police continued with their enquiries. Finally they were charged with fraud and a couple of other crimes and were told they would have to appear at the Old Bailey.

Mario continued living in his Mews flat and always had plenty of money, sometimes to the point of embarrassment as he would never let me or anybody else pay for a drink or a meal. To be able to rent an apartment in swanky Belgravia, one needs to be very well-heeled. You cannot buy property in Belgravia as it all belongs to the Duchy of Cornwall, or did at that time; I think it has now been passed to the current Prince Charles. Mario told me his brother was the head of American Steel and Mario himself was the godfather to Frank Sinatra Jnr. How true that was I never did find out.

On Christmas Eve, we spent the evening in The New Horse & Groom near Mario's flat. About eleven o'clock, Mario suddenly said "Right! We are all going to midnight mass in a nearby church. OK, Roy?" I said, "Not for me. I'll see you when you get back." When he insisted, I said, "Mario, you are Catholic, and Chrissie and I are Church of England. We don't do mass." He reluctantly agreed but asked us to wait until they got back to have after-hours drinks, which he had arranged with the Governor. After an hour or so, they all returned and we continued drinking to the early hours of the morning. We became firm friends with one of the guys there, Barry, and his girlfriend Annabelle. Mario suddenly called for silence and we all wondered what he was going to announce. He called Chrissie and Annabelle together and said he had a small Christmas present for them. He produced two pieces of jeweller's paper wrapped around two big diamonds. We could not believe it. He thought an awful lot of both of the girls and would refer to Chrissie as my little cockney bird; he probably had no idea what a cockney was and had picked it up somewhere. The evening finally came to a close and Chrissie and I headed home to our flat in North London, full of wonder at what Mario had given the girls as a present.

We got to know a couple of guys from Romford who were in the motor trade and sold good-condition vehicles. One evening, Mario said to one of them, "John, could you get Roy a nice car? I'll pay you for it!"

I said, "Mario, I don't need a car. I have an Embassy car home every night."

"Don't worry about that. It's nice to have your own car."

We argued back and forth, and eventually I said, "Ok, if that's what you want, thank you."

A week later a Ford Cortina in very good condition was delivered to the pub. Mario asked John how much he owed him, while pulling out a roll of banknotes that would choke a horse. John gave him the price less discount for family and friends. He must have thought Mario and I came up with the milk this morning. Family and friends, indeed! I could have told John and his partner that I had pulled more strokes than the Oxford and Cambridge boat race crews put together, the adage being "Don't try to kid a kidder." Mario showed him the bankroll and said, "Or would you rather have these?" He opened up a small wrap full of diamonds. Did John's eyes light up! Mario explained that two of these were probably worth twice the price of the car, and brought them along nicely by saying, "The choice is yours, John! It makes no difference to me." "I'll take the diamonds," said John a bit lively, and Mario handed over two of the larger ones, which John deftly deposited in the top pocket of his jacket, handshakes all round.

One week later, John and his partner turned up at the embassy and said, "We have to take the car back, Roy, as those diamonds Mario gave us are not diamonds but zircons, which are worthless by comparison. We have had them assessed by a jeweller friend of ours and we are taking the car back. I apologise for what has happened, and it is nothing to do with you."

I rushed round to Mario's flat, let myself in with the key he'd had cut for me and saw packets of the so-called diamonds spread all over the dining room table. He was nowhere to be seen. I shouted out his name, the bedroom door opened and a completely naked girl stepped out and bade me good morning. Then Mario entered the room and she disappeared into the shower. "Who is she?" I asked. "Some girl I picked up from the club last night," he said. "She looks like some old brass to me. Are you mad? You don't know who she is and you have a table full of diamonds. She could have helped herself!" "She's OK," he said and that's all, while I waited for him to tell me they were just zircons, but I waited in vain. Finally, I told him John had been to see me and taken the car back. "Don't worry," he said, not at all perturbed, "we will get you another one." Another one, with the same procedure! I'll give that a rapid miss, thank you. My thoughts then turned to the Christmas presents he had given to Chrissie and Annabelle. They were probably wrong 'uns as well, which we confirmed when I had them valued in a nearby jewellery shop, and Barry and Annabelle received the same result.

About a week later, Mario introduced me to three American guys who were in the blood bank business. They collected blood and sold it on the blood bank market. They said it could be very lucrative and were wondering whether I, with my embassy connections, could help them get into Africa. I said I had no influence in that department but I could put them in touch with our Commercial Attaché, Mr Aggousie. They thanked me and said if they were successful, I would be given a substantial finder's fee, which would be ongoing. After they left, Mario asked me whether I had a Swiss bank account as I would need it if the venture took off. They had told him they would pay one cent into my account for every pint of blood they took, and there were millions of people in Africa. Blood's blood, whether it is from black or white people, and these guys sold it all over the world once it had been cleared as safe. The three guys were all millionaires.

I had a meeting with Mr Aggousie and gave him a brief outline of the proposal. He said he would be prepared to engage with them if they would contact him by telephone and make an appointment. I passed the message on to Mario, then sat back and waited and waited, but I never heard anything more.

Just before I left Eastchurch, I became friendly with a London guy by the name of Murphy, who, like most Murphys, was known as Spud. When he was released, he and his Spanish partner opened a club in the West End called Le Foyer. The club was for gay people as with this type of club, there were never any problems or violence and the weekly take was tremendous. One evening, Mario and I walked into the club and were welcomed by Spud, who introduced us to his partner. There was a small drinks bar set up for the clientele and a dance floor the size of a postage stamp with a few guys dancing with each other. We made three or four visits to the club after that, but one day Spud told me he could not afford to have us anymore as we were frightening the life out of the clientele. He explained that it wasn't so much me as Mario they were scared of – Mario, sitting at the bar with his fedora hat and vicuna overcoat, with shoulders as wide as a barn door, which would have been a good day's march across his back for any ant. Spud said, "I don't want to lose touch, Roy. You are always welcome, but if you do come to the club, try to bring a young lady with you." I then told Mario that the club was going to change hands and Spud and his partner were moving on, so we would not be going there anymore. I continued taking Chrissie to the club for a while, just to keep in touch with Spud.

I was looking in a jeweller's window in Bond Street once and saw a beautiful gold Omega De Ville watch with an elongated face as opposed to the usual round type. I asked the young salesgirl whether there was any concession for diplomatic staff, and when I explained my position in the embassy, she said if I could bring a letter stating that I was attached to the embassy, she would give me the diplomatic discount. I knew that Leah would give me a letter, or failing that she would accompany me to the shop and buy it after showing her ID, but she typed the letter in question and I purchased the watch. I'd had it about six months when Chrissie and I visited Spud's club and left in the early hours of the morning. We caught a cab home and woke up the following morning minus the watch. I rang Spud in case it had slipped off my wrist, then rang the Public Carriage Office, the governing body of the black cabs, and told them what had happened. They said they would contact me if any driver handed it in, which was most unlikely because if I had lost it in the cab, the next punter to get into the cab would have found it before the driver did. It was never recovered, and I lost it for good.

One evening in The New Horse & Groom, Mario introduced me to various people, including an ex Luftwaffe pilot who was still flying as a cargo pilot. He was of Italian extraction and went by the name of Vitorio. He was very friendly, spoke perfect English and was quite entertaining. Another guy, Barry, who'd heard Mario introducing me, told me he was the chauffeur for the millionaire financier Bernie Cornfield, who was quite often in the news and always flying round the world doing deals, albeit some of them shady, according to the newspapers. Barry said that he was looking after Mr Cornfield's house in Belgrave Square and asked whether I would like to see it. I said maybe later, as we had just arrived. Vitorio made his way over to Chrissie and me and started to tell us about some of the trips he had been on. One of them was a regular run to Goose Bay in Newfoundland in Canada, and he said that if we would like to see it, we would be welcome to accompany him the next time he had some cargo to drop off. With that, over came Barry again, asking whether I was ready to look at the house. I said "Barry, I am in the middle of a conversation with Vitorio. Leave it till later!" He gave Vitorio a glare and walked off. I said to Mario, "What's the strength of that ice cream, Barry?" He had no idea what I was talking about and I had to explain: ice cream freezer = geezer. "Why?" he said. "Is he straight or a nodder and smiler?" "No," said Mario, "I have seen him in here a few times with a girl – why?" I told him how insistent he was about showing me his boss's house, but Mario said he probably just wanted to show it off. As the evening wore on, I told him I was ready to go, and off we went to this magnificent house. In the basement there was a screen on the wall and rows and rows of red padded seats, with an aisle running between them. It was beautifully designed and must have cost a fortune. It just needed an usherette in uniform and an ice cream lady walking down the aisle as I was used to at the old Hoxton Cinema, but I'd bet there'd be no empty ice cream tubs and half-eaten sandwiches raining down on Bernie Cornfield's guests. Before we left, Barry said, "What do you think of that Vitorio?" I said, "He seems a nice guy and does a very interesting job." Barry said, "I fucking hate him!" "Why?" I asked. "I'll tell you later," he said. "We had better be getting back." I was telling Chrissie, Mario and Vitorio about the house I had just been in when Barry came over with a look on his face that spelt trouble. "So you were in the German Airforce?" he said to Vitorio. "I was," came the reply. "Bombing the shit out of London," said Barry. I thought things were going to get out of hand, and I tried to calm him down by saying, "Didn't we do the same to Berlin and Dresden, Barry?" but he wouldn't have it and ranted on. Then he said, "My brother was riding his bike during the war and a German bomb blew him off his bike and smashed the bike up. I'd bet it was you that dropped that bomb!" Vitorio said with a straight face, "Was it a blue-coloured bike?" We all burst out laughing at his quick and witty response, and Barry slunk away, telling Vitorio to fuck off. Unfortunately, Chrissie and I never did get that trip to Goose Bay.

CHAPTER 32

MARIO'S TRIAL

Mario had outlined on more than one occasion what was in the pipeline for us once the trial was out of the way. He said, "When this trial is over, Roy, we are going to Portofino!"

"Where is that?" I asked. "And what are we going to do there?"

"It is a beautiful place in Genoa, and we are going to open a restaurant there. I will be the chef with two or three commis chefs assisting me."

"Mario, I know nothing about the restaurant business or food! What will be my position there?"

"You will be the manager, wearing a white suit, meeting and greeting the customers. You will look the part as you are always very well dressed, and you will be in charge of the waiters and waitresses and the day-to-day running of the restaurant."

"Ok. Let us see how the trial pans out."

"Don't worry about that! It is all taken care of, and I have more money than you would believe coming from the States to finance the venture."

On the morning of the trial, a few of his friends and I went to the Old Bailey to support him. Mario, the other American guy and one of the two English guys stood in the dock; the other English guy who was working for a television network was told all charges against him had been dropped. All three had submitted a plea of not guilty, but all three were found guilty. The American received a four-year sentence, the English guy walked away with three and Mario was given a five-year sentence. We were all dumbstruck, but worse was to come. Keeping the five-year sentence company was a deportation order. He would have to complete two-thirds of the sentence, and with good behaviour he could be released, so Mario could be out in three years and three months. Six months before his release, he would be transferred to an open prison, and then picked up by the police, put on a plane and deported back to the States. I went down to the cells below the court to see him, and he was somewhat deflated. I tried to cheer him up and asked him what I should do about all his possessions in the Belgravia flat. "Take everything you need," he said, "You have the key." I said, "Drop me a line and let me know where you are, and I will write to you." Alas, I never heard from him again and there was no way of keeping in touch. Chrissie and I went to his flat and loaded up our car with things we thought would be of some use, and all his clothes went to a charity shop. I became quite emotional in that empty flat that held so many happy memories of dinner parties and the interesting people I had met. At the time of writing, all I have left is the large pasta bowl in which he would serve up the tagliatelle. I am pleased that Mario and I were pals for those couple of years and believe my life was richer for knowing him.

CHAPTER 33

CHANGING OF THE GUARD

Mobio received instructions from his Government that he was to be transferred to the Ivory Coast Embassy in Brussels, and his replacement would be transferred from the Paris Embassy. When the new Financial Attaché arrived, Mobio called me to his office to meet him. He seemed a nice guy, and when Mobio introduced us, he said, "If there is anything you need help with, Roy is the one to speak to. We have been good friends for some years and he is a good man." Later that day, the three of us had a drink together in our local pub.

Before Mobio left the office for Brussels, he asked me whether I would drive his car to the Brussels embassy if he bought me an air ticket back. The thought of driving his BMW there was very attractive. Chrissie accompanied me on the journey, and I had purchased a flight ticket for her for our return. At the embassy, Mobio thanked us both warmly. He had met Chrissie on a couple of occasions when he had invited us to dinner with his wife, Josephine, at his house in Olympia. It was quite emotional when we shook hands and hugged for the last time. We'd had a lot of laughs together, and I had, as usual, pulled a few strokes for him. When we had our last drink together with the usual gang in The Horse & Groom, we presented him with a glass tankard inscribed with his name.

A week later, I was called to the new man's office and told his Peugeot 504 was still at the Paris Embassy. He asked me whether I would like to fly there to pick it up and drive it home, if he paid for the flight there. I readily agreed, and another nice trip was enjoyed.

Leah called me to her office one day and informed me that the Ambassador's wife's baby, who had been named Stephanie, was due to be baptised in the French Notre Dame Catholic Church in the West End on the following Saturday. Paul, Ray and I would be needed to drive invited guests as well as some diplomatic staff to the church and return them to the embassy for the planned celebrations. When I relayed this back to Paul and Ray, I suggested we have an audience with His Excellency to discuss our pay for the Saturday. Paul said he was about to wash a couple of the cars, but I could go ahead. Ray looked like a bottle of milk at the very thought of confronting the Ambassador face to face and said, "We will leave it to you, Roy!" I had no backup from these two gutless workmates, which might have made our case stronger. I went to see His Excellency and asked for a moment of his time.

I said, "I understand you would like your three drivers to work this coming Saturday for the baptism of your daughter?"

"Oui."

"May I ask you, Excellency, how much you will be paying for us working on Saturday?"

"I am not offering any pay for Saturday!"

"Why is that, Your Excellency?"

"I don't receive any pay for working Saturday!"

"With respect, Your Excellency, you are an Ivorian representing your country, but I am an Englishman, and here in England, if we work extra hours, we would expect payment for those hours. When the window cleaner comes to the embassy to clean all of the windows and the plumber comes if there is a problem in the kitchen, do you pay them?"

"Oui."

"Then why would you not pay us for working outside of the hours agreed with Mr Mobio?"

This was met with a shrug of the shoulders, a response that was hardly becoming for a man in his position. Rising from the chair, I said, "Thank you for your time, Your Excellency, but I have to tell you if we aren't to be paid, we will not be working!" Another shrug of the shoulders! I returned to the chauffeurs' room and the other two, all ears, wanted to know how I'd got on. "He is not going to pay us," I said, "so we have to make a stand. Let's agree now we will not work on Saturday, is that right?" and they both agreed we would not work. When I got to work on the Monday morning, I learnt both of them had worked for no pay, despite my fighting their corner, and Roberto, the butler had driven my car. I was well wound up and told them their fortune! They stood there like two naughty schoolboys. If it had been an industrial dispute, these two would have been labelled as scabs. They were like two big Easter Eggs, nice on the outside and fuck all inside!

At this point, I would like to include part of a letter I wrote to a friend some years ago describing an incident that happened to me whilst I was at the Embassy. It may appeal to those of a romantic inclination.

A couple of weeks ago, I was watching a film on television, Indecent Proposal, starring Robert Redford and Demi Moore. In one particular scene, he relates to her a story about travelling on a train and totally losing his heart to the most beautiful girl he had ever seen. He finally had to leave the train without knowing who she was or making contact. He waited every day after that, hoping that he would see her again, but he never did and never forgot that beautiful face. I found myself reaching back for yesterday, searching till a long-forgotten love appeared, although what I am about to relate was hardly an affair but something very special, and when it comes to mind, I always become emotional and feel some silver springing up in my eyes. The film was made in 1973, and the incident that happened to me was three years earlier. It was almost identical, but this was no ordinary girl. This is just the prelude to my story.

My Story

I shall call it "A Journey Home on a Downtown Train".

When I was working as chauffeur and aide to His Excellency, the Ambassador of the Ivory Coast Republic, I would invariably have an embassy car to drive myself home. It afforded me all the privileges of working for a foreign government: CD on the number plates, as well as a tax disc that said "Exempt", which allowed me to park anywhere with no retaliation from parking attendants or police.

On this particular day, there was no car available for me to take home and I was forced to take a tube train from Hyde Park Corner to Old Street and change at King's Cross on the Northern Line.

The train pulled into Hyde Park Station and I settled down ready for the journey ahead. At the next stop, which was Green Park, people entered the carriage while I was totally engrossed in the newspaper I had started to read. The train pulled out and I peeped over the top of my newspaper. Opposite me was the most beautiful face I had ever seen, framed by a nun's cowl, the usual black and white, and below that she wore a full nun's habit with a crucifix resting on her chest denoting the anchoritic life she had chosen. To the point of rudeness, I found it almost impossible to avert my eyes.

She, on more than one occasion, caught me looking at her and coyly, as only a woman can, lowered her eyes to the floor. I feel sure that other men on that train must have been transfixed by her beauty, but I felt that each returned gaze from her was just for me.

The train rumbled on towards King's Cross and I hoped it would break down or experience some delay to stop it reaching its destination so I would have more time to spend in that carriage with her. I caught her looking at me on one occasion and held her eyes, and this time she did not look away. I started to feel those butterflies that one gets at the first stirrings of love.

The train winged its way across town and finally King's Cross Station loomed in the near distance. I knew I would have to leave and pick up my connection for Old Street. The train stopped and I made a move to leave. I could feel her watching me, I locked onto her eyes and winked at her, and she gave a beautiful smile and dropped her eyes to the floor.

I stepped out of the train and stood on the platform willing her to look up. She did, and our eyes met again as the train pulled out of sight, and then she was gone. For the first time in my life, my breath was taken away, and for that short time, I fell totally in love with that beautiful person.

I travelled that same route many times in the coming years and always hoped I would see her again, but alas, I never did. I always wondered what her name was, what order she belonged to and where she lived. I guess I will never know.

I have never forgotten that vision of loveliness that fate put in front of me, and I feel sure that we both shared a special moment on that "Journey Home on a Downtown Train".

The Ambassador was recalled to his country and promoted to Director-General which I understand is something to do with internal security. That left my old adversary, Mr Viera, in command as acting Ambassador. I was called to his office one morning and told that two visiting diplomats would need to be met at Heathrow at 6 am the following morning. "Very good, Mr

Viera," I replied, "I will take one of the embassy cars home this evening so I can get an early start in the morning."

"No, I don't want you to take an embassy car home!"

"I have no other way to get here to pick up a car. The underground trains do not run all night, and I would have to leave my home anyway at about four-thirty to be at Heathrow by six. How would I get to the Embassy to pick up a car and get there in time?"

"It is not my problem," he said.

"You are giving me an impossible task! I have always taken an embassy car home with the approval of His Excellency, as well as Mr Mobio."

He shrugged his shoulders, being as bloody-minded as possible and probably remembering I had got the better of him on a couple of occasions; the Ambassador had given me right and torn a strip off him.

"If you cannot do the job in the morning," he said, "you must resign."

Never one to back down, I said, "As you like," and walked out.

And that was how five years with the Embassy came to an end. This no-good little weasel had finally got the better of me. I would have liked to meet him on a dark night in an alleyway or gone to where he parked his car at night, armed with a bradawl for the four tyres and a can of paint stripper, and made a fuss of his shiny new Jaguar. I came out of his office and on the way down saw Leah and told her what had happened. She put her arms round me and started to cry. Nicole was also very upset, as was our receptionist, Luciana.

CHAPTER 34

"I DO."

A couple of months before I terminated with the embassy, I started to play host to a gang of construction workers who had been engaged to renovate the inside of an office building on the corner of Grosvenor Avenue. There was a preservation order on the outside of the building as it was a listed building. The gang consisted of about six Irish guys who were all very amiable and would be in the pub every lunchtime. One of them, Tom, was an enormous man, about six feet six and almost as wide. When he overheard me speaking with one of my pals using various slang terms, he came over to us and said he also spoke a lot of cockney slang. He had me teach him more and often said, "I have always mixed with cockney people but have never met anybody who knows as much as you do." The trouble with Tom was that he was always skint. He was paid on Friday and by Monday was potless. One Monday lunchtime, he said to me in the term he used, "Can I beg you?" I said, "What do you want, Tom?" He said, "Can you oblige me with a few quid until Friday?" so I gave him a tenner, and come Friday, the tenner was put back. The same thing Monday morning, so I said, "Tom, I do not loan money to friends, I give!" and gave him a ten-pound note. He was so appreciative and said it would be back on Monday. "No, Tom," I said, "I am giving you that tenner. It is not a loan, and anytime you are short, you come and ask me before anybody else." I knew that he would never ask me again. He had no problem borrowing the money because he could always put it back but would feel awkward asking for another gift of £10 knowing I would not take his money. He said, "Love you, Roy!" and putting his hands under my arms, he lifted me right off the floor, kissed me in the middle of my forehead and then lowered me onto my feet, all this in front of other customers in the pub. We came to be good pals and he never got into me again for a loan. I was also good friends with his cousin, Bill, who was the ganger man.

These Irish boys would spend an awful lot of money every lunchtime, five days a week, and after a couple of weeks I was pulled to one side by the guv'nor of the pub whom I'd come to regard as a good friend. He said apologetically, "Roy, I cannot afford to have these Irish boys in the pub anymore. I know they are all your friends and they spend more money than the rest of the punters here put together, but these are my regular punters, and by the time the job Bill and Tom are working on comes to an end, I will have lost all my regular customers. Some of them have complained to me about the way the boys are dressed."

"Jimmy, they are hard-working guys and have never said a word out of place."

"I know, but they are coming in here in wellington boots with dried concrete on their clothes. It is upsetting some of the customers who sometimes have their wives and girlfriends with them, as well as all the office workers."

"I assume then, Jimmy, you want me to break the news to them?"

"Would you mind? I know how well you get on with them."

"OK," I said, and from then we started to drink in another pub close by the embassy.

Bill the ganger man said, "I hear you are finished with the embassy. If you are looking for something just to fill in until something permanent comes along, there is always a job for you with me on the site. So a week later I started on with Bill and about fifty other workers rebuilding the listed building. The wages were just like the embassy, money in your hand every Friday, and good wages at that! All the original floors had been demolished and cleared, and all that remained were the outside walls. In came the iron fighters and the foundations were laid, then each floor was put in using RSJs (rolled steel joists), one floor at a time upwards. I would walk across these steel girders which were about eight inches wide, and I was OK for the first couple of floors, but as it became higher and higher I used to sit down and straddle them to cross from one side of the building to the other. There was nothing in between the steel joists because the flooring had yet to be fitted, and when you stood on the top you could look right down to the basement. By the time the top floor was installed, I had become an old hand and was strolling across the joists as if I was strolling through Hyde Park, with no fear of heights at all.

Bill asked me one day to help him load some building items into a guy's van, and I never thought any more about it. Having a drink with Bill after work that day, he put a hundred pounds in my hand and said, "That is for helping me with that bit of business today, and I will be putting you in for more." Tom said to me when Bill had gone to the toilet, "How was that, Roy, a nice little tickle?" I said I'd never expected it, but he said, "Bill thinks the world of you, Roy, and he will always put you in for your whack." Then I sussed it: Bill was selling off various building supplies to some private builder and was putting Tom and me in for our whack. This started to happen on a regular basis.

A friend of mine mentioned that a company located in Belgrave Square was looking to engage someone to take over the running and cleaning of the building and provide tea and refreshments to the staff at morning and afternoon break. It might suit a woman candidate, and a penthouse flat would be provided. I mentioned this to Chrissie, so she applied for an interview and successfully secured the job. It was a firm of architects and surveyors whose offices displayed a large bust of Sir Edwin Landseer Lutyens, who was famous for designing many up-market country houses. Chrissie and I moved into the penthouse flat. It was a beautiful building with lots of wood panelling and original features. The manager was a Mr Gallagher, who asked us to pop down to his office where he presented us with a key to the park in the middle of Belgrave Square. Only residents of the square were eligible to carry a key. In the park were statues of historical people as well as a lovely mausoleum with an open front with seating where one could while away the hours and take time for reflection, with just the sound of the birds for company.

Chrissie's job included dusting and emptying baskets in the computer room on the lower ground floor and the manager's office on the ground floor. I would help Chrissie do this when I came home from the building site. During this period, we decided to get married and were married at the Caxton Hall Registry Office in Westminster where people of high society and celebrities such as Elizabeth Taylor and Ringo Starr were married. After the ceremony, we retired to a little pub in Lower Belgrave Street called The Plumbers Arms. It was situated opposite the house of Lord Lucan, who would frequent it before he went on the missing list. We obtained permission to hold the reception in the large room on the ground floor of the building where we lived. Many friends and family attended, and it all went very well.

The manager approached me one day to find out whether I knew anyone who could scrub off the front steps of the building that by now were looking a bit the worse for wear. I informed him that I had at one time been a supervisor for a cleaning company in Hatton Garden and had scrubbed off many floors. He asked me I could see to it over the weekend, after we inspected the job together. Because the floor was marble, it needed specialist cleaning, and I asked my Dad to help me, not that I needed it but just to put a few quid his way. I showed Dad how to operate a scrubbing machine that I had hired for the day and we were finished by the afternoon. We scrubbed it off, let it dry and then poured bleach all over the marble. The bleach brought up all the white marble beautifully and emphasised all the coloured stone as well. On Monday when I arrived home from the site, Chrissie said Mr Gallagher wanted to see me in his office. He said, "Wonderful job, Roy! The front steps are a credit to you. You must have worked hard over the weekend." I agreed with him and laid it on a bit thick. I said I only finished late on Sunday evening, whereas it had been game shot at 4pm on Saturday afternoon. He paid me in cash and then asked me to scrub off the floor of the computer room and the main office, which had a large wooden parquet floor, which would be the earner.

I scrubbed and polished the floor of the computer room and then it was onto the main office. Dad helped me on this one, stripped the old polish off, resealed it and then applied two coats of non-slip emulsion polish, all the time keeping Gallagher abreast of the progress and how much work was involved. He was delighted upon inspection and paid in cash as usual. "You and your dad must have worked hard over the weekend," he said, "and it looks very nice for the president's visit next week." In actual fact, the job had been finished on Saturday afternoon!

The following Thursday, the company president was expected at 2 pm and all the staff were under starter's orders, looking their best, albeit somewhat nervous. Chrissie was extra busy doing sandwiches and cakes and large pots of tea which were to be served after he had done his inspection and met all the staff from the different departments. Gallagher had lined up all the staff, like at a Royal Command Performance, and they were talking quietly among themselves, awaiting this top jockey to make his entrance. Gallagher was buzzing around like a dog with two dicks and came down in the lift to the kitchen to let us know that the staff inspection was imminent. The three of us entered the lift and started to ascend to the main office. Gallagher said to me, "The president is a bit of a card, you know."

"How do you mean?" I asked.

"He likes to joke around with the ladies and pat their bums."

"If your president touches the bum, as you put it, of my wife, I will, president or no president, knock him out on the spot!"

He almost swooned when he heard this. "Oh Mr Wild, don't talk like that!" he said and threw his hands up to his face.

"Well, you had better mark his card, then. How would he feel if I touched up his old woman?"

We alighted from the lift and joined the line-up. Enter the president, a fat old boy in a cheap three-piece suit with the chain of office around his neck, looking like a refugee from the offices of Barnsley District Council. Chrissie and I were at the end of the queue, and when he came to us, Gallagher looked extremely anxious. "And who have we here?" asked the president. Gallagher said, "This is Chrissie, who looks after us with the teas during the day and keeps the offices looking nice, and this is her partner, Roy, who helps out. He shook our hands and then walked away with Gallagher. Maybe his card had been marked.

When it was time for refreshments, Chrissie and I retired to the kitchen to fetch the tea and eats. The floor of the small lift never aligned with the floor of the kitchen, and trolleys had to be lifted into the lift. Chrissie forgot about the uneven surface and the trolley she was pushing tipped over, scattering the food all over the lift and kitchen floor. "Don't worry about that," I said to Chrissie, who was almost in tears. We picked up all the buns, sandwiches and cakes, dusted them off and put them back on the trolley, a couple of them a bit wet from the large pot of tea that had also tipped over. I said, "Take the sandwiches up to them, and I will be making another pot of tea. Tell them we didn't have enough room on the trolley." So the sandwiches and everything else were royally served up and no one knew the difference, least of all his nibs. Chrissie and I laughed about it for weeks, but dark clouds were gathering on the horizon.

One morning in late September when I was passing Gallagher on the staircase, he stopped and said to me, "October the 1st this coming Monday."

I thought he was having one of his turns. "Why do you tell me that?" I asked.

"The boiler has to be lit now that winter is about to descend on us."

"I understand that, but why are you telling me?"

"It is your job to see to it and make sure it is always alight to keep the offices warm during the day."

"What are you talking about – 'my job'? I am not employed by you or your company, so where do you get that idea from?"

"It is part of your wife's duties, but I don't expect her to do it, so I think it is your responsibility as her husband."

"Listen to me. I do not need you telling me what my duties are as far as my wife is concerned. And when she first took this job, nothing was said about any boiler duties. In fact, we did not even know there was a boiler in this building."

"It is below ground, in the basement."

"Has it been cleaned out since last year, when I assume it was last used? All ash or clinker has to be removed before it can be freshly lit. I only know these things because I was in the asphalting business and was a cooker man, and that works on the same principle."

"I don't know."

"To start it up, you will have to have some firelighters, paper and wood kindling and then a small amount of coal to get it going. Then shovel more coal on until it starts to heat the water. At night, the fire has to be banked up so it is still alight in the morning. So where are you getting all these things needed to get it started?"

"I thought you could bring home some wood from the building site you work on."

With this, I nearly exploded. "This is nothing whatsoever to do with me or my wife, and what if she had taken the job and I was not living here, what would you have done then? You would have been forced to employ someone who knew something about stoking a boiler," and at that point, I walked away.

When I returned home from the site the following evening, I said to Chrissie, "The building seems warm. Who has been looking after the boiler?" She said, "I went downstairs to the kitchen this morning and heard some noise from the boiler room. I peeped in and Gallagher was in his shirtsleeves, shovelling coal into the boiler!"

"That's about right," I said.

One evening whilst watching television in our flat, we were surprised by a knock on the door. This was most unusual as the offices were all closed and the building locked up, with us two the only ones in attendance. I opened the door with some trepidation and standing there were two police officers, one in uniform and the other in plain clothes. I asked them what their business was and the plainclothes guy replied, "We have been informed that there are some books missing from the library downstairs."

"Why are you telling me?" I ask.

"It has been alleged that the missing items may be within these premises."

"Who alleged this?"

"We are not at liberty to divulge that information," he said. I sussed it almost at once: it was that weasel Gallagher. "Do you mind if we come in and look around?"

"Do you have a warrant to search these premises?"

"I can get one if that is what you want."

"At this time of night? It has to have the magistrate's court stamp and be signed by the magistrate himself for it to be legal."

"Yes, that is right, and it can take some time."

I just wanted to let them know they were not dealing with a mug. "Ok, come in. I have nothing to hide." They had a quick look around, thanked me for my cooperation and left.

The following morning, I waited in the main office for the weasel to arrive. After waiting close to an hour, I asked one of the office staff whether he was due in that morning. She told me he had come in early and was in his office at the moment. I banged on his door and proceeded to push it open – locked! "I want to see you, you piece of garbage," I said. "Open this door!" "I have nothing to say to you," he said. "I've plenty to say to you, you gutless piece of shit!" He then threatened to call the police and I was forced to back off. I then went up to our flat and told Chrissie to start packing as we were leaving and going back to Harlow. We'd live on our boat until such time as I sorted something out. I went round to the site I had been working on and told Irish Bill I was leaving. I thanked him for everything he had done for me, shook his hand and baled out.

CHAPTER 35

BRITISH WATERWAYS

We arrived back at Harlow Mill Lock where our boat was moored. The lock-keeper, Frank Carr, had been a good friend to us for quite some time and looked after our boat, which helped us to bypass any mooring fees that we might have accrued. He and his wife, Flo, were about to go on holiday, and out of the goodness of his heart, he left us the keys to his lock cottage in case we needed fresh water or needed to make a phone call, as well as the use of his refrigerator.

Frank and Flo returned in just over a week, and Frank mentioned that the lock-keeper further upriver had retired due to the amputation of one of his legs. He suggested that I apply for the job. This was at Sheering Mill Lock in Sawbridgeworth, Herts. I called the office of British Waterways, which was in Enfield, asked for the Section Inspector, a certain Bill Knight, and applied for the job. He said the job was not available just yet and there had been other applicants. (What follows was my plan of action!) When I left the embassy, I asked Leah if I could have half a dozen embassy letter-headed plain sheets, which I thought might come in handy in the future, and she duly obliged. I typed out a blinding reference for myself, with the official embassy stamp on it, as well as the logo of Ivory Coast, which was the head of an elephant all picked out in gold and green. It really looked the part. I included some information about my duties within the Diplomatic Corps and signed it His Excellency the Ambassador.

I included a covering letter from myself, stating that should the job of lock-keeper become available, this was the calibre of person who would carry out his duties diligently and enjoy working for British Waterways. Within three days I was invited to attend an interview in Enfield and shortly after was informed that I had secured the job as lock-keeper. No way could you have had a better reference than the one I submitted, and the Section

Inspector was very impressed. Thinking about it all these years later, that old adage springs to mind: "Up there for thinking, down there for dancing."

Chrissie and I moved into the lock cottage that looked like something one would see on a Christmas card, especially when it was covered in snow. It was built in 1899 and above the front door was a plaque with a red hand on it, denoting the soreness of the hands that belonged to the men who dug the navigation, which is waterway parlance for the river. It was the River Stort, which runs twenty-two miles from Bishop's Stortford in Hertfordshire down through Harlow, joins the River Lea further down and terminates at Limehouse Reach, becoming tidal as it enters the Thames. I was responsible for six miles of river, three miles upriver from the lock cottage to Bishop's Stortford and three miles downriver to Harlow Mill, checking bank erosion, keeping an eye on the wildlife and during heavy rain being on flood control. With excessive rain, the river level would rise and I would have to open the weir and the lock gates to get rid of the water, otherwise the small village of Sawbridgeworth would flood. Each time I sent large volumes of water downriver, I would ring Frank to let him know that a lot of water was on its way down to him, and he would open his sluice and lock gates and then ring the next lock-keeper downriver and so on until the excessive water was got rid of into the Thames.

During flood control, I had to be up all night checking the water levels in the pound as it is called, that is the stretch of river in between each lock, every hour throughout the night, so it was just a doze in the armchair for an hour and then back into the oilskins and sou'wester. I would liaise with Frank the following morning so we both booked the same amount of overtime on our timesheets, and he would do the same thing with the lock-keeper further downriver. We depended on the overtime paid as the basic wage was quite poor, probably on a par with a school caretaker's wage. The timesheets would be collected every week by a lengthsman foreman and submitted for payment. Invariably they would be questioned by the section inspector, who would often delete some hours we had worked during the night, and Frank and I had a running battle with him. He passed away many years ago, and I don't wish to speak ill of the dead, but he was a nasty piece of work to deal with. On one occasion, after having a row with him over the phone, he said he was coming down to see me and then onto Frank.

He turned up one morning and came into the lock cottage producing my timesheets, and we went through them together.

"A bit excessive, this overtime you have booked," he said in an acerbic tone.

"I worked all through the day with my normal duties and then all through the night on flood control. While you were tucked up in your nice warm bed, I was up every hour out in the pouring rain, so I think I am more than entitled to the hours I have booked."

"Sometimes job satisfaction compensates for lack of money."

"Is that right?" I said. "How do you mean?"

"The lovely environment you work in, the trees, the flowers, the wildlife."

"I can't put flowers, trees and wildlife in my food cupboard and feed my family, and why would you possibly question the hours I have worked? If I had not been doing my job all through the night, the village would now be under water."

"I've not come down here to have a row!" he said.

"Well, you are not doing a bad job so far, it seems."

After he left, he never bothered to visit Frank, and we both got paid the hours we had booked.

It was true it was a lovely environment to work in, walking the towpath with my two dogs, Simon and Ben, upriver three miles and downriver to Harlow, pop in and see Frank and have a cup of tea, chat with the fishermen on the way, and it was quite easy to lose yourself by having a snooze in a field. One day I received a call from the section inspector who was quite taken up with riding around in his British Waterway van and keeping an eye on things. He said, "I came to visit you yesterday and could not find you." I said, "I was up at Bishop's Stortford; where were you?" He said, "I drove up there." I said, "That is how you missed me! I was walking the towpath." And on another occasion, when he said he walked the towpath, I said, "I drove up there; that's how you missed me!" so I was a no-win situation for him. You had to be up a bit earlier than that, pal, to catch me! I had forgotten more strokes than he ever learnt.

Some months later, Chrissie announced that she was pregnant, and one evening when the birth of our baby was imminent, I rang Harlow Hospital and asked for an ambulance. "What side of the river are you on?" they asked. When I told them, I was told we did not come under Essex; I would have to ring Bishop's Stortford, which is Hertfordshire. When I rang them, they told me we were out of their jurisdiction and came under Harlow! So I rang Harlow back in the midst of Chrissie's groans of pain and told them they'd better get someone there a bit lively as the baby was about to be born. No more arguments, they dispatched an ambulance and Chrissie was taken to Harlow Hospital, telling me she would ring me in the morning. Harlow was right: our lock cottage was on the side of the river that was Hertfordshire. Early the next morning, I arrived at the hospital and was directed to Chrissie's ward. I was about to push the doors open when a nurse came towards the same ward with a baby cradled in her arms. I looked at the baby, who had a lovely mop of black hair, and said to the nurse, "That is a lovely baby." "Are you Mr Wild?" she asked. When I said yes, she said, "This is your baby daughter!" We walked through the doors together, she placed the baby in Chrissie's arms and I became very emotional.

After a few days, Chrissie and baby returned home and then we had to decide on a name for her. We used to watch a series on the television called *Rich Man Poor Man* that we enjoyed so much that I bought the book that the series was based on. In the book, one of the daughters of the Jordache family is named Gretchen, although that was not featured in the television production, and I knew as soon as I saw that name I wanted it for my daughter. Chrissie was also pleased with it, and for her second name we chose Farady, which is American. I think it sounds kind of nice: Gretchen Farady Wild.

We applied to the local St Mary's Church to have Gretchen christened there. I knocked on the door of the Rectory, which was opened by the rather portly figure of the vicar whose name was Mr Rupert Childs. He made an appointment to visit Chrissie and me at the lock cottage and asked about our backgrounds. I asked him during our chat whether he would like a cup of tea or a drop of Scotch. He opted for the glass of Scotch, which soon disappeared and was promptly replaced with a second glass. Rupert was a man in his fifties, very ebullient and laughed easily, and sometimes he would come down to the river for a walk and knock on the door just to say hello. I was never sure whether it was concern for our well-being or he knew that another glass of Scotch was in the offing. Either way, he was always most welcome.

The day of the christening was suddenly upon us, and Mum and Dad came down from London. Many friends attended, and the day went off perfectly. Gretchen was about six months old when I asked Rupert whether he would "church" Chrissie. He looked at me dumbstruck and said, "How on earth do you know that phrase? Do you know what it means?"

"Of course! My mother told me many years ago. She was churched not long after I was born. It is a known thing in the East End. It means giving thanks to God for bringing the mother and child safely through the birth!"

"That is right," he said. "Since I have been at Great St Mary's, which is many years, no one has ever asked me for that ceremony, and it has taken an East Ender from London to bring that back to mind. It is a Northern thing! I would be honoured to carry that out for you."

On the day it took place, there was just Chrissie, Gretchen and me. Chrissie had to kneel in front of the altar, and Rupert performed a lovely, if short, ceremony. I think he was very pleased to do it as it was his first one in that beautiful old church that was built in the thirteenth century, with the church bells installed in 1664.

Coming off the main river was a small tributary that ran underneath the road, wound round behind the lock cottage and then flowed back into the navigation. Its purpose was to lower the river level above and then feed it back into the river further downstream. We decided to buy two donkeys from a sanctuary in Malden in Essex, a mother and her foal. Behind the cottage was a large field that was owned by a local farmer, Mr Marsh, who had a dozen or so cows grazing there. I asked him whether he would let me graze the two donkeys in the same field, and he was happy with that, with no cost involved, possibly because I was of some authority being the lock-keeper, plus I would keep an eye on his cows as far as vandalism was concerned. There was also the calming influence donkeys have on pregnant cows, which most farmers are familiar with. I set about building a stable at the rear of the premises, as well as another shed adjoining it for the winter hay and bedding straw they would need. Suddenly the day arrived for their delivery and we were so excited. They were led round to the back of the lock cottage where the stable had been built and hay and straw had been delivered by Mr Marsh, and they settled in immediately. We named the foal Nathan and his mum Liberty. However, there was no way of getting them into the field as the back stream separated the cottage from the field, so it made sense for me to make a bridge across the stream that they could just stroll over. This illustrates my limited knowledge of donkey husbandry. I purchased three extra-long lengths of railway sleepers and managed to ford the stream. Hand rails were fitted, and when all was completed, I said, "Come on Liberty," and started to lead her across the bridge, thinking little Nathan would follow his mother. The idea was great, but putting it into practice was a different thing. She would not budge. I was later to learn that donkeys do not like crossing water! Suddenly, a light-bulb moment! I picked up little Nathan in my arms and carried him across the bridge with mum watching. I put him down on the grass, he gave a little cry and she came over the bridge a bit rapid. Moral of the story: brain will always beat brawn. It was a lovely little bridge and enhanced the rear of the lock cottage admirably, especially in winter when it was covered, like the stable, in snow. Some people only see these beautiful scenes on Christmas cards, but we were fortunate to have the real thing. I think Isambard Kingdom Brunel would have been proud of me if he had seen my bridge.

I managed to acquire a large white butler sink, made a frame for it to sit on and put it in one corner of the stable where it was always filled with clean water for them. I had fitted some pipe work underneath the sink so that any soiled water could be drained straight into the back stream. I also fitted up a light in their stable and a salt lick container screwed to the wall, and I caught them quite often licking that large bar of salt that donkeys love. It was so cosy for them of a night time with the light on and the fresh, dry straw; I would go out there and loved joining them lying down. On winter nights the stable doors would be locked, keeping out the cold.

There was a knock on the cottage door one morning by a member of the public who told me that there was a guy on the towpath with an airgun rifle, and they were concerned that he was shooting wildlife. Any kind of weaponry is strictly prohibited on the towpath and adjoining fields owned by British Waterways, so I rushed out and saw a Chinese guy whom I recognised from the Chinese restaurant up in the village. I asked him what he was doing with the rifle on the towpath, and he replied in broken English, "I come here to shoot the ducks." I explained that shooting was not allowed, but he started to argue with me. I told him that if he shot a duck, I would throw him and his gun into the river and call the police. He backed off a bit lively and left, with me telling him I knew where he worked and the police would be up to see his governor at the restaurant if I saw him again with his gun. That exchange seemed to work as I never saw him again.

When my mum and dad would come to visit, Dad loved the flowers blooming in the fields and around the lock and would often comment how he would like to live in that environment. All he had ever had was a window box in their flat in Bethnal Green, and he lovingly cared for his flowers, his favourites being geraniums and chrysanthemums. One day I happened to mention this to Rupert, the sky pilot (vicar), who said he was looking for someone to look after the flowers around the church and someone to keep the inside of the church looking nice and there was a flat that could be offered as well. I thought this would be lovely for Mum and Dad as they were both retired and they would be close by me. We visited them at their flat and I mentioned this excitedly to Dad. He was all for it and said they would think about it. I called Dad a week later and he said that Mum did not want to move because she was too used to Hoxton and now Bethnal Green, but I could tell he was disappointed by Mum's refusal to move. I felt so sad for him; he would have been in his element in the lovely rural environment that I enjoyed so much.

During the summer months when there was no call for flood control, my wages dropped drastically because no overtime was booked, and on speaking one day to a guy I knew from the village, he mentioned that he did some security work for a company based in Harlow and suggested I give them a call. I spoke to the owner of the company, and when I told him of my history with the Diplomatic Corps, he invited me round to his house for a chat. He offered me regular weekend work after I'd told him I was employed by British Waterways as a lock-keeper and could not work during the week. The following week he rang me and asked if I could go to London and pick up two uniforms for myself, as well as a hat and a couple of shirts.

The uniforms were airforce blue with a matching cap and looked very smart. Should anybody have seen me in this uniform, they could have mistaken me for Wing Commander Johnny Johnson from the Battle of Britain. My first job was at Schreiber, the furniture manufacturer in Hoddesdon, about a twenty-minute drive from the lock cottage, to relieve the current security guard. On Saturdays, my hours were 2 pm to 10 pm. On Sundays, I would relieve the guard at a company that made cluster bombs for the Ministry of Defence, Hunting Engineering, which was also in Hoddesdon, but this was from 6 am to 2 pm.

I did very well with the company and was well thought of by the owner, Alex. He always paid my wage in cash in my hand, which suited me, and said, "I am buying some stripes for your uniform which I would like you to wear, three on each arm."

"Making me a sergeant!"

"It is a good advert for the company."

"How many sergeants are there on the firm?"

"You are the only one, and get rid of the blue shirts you wear with the uniform. In future, you will wear a white shirt, which will make you stand out from the other security guys I employ."

I said jokingly "I can start ordering my wife about! If she objects, I will draw her attention to the three stripes and tell her I outrank her."

"That is a good idea! I never thought of that."

As soon as Alex had a large cheque come in, he and his wife went jetting off somewhere and it was a case of "Roy, hold the fort until I return," for which he paid me extra for the responsibility. After a while, he asked me to work full time for him, but I explained my job with the Waterways entailed a tied cottage and if I terminated with British Waterways, I would be out of house and home. He said he understood but lots more work was coming in and he would have to employ a manager. I said, "Go ahead and do that."

One evening about two weeks later at Hunting Engineering, the bell rang on the large company gates and there stood a guy who introduced himself as Mark, the new manager Alex had appointed. He came in and had a cup of tea and we chatted for some time, and then he left, saying he would pop in to see me the following week. This continued for a couple of months, and on one of these visits he said that I was the smartest security guy he had ever seen and he very much liked my style; would I be interested in putting something together with him?

"What have you got in mind?"

"Before I took this job, I worked for a company, half of which supplied security and the other half supplied relief management to pubs owned by the big breweries. If a manager was sacked, went on holiday, or was taken ill, the brewery would ring the company and request a manager to take over the pub and pay the company an agency fee." "Mark, it sounds swell, but the only thing I know about pubs is when my belly is up against the bar!" "Don't worry, you will soon pick it up."

Unfortunately, he had a falling out with Alex and left, and nothing came of that venture at the time.

I continued working weekends for Alex, and one day he asked me to switch from Schreiber and report to a photographic studio in Harlow Town by the name of AK Studios. This company supplied household items that you would see in television adverts such as leather chairs, vases, TVs (devoid of any internal workings), and kitchen equipment. All these things were hired by the day, and when the adverts had been shot, they would be returned to AK Studios. I became very friendly with the owner and mentioned that I would like to put my daughter Gretchen into modelling as she was such a beautiful child. He suggested I contact the Elizabeth Smith Agency that was owned by a friend of his. I called the agency a couple of days later and was asked to attend an interview with Gretchen, so Chrissie and I went along. We walked into a large office full of girl typists, and we were approached by the office manager and made welcome. By this time, many of the office girls had come over and were totally enchanted by Gretchen, remarking how beautiful she was and making a fuss of her. We were told they would have no hesitation in having Gretchen on their books and representing her. They sent us to a photography studio in Ilford, and professional photos were taken of her in different poses. These were sent back to the agency, who then submitted them to various companies that wished to use a child to advertise their products. The work came in thick and fast. Gretchen modelled for *Woman's Weekly*, *Woman's Realm* and *Woman's Own* magazines, which were very popular at the time and read nationwide. She modelled for Kangol children's car seats in Pimlico; they had to remove the four doors of the car to enable them to get the lighting and cameras into the car. She also appeared in the Munch Bunch advertisement on television and Baby Boots. A sad job she had to do was when *Woman's Weekly* was running a feature on children in hospital and how they were missing their parents and family. We met the film crew at Westminster Children's Hospital and were led to a ward of sick children. Gretchen was put into a hospital gown, and I lifted her into a cot. The director said, Gretchen, I want you to look really sad; pretend that you are missing Mum and Dad while you are in hospital. You're not really going to stay here. This is just for the camera." She was just two-and-a-half years of age, and we didn't want her to think we were leaving her there! She was a natural. We couldn't wait, each time she'd modelled, to rush out and buy the magazine she had modelled for; we have them to this day. She also modelled with Emma Bunton of Spice Girl fame, who was about the same age as Gretchen. I took her out of modelling when she turned five as she was ready to start school. Gretchen and I have discussed many times where modelling could have led her. With her lovely looks and personality, she might have been a television presenter. We will never know, but she has carved out a career for herself in dentistry. She has passed many examinations at King's College and at the time of writing is a head nurse. I explained to her I had to take her out from the world of modelling because I would have been failing in my duty as her father if I had denied her an education. I have also educated her in the ways of the world and what to side-step, and I am so pleased and proud that she has used me as the template for the future men in her life.

Early one evening, there was a knock on the door and there stood a guy who introduced himself as the Headmaster of Readings School, which was just the other side of the village.

"How can I help you?" I said.

"I see you have a couple of donkeys in your back field, and I wondered whether you might loan them to us for the day, as we have the school fete in two weeks' time."

"In what capacity do you need them?"

"To give the children donkey rides, like on the beach."

This is something I have always been totally against, the exploitation of animals that have no say in the matter. I support many charities financially that care for donkeys, mules and horses that are forced to work in terrible conditions in the Middle East. My contention is, love animals for what they are, not for what they can do for you, so I said to him, "I'll tell you what. Why don't you jump over the wire fence and ask them if they don't mind walking up and down all day in the hot sun with different children on their backs, and if they agree, you can come and collect them on the day of the fete. If they refuse to speak with you, take it as a no."

He stood there with a stupid look on his face, turned on his heel and left. I was in the near future to have another run-in with this idiot, and again he came off second-best.

One weekday morning, there was a knock on the door and there stood the Headmaster again. Have you come back for seconds? I thought.

"Yes?" I said.

"Can you put us through the lock?" he said.

What I never knew was that the school had its own narrow boat that he would sometimes steer down the river.

I said, "Are you not familiar with how the lock works? Close the gate on the lower river, fill the lock with water, and when it is the same level, open the gates on the top river. Pull the boat in so now you are in between both lock gates, drain the lock, the boat will drop until it is at the same level as the downriver, open the gate and steer the boat out. Have you got that?"

"I know all of that!"

"Then why are you bothering me by knocking on my door? I am here as the lock-keeper and only too pleased to help out anybody who does not understand how the lock works, but seeing that by your own admission you know how the lock works, I ask you again, why are you knocking on my door?"

Again, tail-between-the-legs time and he slunk back to the boat and locked himself through.

I relented in as much as I took Liberty to the school fete, knowing I would be there for her welfare and having learnt there were prizes to be given for the best turned-out animals. People brought their cats and dogs, somebody brought a pet chicken, and we also took Jemima, our pet Muscovy duck, who wore a blue bow around her neck. I think the judging was carried out by two or three people from the school PTA. Suffice to say, Liberty won first prize and was presented with a nice rosette which she wore on the side of her head harness. I had blackened and polished her hooves and brushed her just before we left for the fete, and she looked a picture. Jemima walked away, or should I say waddled away, with a prize for best bird. And my prize was that the Headmaster blanked me all day. That'll do for me, cocker!

Chrissie and I were friendly with a young couple who lived in the village. The wife worked for Don Miller, the bakers in Bishop's Stortford, and they were looking for a cleaner to sweep up and tidy the bakery at the end of the day's trading. I attended an interview, and when I made the manager aware of my experience in the cleaning game, I was given the job. Chrissie and I started one Monday evening, just after the staff had left. I noticed that there were many large bags full of loaves of bread, donuts and all kinds of cakes. I asked the manager what he wanted us to do with all these bags, and he said it was all the stuff that hadn't been sold that day. He told us to throw it in the large skip downstairs! I explained that I was the lock-keeper and all those bags of bread, etc. would feed the wildlife. He said we could take them, so every night we loaded up the car and the wildlife had a feast, especially the foxes.

I always marvelled at the idyllic surroundings we lived in – the river, the fields, the wildlife, the song of the birds on waking every morning – but the downside was the lock cottage itself. The walls had been made all those years ago out of horsehair, plaster and old-fashioned wood lathes, and in winter it was freezing in there. We had no central heating, just a fire, a paraffin heater and a gas fire, and still it was cold. There was no toilet, either, at least not within the confines of the cottage. You had to step outside, and round the back was a cubicle that doubled as a toilet, not one that flushed, but a chemical toilet that had to be emptied by an effluent vehicle that would arrive once a month with a large-bore suction hose. Because the small bathroom was below the river level, it would flood, and many a time

I shaved in front of the mirror with the water lapping around the top of the pair of Wellington boots I was wearing. No way would we have moved into the cottage if we had been made aware of the conditions and sanitary arrangement we had to endure.

One of the nicest memories, though, was one Christmas Eve when everything was covered in snow. We had the tree lights twinkling in the front room and Gretchen was looking forward to Father Christmas popping in during the night with the goodies. I said to Chrissie, "I am going to bring Nathan and Liberty in to complete the picture!" I put a harness on each of them and led them into the front room. Liberty put a couple of her hooves through some of the presents around the Christmas tree, but on the whole they were well behaved. It is an indelible memory that seeps into my mind whenever I hear that lovely Christmas carol, "Away in a Manger".

I complained endlessly to my section inspector about our terrible living conditions and said if something was not done about it, I would take things into my own hands, starting with "bucket and chuck it". It was just an empty threat as no way would I have emptied effluent into the river, but he didn't know that. "I will send somebody down from head office," he said. A week later an official-looking letter came from the head office of British Waterways stating that I would be visited in a couple of days' time. When the guy arrived, he introduced himself and said he was a civil engineer. He asked me to take him around the property. He also said that if I dug a hole at the back of the cottage and the hole filled up with water, it meant that the cottage was below the water level and there was really nothing that could be done. "Nothing that could be done!" I said. "In this day and age when a person's heart can be taken out, put in a cold box, flown to the other side of the country and put in the chest of somebody else, and they are walking around in a couple of days, let alone sending astronauts to the moon and back? All I'm asking for is an inside flush toilet. You are a civil engineer. Where did you take your training? Kellogg's Corn Flakes factory?" "I am sorry," he said, got back into his car and drove off.

The weir on the stream close to our lock cottage was a favourite place for fishermen as there would usually be an abundance of fish there, but I never allowed anybody to fish there as we would have been inundated with people every weekend. I became friendly with a young guy named John

Saunders, who would at times fish in the main river. The day after the visit from the engineer, John was fishing off the small island next to the weir and I told him the outcome of our meeting.

"Which company owns the cottage?" he asked.

"British Waterways," I replied.

"How do you feel about being rehoused?"

"How could that happen?"

"Not a problem. I am the Environmental Health Officer and I work for EFDC (Epping Forest District Council). I will have this property closed within two weeks as unfit for human habitation, especially as a child is involved."

"Can you do that?"

"You betcha!"

I relayed John's comments to my section inspector who said, "Don't make me laugh! He can't close your lock cottage! We are British Waterways, and he just works for a local authority!"

When I reported this to John, he smiled and said "Just watch." Within two weeks the lock cottage was closed.

Within a week, we were offered a very nice three-bedroom house in the lovely village of Epping Green about four miles from the lock cottage. The letter also stated that if we wished to purchase the property, the price would be £18,000. It was a lovely property with a very large garden that you needed a minicab to get to the end of. John closed the lock cottage as he said he would, and one day, before I left for the river and my patch, he turned up to see how we had settled in. He asked me whether we were going to purchase the property. I told him about the letter we had received with the asking price of £18,000 and said we were going to purchase at that price. He said, "You do nothing until I ring you!" A couple of days later, we received another letter with another offer of £12,000 which we quickly accepted. I called John at his desk and told him about the new offer and said, "How did you swing that?" He laughed and said the housing officer was a good friend of his. I met John at his favourite fishing spot at the weir a couple of days later and said, "John, I can never repay what you have done for my family. What can I offer you as a heartfelt thank you?" He said, "Nothing, Roy, it's what I do. Maybe a bottle of wine would be nice for me and the wife to enjoy!" I felt I owed him so much more but could only abide by what he'd suggested.

The joy of being rehoused in the village was clouded with the sadness that Nathan and Liberty had to be returned to the sanctuary. On the day they were loaded into a horsebox provided by the sanctuary, there were many tears shed by all of us. The sign I made with their names on it, which hung on the stable door, now has pride of place in my study, and they have a special place safely tucked away in my heart.

I was still employed as the lock-keeper; it just meant that I had to drive to my patch of river. That was no hardship and it gave me more scope to be on the missing list when the section inspector was on the prowl. I was not one of his favourite people after bringing in the troops, in the shape of John Saunders, and getting the lock cottage closed.

At the corner of our lane was a petrol filling station that also sold chocolates, confectionary and flowers, and Chrissie would quite often walk Gretchen round there to buy her some sweets. On one occasion, they were just coming out of the petrol office when a car pulled in and Mark (who had fallen out with Alex) left the car and approached Chrissie. "Aren't you Roy's wife?" he asked. "I have been looking for him the last couple of years. Where are you living now? I know the lock cottage is closed." Chrissie said, "We live just round the corner, and Roy is in now if you want to see him." Mark came and outlined what he had in mind, more or less what he had told me before, which was starting up in the licenced trade. I said, "If you are sure, let's do it." I continued driving back and forth to the lock and my patch and one day received a phone call from the section inspector that I was to report further downriver, completely off my three miles of river, and join a work boat. "Nope!" I said. "I joined British Waterways as a lock-keeper, and just because I do not now live in the lock cottage, it does not alter my job description. If you insist, I will take my case to the union I belong to." That made him back off a bit lively and it was never mentioned again. Mark visited me a couple of times and said things were starting to move. He had been in contact with some brewery people he knew and they were willing to put some pubs our way that would need relief management in the near future, so that was something to look forward to.

CHAPTER 36

MARKENROY

He called me one evening, very excited, and asked if we could meet at the lock as we had been given our first pub. He asked me to go to The Nag's Head in North London and meet our relief couple who would be taking over from the resident manager and his wife, who were about to start two weeks' holiday. I reminded him I knew nothing about pubs, and again he said, "You are a very confident guy, Roy. You'll get by. Here is a contract we are going to use for those who work for us. Make sure you get it signed. The District Sales Manager you have to meet there is a real nice guy, and I have told him you will meet him there at 9 am." He also gave me the name of our couple who were due to take over the pub and who had worked for Mark before.

I arrived at the pub looking the part, with a new briefcase I had purchased which held nothing but an apple and a couple of sandwiches that Chrissie had made for me. I was met by our couple and the DSM (District Sales Manager) who introduced himself as Steve, and shortly after the stocktaker arrived and began taking the stock figures. This was all new to me, but I never let it show. After a while, Steve said, "Shall we have a look down the cellar?" I had never been down to a pub cellar! He started to shake the barrels and said, "I think about seven gallons in there. What do you think, Roy?" I gave it a shake and said "I think that's about right, Steve," and for the rest of the changeover bluffed my way through.

That first pub became three, then six, and I knew that I had to make a decision: give up the pub trade and business we were now in, or give notice to British Waterways after six years' service. Chrissie and I talked it over and I decided to stick with this new venture. Mark could not visit all the pubs on takeover morning as they were starting to come in thick and fast, and what would we do if two pubs started on the same morning, so I gave in my notice to the Waterways and we started full time in the licensed trade.

We hired an office in The Maltings in the village of Stanstead Abbots, which was a five-mile drive from where I lived. The office we took was on the top floor and very cheap, probably due to the fact that there were no lifts and the office floor sloped. Maybe the building had started to list? I brought a tennis ball to work in my briefcase and said to Mark, "Watch this." I let go of the ball from one wall and it rolled across the office all the way to the opposite wall. After a full day in the office, moving around with a rather ungainly gait, standing on terra firma was a pleasant relief.

We now had to decide on a name for the business, and we agreed to combine our names into Markenroy. We then engaged a firm of solicitors in Harlow to represent us and they promptly registered us at Companies House as Markenroy Relief Management Services Ltd. We further engaged the services of a well-known firm of accountants to take care of our finances. Mark at the time did not have a car of his own and would borrow his dad's old Vauxhall that had seen better days. I had not long taken delivery of a new Citroen Dyanne 6 CV, and we would take turns using our cars. Our first long-distance pub was in Canterbury in Kent, and we used the Citroen as probably being more reliable and less susceptible to breaking down.

After three months we were inundated with breweries ringing us. Some of the breweries we dealt with were Courage, Green King, Charles Wells and Everards, but our lifeblood was Charrington's of Silvertown in the East End (Canning Town), with whom we had a very good relationship. We were doing so well we ordered two brand new Nissan Bluebirds from a Nissan dealership that were delivered to our office.

The next step was to employ a secretary and we advertised in *The Morning Advertiser* for a secretary/Girl Friday. We interviewed half-a-dozen candidates and chose Tracey, who proved to be an absolute asset to the company. Shortly after, we moved into a larger office on the floor below. We stayed in The Maltings, which was ideal for us when first starting out, but alas, not very prestigious when visiting brewery officials came to see us. By this time, we were handling thirty or forty pubs a day all over the country, from Manchester and Liverpool down the M5 into Devon and Somerset. Mark would handle the admin side of the business, and I was better suited to being out on the road and meeting the various area managers, but when there was a quiet day in the office, Mark and I would go out together, visiting some of the pubs in our care. When we were handling between sixty and seventy pubs a day, we both agreed it was time we spread our wings and we took a suite of offices in a very nice building in Harlow where we both were living. Mark's office, at one end, was all wood-panelled, then there was our operations room, then an office for our secretary and finally my office, where we engaged a carpenter who wood-panelled my office, and it looked very prestigious for interviewing pub managers who had applied for a position with our company. Invariably, it was me who did the interviewing. In our operations room was a large 8x4 whiteboard that we had covered with a clear plastic sheet, much like those one sees in a betting shop. Using a chinagraph pencil, we would enter into various boxes the name of a pub, the date we would take over, the date when we were due to come out, the brewery and the name of the relief manager. It was brilliant in its simplicity. The relief coordinator for Charrington's came to visit us to take in a spot of lunch and take in how we were running the business. He took one look at our operations with all the information on the whiteboard, thought it was a marvellous system and promptly adopted the same system back at the brewery. About a month later, we were invited by Keith, the relief coordinator at Charrington's, for a lunch appointment with a couple of brewery directors, who asked us what we had done before we came into the licensed trade. Mark told them of his previous history and then told them of mine. He said Roy worked for British Waterways, and prior to coming into the trade, he knew nothing about the running of pubs. Now he teaches me!" I thought that was the nicest accolade he could have bestowed on me.

We'd had our Bluebirds for about two years and took the advice of our accountants to start spending some money, so we ordered two Nissan Laurels which were delivered. We had our company insured by a large insurance company in Stevenage, and what I am about to relate is rather amusing. At least it was for Mark and me. We had also insured each other, as well as the partnership, and had become very friendly with the local rep for the insurance company, Peter, who would pop in to see us every so often and the three of us would pop out for lunch. Peter would laugh uproariously at some of the tales I would regale him with and always thought I was the rascal of our company. He wasn't far wrong in his estimation.

Chrissie, by this time, had presented me with a healthy son, who was born in Epping Hospital, and I was so proud, like most men, to have a son.

Mark came into my office one morning holding a newspaper displaying an advert for a travel company in Muswell Hill, North London, that was offering cheap flights to San Francisco. He said, "We have worked hard to get where we are today! What about a week's holiday there, just the two of us?" Neither of us had been to America, and San Francisco was somewhere we had only seen on television. California was very appealing and enticing. By this time, we had also engaged a junior typist, Wanda, an elderly gentleman, George, who was our board man, whose job it was to enter all the new pubs that came in, and an office manager, John, so we felt the business was in safe hands. It was only for a week we would be away.

So I said, "Let's do it," and he said, "If you want to run over to the travel agent now, I will countersign the cheque book," which we had agreed would always need both of our signatures. I drove over to Muswell Hill and booked two tickets to San Francisco and then we had to tell our wives. I said, "Leave it to me. I will come up with something." I thought about it all evening and the following morning I called Peter at his desk in the insurance office and invited him over for lunch with Mark and me the following day. Sitting at the lunch table, I asked him whether he could let us have one of his blank letterheads. He asked what for, and I told him we were off to America and as valued customers of his company, we had been invited to its annual shareholders' meeting, which, that year, was to be held in the US. We needed the blank letterhead to type our own invitation to attend. He burst out laughing and said, "Don't worry, I will type and send it to each of you in a couple of days."

I was just leaving for the office one morning when the post came. I could see Peter's letter among the others as it had the company's name and logo. "What's this?" I said and made a business of opening the letter. "Well, what do you know? Mark and I have been invited to San Francisco by Peter's company as valued customers for a week!" Sudden silence! "Are you going then?" said Chrissie. "Well, we could hardly snub a big company like that," I replied. When I arrived at the office, "Did you get the invitation?" was the first thing Mark said. "It's in the bag!" I said. "Terrific idea you had," he said. I said, "Remind me again – where did you say you left your heart?"

From Heathrow we flew to Los Angeles and then picked up a connection to San Francisco. We did all the usual things we had read about, visited Alcatraz Prison across the bay on the ferry, booked a flight in a helicopter that circled twice over Alcatraz, hired a car and crossed over the Golden Gate Bridge into Sausalito and did some sunbathing on the lovely beaches there. We rode in the cable cars, did lots of shopping and had a wonderful time. All the things Tony Bennett sang about it were true.

We returned from America to find all was well with the business and we had inherited more pubs from various breweries. At this point, it is worth mentioning that all the managers that worked for us had to pay a £1000 bond as a safeguard against stock or cash deficits, and this is how it worked. On the morning of changeover, when the returning manager arrived, a stocktake would be done by a brewery stocktaker to determine that the bankings or money taken over the counter matched the liquor sales. A classic example of a stock deficit was the following. We were holding a pub in Berkshire for Courage brewery and on the morning, the stocktake revealed a stock deficit of £400 via our manager. The following morning I drove to the pub to see if I could find the reason for the deficit. The manager, his wife and I sat around a table before opening and I went through the WSOB (weekly statement of business) as well as the stock sheets that had been left behind by the stocktaker at my request. I asked the manager and his wife, "What do you do last thing at night after you have closed the pub?"

"Err! We check the toilets to make sure no one is hiding there to rob the pub later."

"That's good. Then what?"

"We check all the ashtrays to see there are no burning cigarettes that could be a fire hazard.

Very good! Then what?

"We put all the chairs on top of the tables ready for the cleaner in the morning."

"Very good. Then what do you do?"

"We all sit down after a busy night and have a drink."

Who is we?

"Myself, the wife, the bar cellarman, and the two barmaids."

"So you buy drinks for the people you have mentioned every night after the pub closes?"

"No, I don't buy them!"

"So they buy their own drinks, is that right?"

"No, of course not, they don't pay for their own drinks."

"Have you a hospitality allowance?"

"No."

"Have you a spillage allowance?" (Can the reader see where this is going?)

"No."

"Then who the bloody hell is paying for the booze that is being consumed on a nightly, seven-days-a-week binge by yourself and the staff? If that was consumed by the punters who use this pub, the money would have gone into the Jack & Jill (till) and you would not have suffered a deficit, which doesn't look good on our company. I have taken a round trip of 120 miles to come here and sort out your problem. You are the captain of this ship and you are not controlling what I pay you for. The Area Manager has made me aware that it is a £400 deficit. If that is cost price, he could well ask for the retail value on top, which is profit, and it will come to a lot more you will have to pay." Suffice to say, the area manager, because of our friendship, accepted the original cost price of £400.

I could fill another book with the many incidents I witnessed during my almost twenty years in the licensed trade, but I will mention just a couple.

In a dispute, I took on one of the largest banks in the country, who retreated rather ignominiously after swords were crossed. A manager who was working for our company had a very large stock deficit to the tune of £850. I had interviewed this guy and his wife a couple of weeks before he started with us, and he did not, at that point, have a £1000 bond to lodge with us, but he was sure he could raise the amount and then call me, which he did. I put him to work in his first pub and the above deficit is what he returned. He could give no explanation for the deficit and I terminated his contract, thinking, "If this is his first pub for us, what is the future to be like?" Two weeks later, I received a letter from his bank asking for the £1000 they had loaned him. There was no mention of what their £1000 was for; maybe he never told them. I explained that the £1000 was to guard against stock or cash deficit and their arrangement was with him, not our company. They threatened us with all kinds of legal action and said that the money belonged to them. I wrote back to them asking whether, at the time of writing, they were inebriated or on medication. I had no intention of returning their client's bond as he had signed a contract with us and I had paid the brewery for the deficit. Further, I had no interest in where he'd obtained the £1000, whether it had come from an arrangement with their bank or Father Christmas had dropped it down the chimney. I told them we had taken legal advice and been told that the loan was between them and their client and in no way implicated our company. After my letter, we never heard another word from this bank.

We continued to expand and had only one major competitor, a company in Derbyshire who were very well established before our own company was formed. They had adverts in the trade paper claiming to be the biggest in the country. I countered that in our adverts, borrowing a line from Sir Winston Churchill, who, in reply to the USA defence secretary's statement "We have the biggest navy in the world," said, "That is very true, but we have the *best* navy in the world."

CHAPTER 37

THE UPPERCUT CLUB

One of our managers, a guy by the name of Billy Beard, was very much into boxing, and on the last Sunday of the month, he would attend a meeting at the famous Thomas A'Becket pub in Old Kent Road. This was where the Uppercut Club was situated and was attended by many former world champions and boxing *aficionados*.

Billy invited me to accompany him to the next meeting where I would be able to meet many boxers and followers of the sport. We arrived at the Becket to find the pub filling up with people, and I was introduced to various world champions as well as British and European champions, in particular John Conteh, who became a lifelong friend, John H Stracey and my old pal, former middleweight champion Terry Downes. John H and I hit it off immediately when we compared notes and found out we were the only two East Enders in the pub. The rest of the guys were all South Londoners. I was asked by the club secretary whether I would like to become a member of the Uppercut Club, which I accepted forthwith. The club raised money for ex-fighters and anybody else that had fallen on hard times. Funds were raised by ex-boxing champions attending at various pubs, shaking hands with the many fans who had supported them throughout their careers and who loved having their photos taken with their idols. There would also be raffles and small auctions for signed boxing gloves and shorts. It was a great evening out, with all the proceeds going to a most worthy cause.

After about six months in the Uppercut Club, I was taken aside by a committee member and told I was being considered for a committee member; would I be interested? "Of course," I replied, "it would be an honour!" The committee members sat one side of a makeshift bench that was, during the week, a snooker table, and at the next meeting it was announced, in front of about three hundred members, that I was to be enrolled as a new committee member, alongside my two pals, John H Stracey and Terry Downs, Larry O'Connel, a famous referee and Uppercut treasurer, and a successful TV actor, Johnny Shannon. I was delighted and humbled that after so short a time, these friends I had made thought I was the right material to become the fifth committee member. I indeed felt honoured.

One Sunday morning, just after the latest meeting of the Uppercut committee had been concluded, and most members had their bellies up against the bar waiting for a drink, a member sidled up to me, introduced himself and said, "I hear you are in the licensed trade, Roy!" "That's right," I said. Puffing out his chest, he continued, "I have eight pubs," and waited for my response. "Wow! That's a lot of pubs." "How many have you got?" he inquired. "Forty-seven at the moment," I replied.

Stunned silence! "See you later," he said and walked away.

Upstairs in the Becket was the world-famous gym where many fighters trained, most notably the UK's most loved boxer, Henry Cooper. The gym itself was looked after by Danny Holland, who was Henry's corner cut man during a bout, and on many occasions I would pop upstairs and sit and chat with Danny.

As well as attending Uppercut fund-raising evenings, Terry Downes had his own charity that he would raise funds for, The Terry Downes Sunshine Coaches For Disabled Children. Terry, away from the ring, had cemented his place as one of Britain's most popular fighters by his tireless work for disabled children and personally raised over £100,000 for the cause. I am proud as well as humbled to say I was somewhat instrumental in this effort and that we were good pals.

The Governor of the Becket, Gary Davidson, was also a good friend of mine. He was a very good fighter in his own right and went on to become Southern Area Bantam Weight Champion. He was someone else I was proud to have as a good friend, and the whole boxing fraternity was devastated when Gary became ill with motor neurone disease and passed away in the year 2000 aged just 46. I am now, at the time of writing, proud and indeed fortunate to have Gary's son, Gary Jnr, as a friend who resides in Cambridgeshire and runs and trains up-and-coming fighters in his own gym. He has inherited many of his dad's boxing and social skills.

Mark and I, with two other friends, had decided to embark on a trip to New York to see the sights and take in some shopping, and I mentioned this to a couple of Uppercut members one Sunday morning. Shortly after, I was approached by a member who was a boxing referee, a guy known as Paddy Sower, who said I should ring a certain person in the Bronx and let him know we were coming to New York and he would escort us around. This guy, Mickey Katz, was well connected to the world of boxing, as well as having a very high position in the Masonic movement. I rang him just prior to leaving for the States and was greeted by a broad Bronx accent. He was very friendly and said as soon as we landed, we should ring him from our hotel, which was the Roosevelt Hotel on E45th Street in Manhattan.

The four of us all had separate rooms, and after unpacking, I called him. He said he was on his way, and about thirty minutes later he called to say he was in the hotel reception and would I like to come down to say hello. I said, "How will I know you?" He said, "You will know me!" I took the elevator down to the ground floor, and as the doors opened, in front of me stood a little Jewish guy in an overcoat and an Astrakhan hat. We embraced, and by this time, Mark and our other two pals had descended into the hotel foyer and introductions all round. Over coffee, he told us that there was a seventeen-year-old heavyweight on the scene that was knocking out seasoned fighters, and he had arranged for us to meet this young guy and his manager, who was a friend of his. The meet was at the famous Gleason's Gym in Brooklyn, which was now owned by a friendly guy known as Ira Becker but still retained the name of Gleason and was renowned as one of the best gyms in the country. The fighter we were due to meet was none other than Mike Tyson, and his manager and trainer Cus D'Amato. We watched the fighters in action in the gym, and after a short while, Ira took a phone call from Cus D'amato to say that he and Mike could not make it for the meet. We were very disappointed, but before leaving, Ira made me an honourable member of the gym and I made him an honourable member of the Uppercut Club. I gave him my Uppercut badge that I always wore, and he, in return, gave me a badge, or pin as they call them stateside, with Gleason's Gym emblazoned on the surface. We spent the rest of our time shopping and socialising with Mickey and then flew home. It was a memorable trip, and I stayed in touch with Mickey for further trips I made with my family to New York and also when Mickey came to the UK.

Our company, Markenroy, continued to go from strength to strength, and we were heading for the "one hundred pubs a day" rubric. One day, on the way to visiting one of our pubs, we passed Stapleford Abbots Aerodrome and Mark said, "Do you fancy trying for a pilot's licence?" "Sure!" I said, so on the way back, we called into the airfield, made some enquiries and booked our first lesson. We turned up for the first lesson on a lovely sunny day, checked in, were told we had to purchase a flyer's logbook, were taken out by two instructors and had to do a pre-flight inspection of the planes, which were two small, single-engine Cessna aircraft. The pre-flight inspection consisted of walking round the plane checking the ailerons, wing flaps, oil and fuel, as well as the lights. I entered the plane with the instructor, and away we went. He took the craft up into the air and then handed it over to me, after explaining some of the instruments and controls. I learnt how to trim forward to take the nose of the aircraft down and to trim back to bring the nose back up for level flight, as well as the yoke, which was like a car steering wheel cut in half.

After the third lesson, I started to suffer from headaches, which intensified after each lesson. After the seventh or eighth lesson, I decided to discontinue the lessons, which was a shame as I had been doing very well, according to the instructor. I had got as far as taking off in the plane, and the instructor would land it, which, I understand, is the most dangerous part of aviation. Mark had decided to quit as well. I feel sure if we had continued, we would have both attained our pilot's licence and possibly purchased our own light aircraft, which would have been handy for visiting some of our pubs up in the Newcastle area and then down the A5 into Somerset and Devon, as long as we could find a landing place. The headaches never returned, even when I did the long-haul flights to New York and California. Maybe that was probably due to the pressurised cabins on the large 747s.

On the subject of aeroplanes, every year in December, Mark and I would take a flight somewhere to do some Christmas shopping. One year it was to Jersey, and we flew from Southend airport to the Channel Islands, which was about 205 miles and would take roughly 55 minutes. On boarding the aircraft, I remember saying to Mark, "I think this is an old World War Two troop carrier." It took off amid rattles and bangs, and I didn't like the sound of it – shades of *The Flight of the Phoenix*. Near the end of the flight, the cabin hostess came around with a tray of boiled sweets and said, "These will stop your ears popping as we land." I wasn't sure if she meant suck them or put one in each ear! By this time, Mark was completely out of it, sick in a bag and his ears popping, as were mine. I remember remarking that we would have been better sitting on the wing. (Did I say Phoenix?) Worse was to come – the return flight! The less said about that the better.

I returned to New York at Christmastime with Chrissie and the children, and was met at the John F Kennedy Airport by Mickey, who had a cab waiting to take us to the Roosevelt Hotel and then onto his house in the Bronx to meet his wife, Rose. We stayed for a lovely cooked meal and then returned to our hotel. We were met the following morning by Mickey, who took us shopping in and around the Big Apple, and I picked up a couple of boxes of cigars for my old pal Terry Downs, who always smoked a la-di-da. Mickey had booked us on a short trip around the harbour on the Staten Island Ferry. This was when we learnt what cold really was. The wind that blows down Fifth Avenue is unbelievably freezing, but before we left the UK, Mickey had called me and told me to come well wrapped up as there was snow everywhere. I bought the four of us full-length sheepskin coats and warm jumpers, which made extra luggage. On the ferry with Mickey, we were amazed at the size of the Statue of Liberty as we passed close by to her. Mickey said to the children, , whilst winking at me, "At certain times, when the temperature drops even further, the New York Authorities put a large woollen sweater on Miss Liberty to keep her warm."

We had a wonderful time in the Big Apple. We watched the skaters at the Rockerfeller Center and visited Central Park. In the middle is a small area called Strawberry Fields, dedicated to the memory of John Lennon who was shot outside his home in the Dakota building in 1980.

We said goodbye to Mickey and then flew on to Florida. What a complete change of weather! We had to take all our sheepskin coats with us as well, with the temperature about 75 Fahrenheit. I rang Mickey a couple of months later and Rose picked up the phone to give me the devastating news that Mickey had died. I was so upset but kept in touch with Rose, who was now nearing her 90th birthday and was about to move to Florida for the warm weather. She said she would ring with her new phone number, but we never heard from her again. Maybe she lost our phone number, but they were two friends we will never forget and will always hold in the highest esteem. Before he died, Mickey and I always kept in touch, and he would affectionately refer to me as his Limey buddy. He would always close his letter with "Don't count the days, make the days count," and I would always counter with "It's nice to be important, but more important to be nice." My life was much richer for knowing that lovely couple, Mickey and Rose Katz.

CHAPTER 38

STUBBS CLUB

Markenroy was going from strength to strength, taking on more pubs. We heard from one of our managers that a friend of his was instrumental in the running of a club in Romford Road, Stratford, and was looking to give up the club and sell the business on. We gave him a call and made a meet to visit him at the club, which was a members' club called Stubbs Club. It had initially been a Labour Party meeting place. The actual owner of the freehold property was a very wealthy man who had made his fortune in betting shops, and the current guy, whom I will call Rick, had fallen behind in the rent and also owed a substantial amount of money to a local brewery for the beer and spirits.

We had a meeting with him and asked what kind of a deal he was looking for. He wanted us to take care of the back rent he owed to the owner and the money he owed to the brewery, and twenty-five bags of sand (grand) for himself in cash, as well as being retained as the manager, which we agreed to (wrong decision). We demanded to look at the weekly statement of business and could see there was plenty of potential in the club. We said we would think about it and get back to him. We kicked it around a bit on the way home and decided we would give it more thought.

At that time, we were having two villas built in Alicante, Spain, one each, and showing an interest in buying a complex with a clubhouse, swimming pools, a football pitch and hard standing for cars. On a plane home after one of our visits, I mentioned to Mark that we might have to choose between the club and this Spanish venture. I pointed out that the Spanish thing could prove to be awkward as far as keeping an eye on it, due to the distance involved, so we decided to go with the club.

A meeting was scheduled at the club with the owner of the club, the area manager for the brewery and Rick. It was agreed that we would take care of the brewery beer bill he owed, which was about £20,000, and the twelve grand he owed in back rent; he had asked us not to mention the £25,000 for himself as the area manager would demand he settle his beer bill, as would the owner regarding the rent arrears. The owner of the club, in all fairness, said seeing we were paying out a substantial amount of money, he would put the rent arrears on hold and would assign the lease to us when we had paid the rent arrears in full. The area manager said he would give us six months to pay Rick's outstanding beer bill, and the deal was done.

Mark and I would visit once a week to keep an eye on the business and Rick, and over a short period we noticed a falling off in trade which never recovered. We terminated Rick but kept him on as a barman to work under one of our own managers. I was still a committee member in the Uppercut Club, and when we heard that my old pal Terry Downes, the former middleweight world champion, was going to have a birthday in a couple of months' time, Mark and I decided to throw a big party for him at the club. We invited many people from the world of boxing and celebrities that I knew, and I engaged the comedian Mike Read to do a stand-up session. When I asked Terry's wife whether there was anything special Terry would like, she said he would love to see his old trainer who had taken him to the world title and whom he had not seen for years. I said, "Give me his phone number and I will invite him," thinking he might be living somewhere in London. She said, "He lives in Massachusetts." That threw me for a moment, but I still rang him and invited him to the party. He said he could not afford the expense, but I told him I was paying for his flight, and I sent a return ticket to his home. He called me when he arrived, and I picked him up at the airport and hid him away in a hotel until the night of the party. Terry was asked onto the stage and he made a lovely speech, amid a few tears. At the end of it, two ring girls we had hired came bursting through a six-foot birthday card. Then the Master of Ceremonies I had hired for the night stepped in and announced one last surprise. Out of the club kitchen where I had him hidden away stepped Terry's old trainer, and they embraced; that was the first time I had seen Terry break down. Terry was a hard man in and out of the ring, but the emotion got to him. Another nice thing that happened on that eventful night was introducing my mum to Mike Read. She was an avid fan of *EastEnders* that Mike was starring in, and she was thrilled when he put his arms around her and gave her a hug.

Just prior to Terry's birthday, and in the midst of organising everything for the big day, I was approached by a young member of the club who introduced himself as Mark Aaron. He was about nineteen at the time and informed me that he was a very capable caterer. Would I consider letting him take care of the catering? I said there would be roughly two hundred and fifty people attending but he assured me that he worked with a partner and they had carried out numerous successful appointments, with glowing reviews; he could supply references if needed. So Mark and his partner Ted were given the catering for Terry's birthday bash and did a wonderful job.

Terry's wife called me and said that Terry was so touched by the lovely birthday show I had put on for him that to show his appreciation, he wanted to invite Chrissie and me to the Holiday Inn at Hyde Park as his guests on the evening that was to celebrate the forty years that Bob Monkhouse had spent in show business. That night, we were to see many celebrities attending, stars from television, Ted Rogers (Dusty Bin), and one of the nicest people I've ever met, Jim Bowen (Bullseye), who came over to have a chat. He was mesmerised by all the stars, and he said, "I can't wait to get back home to tell the boys in the pub about all the stars I was with today!" I said, "Jim, you are a star yourself!" "Nah," he said, "not like the people here this evening." We were finally called to take our places at the table that Terry had booked for us; we sat with Terry and Barbara, Billy Aird and his wife Angie, and Johnny Bicknell and his wife.

The top table was full of stars, with Bob Monkhouse seated in the middle. As this glorious and glitzy evening was drawing to a close, the Master of Ceremonies, looking splendid in his red uniform, called on Bob Monkhouse to give a speech and everyone started to clap and cheer. Suddenly, Mike Yarwood, the comedian, stood up and did an impression of Bob and it brought the house down. Bob almost slid under the table laughing. It brought to an end a lovely evening with good friends.

I was still instrumental in the Uppercut Club and various ex boxers would pop in to see me, including my good friends John Conteh, John H Stracey and Terry Downes, and Mark was always thrilled to be introduced to them. However, our club was losing custom for no apparent reason and started to absorb funds from Markenroy, which really was keeping the club afloat. Mark was always busy with administration, and I was busy visiting our pubs all over the country and could not devote enough time to the club, so we had a meeting and I decided to terminate with Markenroy and surrender my shares in the company, and Mark surrendered his shares in the club to me; we agreed that I was better suited to running a club than Mark was. I terminated the manager and John H Stracey took over the management of the club. Trade increased for a while, but eventually I knew that I was fighting a losing battle and decided to give up the club.

The area manager for the brewery visited the club one morning and demanded payment for the beer bill that was still outstanding. I asked him to quote from the original agreement which read as follows:

"The new lessee has agreed to pay the outstanding sum of £20,000 on behalf of Mr Rick the outgoing manager of Stubbs Club of Stratford pertaining to a beer and drinks bill." I then asked him, "Who is the lessee?" "You are," he said. I reminded him that the rent bill of £12,000 owed by Rick to the club owner was put on hold as the club owner recognised we were paying a lot of money to get into the club and kindly said he would hold off getting us to sign as the lessee until the £12,000 rent owed by Rick was paid, so on a point of law, we were not the lessee and owed him nothing. He left the club issuing all kinds of threats, but it was "pinch of salt" time and they came to nothing. The club also owed a brewery roughly £60,000, plus gas and electricity and VAT. No way could I afford that amount, and I took advice from my very shrewd solicitor to put the club into liquidation. "It will cost you only £12 to go into liquidation, but do not pay it; it will look better if the brewery puts the club into liquidation," and that's just what they did.

I closed the club and emptied the AWP machines, what the public calls one-armed bandits. (AWP is Amusement with Prizes.) The owner of the club asked me if I wanted to sell him all the stock in the cellar, which I agreed to do. He said he would leave it to me to supply a stocktaker, probably because he did not want to pay £100, which was the going rate at the time. I contacted a pal of mine, a chief stocktaker of a large brewery, who agreed to do the stocktake. "Make sure it comes out right on my side, Mike," I said. "Leave it to me," he said. The stocktake was finished in a couple of hours and he met the owner and me in the bar and gave us a valuation of £6000. He stayed for one drink with us and then had to leave. I walked him to the door, paid him a few quid and said "How did we do?" He winked and said, "There was £4000 down there." "Thank you, Mike," I said and slipped another hundred pounds into his hand. The owner paid me in cash, two grand to the good. I now had to lose the six grand somewhere; I could not show it on any statement.

One morning in the club I received a phone call from the Official Receivers Office,

That gave me a date to attend a meeting with Mr Jameson, one of the examiners, and bring any paperwork, such as delivery notes, wages and stocksheets, that pertained to outgoings. The only problem I had was explaining the £6000 stock money. If he thought I had it, I would have to surrender it to be shared out evenly among the creditors, which was not going to happen! I approached my manager at the time of closing and said, "Do you want to earn a monkey in your hand? (£500)" He jumped at the chance. "All I want from you is a signature on a document stating that you have received from me the sum of £6000 in lieu of wages and holiday pay upon dismissal due to unforeseen circumstances and the club closing." He signed immediately and I paid him the agreed £500. I met Mr Jameson in his office and we went through various aspects of the club and why had it failed. He looked at some of the delivery notes and then he said, "You say you had champion boxers frequent your club?" "Yes," I said. "I am a boxing fan," he said, and the rest of the afternoon we talked boxing. I knew of people in business who would quake in their shoes at the thought of facing the Official Receiver, but for me, it was just another day at the office.

Mr Jameson gave me a date to attend again in a week's time and said I would possibly have to attend five or six times. On my fifth appearance with him, he said that our next meeting would be the final appointment. On that day, he pulled out a brewery delivery note and asked, "Was this delivery sold?" I said that when I had closed the club, the delivery had been in the cellar. "Is it there now?" he asked. I said it was not. "Where is it?" he asked. I said I had sold it to the tune of £6000. "Where is that money now?" he said. I then produced the piece of paper that Rick had signed, accepting the £6000 under the terms that we had agreed on. He said, "You have gone into liquidation to the tune of £84,000. You did not pay the brewery, the gas and electricity, VAT or Inland Revenue. Why would you pay your manager the £6000?" I said, "Because Rick was a preferential creditor. As an employee, he took precedence over every other creditor." He looked at me and gave a wry smile. "You have done your homework, haven't you, Roy?" So Rick was happy with the monkey, and I was happy with the five-and-a-half bags of sand.

He then said, "I am going to report to my boss that I am satisfied that in your case concerning the club there was no intention to defraud or any attempted wrongdoing, nor anything underhanded carried out. I am going to draw a line under the £84,000 and write it off and put it all down to mismanagement." I said, "Thank you very much, Mr Jameson, for your observations and the professional way you have handled this unfortunate event." He said, "You look very pleased." I said, "It is a substantial amount of money you have just written off." He turned in his chair and drew my attention to a table close by that was covered with papers, books and folders, about two feet high. "I have just finished that very complex case and have written off two point five million pounds, so yours doesn't really compare, does it?"

All that remained was to walk round the corner to a solicitor's office and sign a declaration. After paying the solicitor £3 in cash, I had to lay my hand on the Holy Bible and repeat after him the following declaration: "I the undersigned, Royston A Wild, do solemnly declare that the information and account I have given is true and correct to the best of my knowledge and belief."

After this little ceremony was concluded, we shook hands and Mr Jameson and I stepped outside. I thanked him for his considerations, and he thanked me for all the boxing conversations we had indulged in over the last six weeks. The last thing I said to him was, "Am I allowed to form another company and be a director again?" He turned with a twinkle in his eye and said, "Not until tomorrow morning."

Mark and I lost contact, mainly because of moving house. Chrissie and I purchased a house in the small market town of St Neots in Cambridgeshire, and I just sailed along on the breeze for a year or so, decorating the house, gardening and taking it easy. I finally knew I had to get back in the race and told Chrissie I was going to form another company and go back into the licensed trade. I contacted quite a few area and district sales managers I had dealt with in the past, told them I was back in circulation and asked whether I could depend on them putting some work my way. Their response was gratifying, and in no time pubs started to filter through. I already had a list of managers' phone numbers from when I was with Markenroy, and one pub became five and then twenty. Because I was now on my own, I capped it at 48 in the managed house division. Soon I was contacted by area managers from the tenanted division as well, and now we were really cooking. A brand new car was ordered, and I took on an office manager. Then I booked a trip to Florida for the family, taking in all the sights, Disney World, Wet & Wild, the Epcot Centre – too many to mention.

One of our favourite places was Frinton-on-Sea on what was known as the Essex Sunshine Coast. One day visiting Frinton, we were lying on the greensward, just above the beach, with the seagulls careering above in God's blue sky, the waves rolling in and sea spray on our skin, creating a feeling of Shangri-La. Chrissie suddenly remarked, "Wouldn't it be lovely to live here in Frinton?" I said, "We could, if that's what we all want!" "What about the business?" she said. I replied, "With my kind of business, I can run it from a broom cupboard as long as I have access to a telephone and somewhere to plug the computer into." So we sold the house and moved to Frinton, buying a big house very close to the seafront. I also bought a new Calibra sports car that was so futuristic it would turn people's heads. I used this car for visiting the pubs all over the country and also purchased a new Vauxhall Carlton Estate for shopping and running about locally, both cars from Carlton Motors of Clacton. I would leave Frinton at 4.30 am to go to a pub in Bristol or Manchester. It was an early start, but I would be heading home just after 11 am, as soon as the changeover was complete, and looking forward to the smell of the sea and taking our dog Holly for a romp on the beach.

CHAPTER 39

PUB MANAGEMENT PROGRAMME

During my time in the Licensed Trade, I was always looking for another angle to bring more revenue into my company. Then, in a quiet moment, I hit on an idea that proved to be very lucrative. A manager and his wife, who had in the past worked for me, decided to take a pub of their own but still stayed in touch with me; their pub was quite close to my office. I called Bill and asked if I could call in and have a chat with them about an idea I had. After settling ourselves around a table, I asked Bill how many years he had been in the pub business. "About thirty years or so," he replied. I then asked Carol, his wife, how long had she been in catering. "About the same time as Bill," she replied. "We met in a pub." I had always been impressed with her catering skills when they worked for me. "All this knowledge and the skills you both have, as well as my own, are going to waste! Here is an idea I would like to run past you," I said.

"I think we should run a course for people wanting to become pub managers. We have the perfect environment here to teach management in a working pub.

The course could last for ten days, covering bar and cellar management, how to change a barrel, and how to operate an EPOS (Electric Point of Sale) cash till that automatically monitors and orders all your stock. This would be your department, Bill.

"Carol! You could bring your expert advice to bear as far as the catering is concerned, but any manager's wife lacking in culinary skills could always order in ready meals and just pop the food in a microwave oven. There are plenty of companies supplying the licensed trade. There may not always be couples applying for management. Quite often there are managers who prefer to work as a single, in which case the management fee over the ten day period would be set at x amount, but if accompanied by a wife or partner, there would be a fifty percent reduction for the partner.

"The course could start at 10 am. We would supply all food, a break at 11am, then lunch, break at 3.00 and finish at 4.00. You would save staff wages, Bill, by using the trainee managers as bar staff, and this would be a good way to assess each would-be manager."

The three of us agreed it would be worth going ahead with the venture. I then made an appointment to visit the local police station and gained an audience with the police Licensing Officer. I made him aware of what our intention was, and he fully agreed with us that it was a good idea. I then asked him if we could engage the services of a police officer to give a talk on drug crime and trading in pubs and what to look for, and he agreed immediately. I said we were prepared to meet any costs involved. He smiled and said, "We are not allowed to charge for a service like that. It is a very good idea." I said, "Would you be averse to us dropping a couple of bottles of whisky into the police station at Christmas by way of a thank you?" "Not at all!" he said with another broad smile.

My next port of call was the local Fire Station, and I again explained what we had in mind as far as the course was involved. I asked if they could spare a fire prevention officer to give a talk on fire hazards in pubs, such as cigarette stubs left burning in ash trays at last orders being called, and also risks in the kitchen. They, too, were delighted to be given the chance to speak on the dangers of fire and said there would be no charge for their time and advice, but, again, they would be pleased to accept a couple of bottles of whisky at Christmas.

We advertised for trainee pub managers in the trade paper, *The Morning Advertiser*, and soon were inundated with enquiries. We consequently started the course with about ten couples. Bill gave his talk at 10 am until 12:00, break, Carol until 3:00 pm and then I spoke about protection orders and the transfer of a full licence for the pub to trade; I also included what to expect from brewery DSMs (District Sales Managers), Area Managers and BDMs (Business Development Managers). All revenue we gained from this venture was shared among the three of us. I was never short of managers for my own company, which by now was not only in the managed house division, but I had been approached by various breweries to look after some of their houses in the tenanted division. Bill and Carol continued running the course after I had announced that I would be moving home to Frinton-on-Sea and would need to be in my office there. We shook hands, wished each other well and I bailed out. It proved to be an interesting and lucrative enterprise derived from no more than an idea in a quiet moment.

CHAPTER 40

EXCEL RELIEF MANAGEMENT SERVICES LTD

The new company I formed was Excel Relief Management, and it soon made a name in the licensed trade. Chef & Brewer was the company I catered to the most, their parent company being the very large Grand Metropolitan, who had an enormous portfolio of public houses and worked out of their block of offices at Riverside House, Northampton. Their relief coordinator was a good friend of mine from my time at Markenroy and would feed me a lot of work and give me priority over other agencies that were vying for work. And when I sent in invoices for payment, my invoice would be put on the top of the pile for payment.

I was offered a pub to take over that was situated in Moss Side, Manchester. Moss Side was notorious for gang crime, drugs and guns, leading to its latter name of "Gunchester". I met the area manager and we travelled up to Manchester together. Finally, he pulled up outside the pub and said, "Pop in and have a look. See what you think!" I said, "Are you not coming in?" thinking we would possibly have one drink, get the layout of the pub and then leave. He said, "No, I'll wait in the car." I entered the pub, drew some suspicious looks from the clientele, who were obviously not used to seeing someone in a suit, and immediately picked up some bad vibes. I thought I would give it a miss; it was an aggravation pub, and it seemed strange the area manager would not accompany me in. I returned to the car and said I would think about it, knowing I had no intention of putting a management team in there. A couple of days later, he called me and said, "You were right to reserve judgement on that pub in Moss Side. Somebody went into the pub last night and shot somebody in the head while he was sitting at the bar. The bullet exited his head and smashed a couple of bottles on the optics."

Another pub I was asked to take on was over in the Greenford-Perivale area of West London. This pub was also known for its violence and narcotics dealings, and the resident manager wanted out as soon as possible due to threats levelled against him and his wife. I assigned a manager, Tony, who never stood aside for anything, and I had used him on countless occasions in unruly pubs that he always straightened out. I also agreed to increase his weekly wage, with the approval of the area manager. If he had rejected my suggestion, the pub would have closed, and that is looked on by any brewery as sacrilege. The reason the current manager wanted out was that there had been a terrible fight in the pub over a drugs dispute and one guy had been held down on the snooker table and castrated (no puns needed regarding snooker balls). On the morning of takeover, as the pub started to fill up, Tony walked into the room amid hostile glances from the current drinkers and said, "I am the new manager in this pub and it will be run according to my rules. If anything gets out of hand, here is my backup. Standing by Tony's side was the biggest German Shepherd dog I had ever seen. I saw him yawn once, and it was like Tower Bridge opening, with rows of gleaming teeth reminiscent of *Jaws*. Things changed immediately. The clientele could see that this guy was not easily intimidated. The area manager replaced the snooker table, Tony was invited onto the pub snooker team and peace prevailed from then onwards. I approached the area manager for a small bonus for Tony, which he gladly gave.

On a lighter note, when Tony vacated the pub and a resident manager was appointed, I gave Tony another pub to hold in Mitcham, South London. It was a nice family pub, and around the walls in the saloon bar was a picture rail displaying all kinds of plates, willow pattern and various rural scenes. One day just after opening, a guy came in, ordered a drink and started to show some interest in the plates. He suddenly asked Tony whether he could look at one particular plate. Tony stood on a stool, removed the plate and handed it to him. After examining the plate he offered Tony £150 for it. Tony said, "It is not mine to sell," knowing that if this guy, who was obviously a collector, was prepared to buy it there and then, it was probably worth a lot more. That afternoon, Tony rang an antique dealer in his shop in the West End, took the plate and sold it to the antique dealer for £600. Then he went to Brixton Market and bought an old plate from a market trader for £5 to fill the space left by the former expensive plate, and nobody knew the difference. When he told me this story, I asked him for my whack. "Leave off, Roy," he said. "You would never have known if I had not mentioned it to you, and it is my pub." I said, tongue in cheek, "No, Tony! It is my pub. I put you in here and I can have you out tomorrow, so again I ask you, where is my whack?" "What do you want, then?" he said. I replied, "I will call in next week to see you, and that lovely wife of yours is going to cook me a nice meal. That, Tony, is my whack. Have we got a deal?" He smiled with relief and shook my hand, and I said, "When I return, I expect to see the plate rail as full as it was when we first took over." I had no intention of taking any money from Tony. I was earning so much Gene Tunney (money) for my company we used to sit around the barbeque weekends burning twenty-pound notes instead of charcoal briquettes. (Only joking.)

For the next couple of years, we took on so much work that we could afford to go to Orlando and travelled to the Florida Keys. I had always wanted to see Key Largo after watching the famous film of the same name starring Edward G Robinson, Humphrey Bogart and Lauren Bacall. After that trip, we decided to suspend any more visits to Florida for five years. We had seen all that it had to offer, so the following year we flew to Los Angeles.

We hired a car and drove through the Mohave Desert and into Death Valley, reputedly the hottest place on earth. We stopped at a place aptly named Furnace Creek and purchased some cold drinks and ice cream cornets, but before we had made it back to the car, the ice cream had melted and dripped down our arms and off our elbows. It was 137 degrees Fahrenheit but a dry heat, so you never really felt fatigued, unlike Florida, which was humid and very strength-sapping. We drove up to Fresno and through Yosemite National Park, visited Sacramento, the capital of California, and then headed for San Francisco. I took Chrissie and the children to Alcatraz and discovered that the helicopter that Mark and I had flown in had been taken out of commission and a submarine was now berthed at the dockside next to the ferry that carried us over to the island. I would encourage anybody to visit Alcatraz should they find themselves in San Francisco. When disembarking from the ferry, you are met by the Rangers, who will take you on a tour of the prison unless you wish to make your own way around. We visited all the cell blocks, the dining hall, the large exercise yards and Al Capone's cell. It is really interesting and reveals the harsh regime those prisoners had to live under. We spent a lovely week in San Francisco, shopping, walking over the Golden Gate Bridge to a picnic area and riding on the famous cable cars. At the end of the week, we drove down the west coast to Santa Barbara, visited the world-famous aquarium in Monterey and then returned the car in Los Angeles. It was a wonderful holiday.

The following year we visited Disney Land in Anaheim, California, which we found was not as nice as Disney World in Florida. In Florida, you could access the park by monorail or take the ferry across Lake Bona Vista, whereas in Anaheim you walk in off the street, but it was still a memorable trip. We also visited Knott's Berry Farm, which was lovely.

Gretchen and I returned to the USA in 2015. She had remarked that we had seen many parts of the USA and suggested that we visit Chicago and spend Christmas there, although the weather report for December was sixteen below and eight inches of snow was forecast. We landed at O'Hare Airport in a snowstorm and took a cab to our hotel where we settled in and waited for the morning. We visited the popular tourist spots, including the famous Wrigley Building in Michigan Avenue, and looked out of the observation floor on the John Hancock Building and the Sears Tower, which were, at the time, the two highest buildings in America. I'd thought the Empire State in New York was high as I stood on the observation deck with Mickey Katz and looked down onto the East River and the Hudson River after taking the elevator up to the 86th floor, which takes one minute, and then taking another lift up to the top floor, which is the 102nd, but these two in Chicago were even higher.

Next to our hotel in Chicago was a larger hotel that had warm air escaping from a vent in the side of the building, and we noticed that a flock of pigeons would gather on the sidewalk day and night to absorb the warm air during the freezing weather. One day returning from a day out, we noticed that one poor pigeon was almost on its side and would not have survived the freezing night air, so we gathered him up and took him up to our room, wrapped him in a warm towel and fed him every day for a week or so. We kept him in one of the drawers we had emptied, and one morning we were so emotional to see he had fluffed up his feathers, was making a fuss of himself and had fully recovered. We took him downstairs as we were going out and let him go. He flew magnificently, circled and was gone. Hopefully, God was watching. All God's creatures…

In 2015 Gretchen and I made yet another trip to the USA. We flew to Las Vegas, stayed a couple of days, hired a car and headed for Arizona. On previous visits to the States, Gretchen had been a child, but this time she was now a driver and it was a great help to share the driving through the vast expanses of desert and deep canyons that were very hot. We took in Monument Valley and visited cowboy towns that were exactly as you see them when portrayed in Western Films, with mock gunfights, banks being robbed, and mules, donkeys and horses wandering around. Even when I was looking around a shop, I was jostled by a donkey nudging me. They were everywhere and all protected by federal law. We also travelled the famed Route 66 and visited the Grand Canyon, which has to be seen to be believed, so very deep with the Colorado River running along the bottom. Absolutely awesome.

We then headed for Utah as we wanted to visit an animal sanctuary there that we had read about before we left. It was situated in Angel Canyon and was full of cats, dogs and other rescued animals. You were allowed to interact with the animals, and children were cuddling the cats and dogs. There was a lovely restaurant and a beautifully kept animal cemetery where animal lovers had, with the permission of the sanctuary, laid their much-loved animals to rest. There were numerous wind chimes, and when the desert wind gently blew, it was the most lovely and peaceful sound in this most serene of places. We wandered about reading the epitaphs on small but lovely gravestones with our eyes full of tears.

Returning home marked the completion of our twentieth visit to the USA, and at the time of writing, I have one final quest: to visit the grave of my teenage idol, Frank Sinatra, who is buried in a cemetery in Cathedral City in California, to pay my respects and thank him for all his music and all the times I lay with a girl in my arms and listened to his beautiful voice. Hopefully, the epitaph on Frank's grave is true and one day will apply to me when it is my turn to toddle off into antiquity: "The Best Is Yet to Come."

CHAPTER 41

CELTIC SURVEYOR

I was introduced to a guy whose business had been underwater salvage in various oceans. He had a very large boat named *Celtic Surveyor* that was lying idle in London's dockland; he did not know what to do with it as he had finished with deep-sea exploration. He asked me whether I had any ideas as to what to do with it, and I suggested turning it into a floating nightclub. He said he knew nothing about nightclubs and would I be interested in taking it on as such if we could do a deal regarding my leasing the boat from him. I went down to see this boat, which was enormous inside, beautifully wood-panelled throughout, with a bar and a large area that would have been ideal for a dance floor.

Over the next few months, I took him to many boxing matches and introduced him to many world champions, and being a boxing fan, he revelled in their company. I took him to a very swish boxing evening at the Royal Garden Hotel that was attended by many world champions whom he was thrilled to shake hands with. He thanked me for the introductions but said, "I only wish, Roy, that my idol had been here this evening." "Who is that?" I asked. "Howard Winstone, the World Featherweight Champion." I took his arm, guided him over to Howard and said, "Here is a great fan of yours, Howard. He would like to say hello to you." I walked away and left them talking, and he came back to me sometime later and thanked me profusely.

I approached one of the breweries that I catered to and asked whether they were interested in doing a deal regarding my selling their beer and spirits on the boat. An area manager from the brewery met me at the boat and could see the potential of the boat becoming a floating nightclub. I told him that the boat would be renamed the *John H Stracey* and he would manage the business. I had cleared this with the boat owner, who had agreed after I told him this would bring in a lot of trade from the boxing fraternity. The brewery agreed to advance me £90,000 for various alterations I would need to carry out on the boat for an agreed amount of barrelage and spirits I would sell when the venue became operable, and we shook hands on that. So I had raised £90,000 and had also agreed with the owner a monthly rental, which would be paid in cash at my suggestion and he could declare whichever amount he chose. He called me a couple of days later and asked me to meet him at his office in the West End and then dropped the bombshell that he had been given a better offer and would not be going ahead with our agreement. He threw our friendship out of the window after all that I had done for him, the revenue I had raised from the brewery and the different places and people I had introduced him to. I was devastated and angry but could do nothing to change his mind. An old adage that a relation left me before he died came back to haunt me: "Pound notes will always make bad friends."

CHAPTER 42

GOOD FRIENDS

One of the members of the Uppercut Club and a good friend was a certain Mickey Moynahan, who was the locations manager for Euston Films, a company that made films for TV including *Widows*, *Minder*, with George Cole and Dennis Waterman, and *The Sweeney* with John Thaw. I had just returned with my family from Florida and rang Mickey, who was shooting a picture on the Isle of Dogs in the East End. He invited me onto the film set and said, "Bring the family with you!" Chrissie, the children and I were shown into his office, and he was making a fuss of the children when the phone on his desk rang. He excused himself to take the call, and the conversation went something like this: "Hello Alan, how are you? Yes! I told you I would speak to him on your behalf. In fact, he is sitting opposite me now with his family." With that, he passed the phone to me, and it was Alan Mullery, the footballer. "Hi Roy," he said. "Mickey has told me about you and I need some advice on how to go about buying a pub and the pitfalls involved." "There are many, Alan, but if you keep on top of it, you can earn a good living. But there is no better place for being ripped off than your own pub. Maybe we could meet and I will explain more." We agreed to meet up in a couple of days. Alan, by this time, had retired after a very successful career in English football, playing for Fulham FC and Tottenham Hotspurs FC and helping Spurs win the F.A. Cup in 1967, beating Chelsea 2-1. Alan also played for England and was a very successful manager for Brighton and Hove Albion.

We met outside one of my pubs in Cannon Street in the City of London. Also in Cannon Street was a very exclusive club owned by a guy I had become friends with, a certain Ray Hudson. I had met Ray through his cousin Tony who was a good pal of mine and one of the nicest guys I had ever met, a real stand-up, twenty-two-carat guy, the kind of guy that if I had

Goliath on my back, Tony would be the one with the slingshot! I had told Ray I would be coming to the club with Alan Mullery and asked whether he could arrange a nice lunch for us. Ray must have mentioned to some of the clientele that Alan would be coming into the club for lunch, and when we arrived, we were surrounded by guys who wanted to shake his hand and say hello. We were finally ushered into the restaurant and our meal was served, but I don't think Alan had a chance to pick up his knife and fork, as people were still coming into the restaurant to shake his hand. Alan and I became friends straight away and we would meet with our wives for a meal now and then. Then Alan called me and said he was shelving the idea of buying a free house as he had been asked to join Sky Television as a football pundit. After that, I would look forward to seeing him every week on Sky Sports.

Mickey Moynahan was a very popular guy; the number of people he knew never failed to amaze me. I always said that if Mickey had been dropped into the middle of the Borneo jungle, someone would say, "Hello Mick, what are you doing here?" He would always compliment me on my dress and one day said, "I have a couple of friends who have a large warehouse in Docklands and they import Italian suits and clothes. Pop in to see them and tell them Mickey sent you."

The warehouse was one of the largest I had ever seen, with rows and rows of suits and overcoats stretching as far as the eye could see, and the owners were expecting me. I purchased three double-breasted and two single-breasted suits, as well as two overcoats that were beautifully tailored. These were the first suits that I had bought off the hook rather than made to measure, and they were given at a special price as I was a friend of Mickey's.

My good pal John H Stracey mentioned to me that the WBC were putting on a show at the Royal Lancaster Hotel in Bayswater Road to honour past British world champions and asked whether I would like to go on his behalf to accept the award as he had another engagement. He was flying out to Cyprus for Combined Services Entertainment with the Liverpool footballer Emlyn Hughes and the humorous pop group The Barron Knights to entertain various regiments of the British Army. Chrissie and I attended this special evening and shared a table with my other old pal, Terry Downes, and his wife Barbara. It was a glittering evening attended by many British world champions who stepped up on the stage to accept their awards. Then John's name was called out and everyone clapped. Bobby Naidoo, the announcer, explained that John could not be there due to a prior commitment but his good friend Roy Wild would accept the award on John's behalf. I stepped up to accept the award, which was a large silver plate inscribed with John's name. I never did find out whether the clapping and whistling were for me, as I knew an awful lot of the boxing world, or for John's achievements. No doubt the applause was for John, especially considering what he'd had to overcome when he won the world title in Mexico.

CHAPTER 43

GIZZY, SMOKEY AND WILLOW

I was asked by the Green King Brewery to take on and hold a pub in Leicestershire until permanent management could be found. I attended on the morning and waited while the changeover was completed and for my couple to arrive. I received a phone call from the couple saying that an emergency had arisen and they would not be able to take over the pub, so I quickly assigned another couple that were waiting for a pub but could not be with me until two days later. This meant I had to run the pub with the help of the resident barmaid. Upon opening the door of the kitchen fridge, I noticed there were many tins of cat food, and the barmaid told me the couple that had left had not taken their cat with them.

On the following morning, just after opening, a lovely looking tabby cat wandered into the pub looking for her breakfast. After being fed, she wandered out and I followed her until she made her way down the steps of an old disused boiler house. There was a wooden door with a small hole in the bottom that I saw her squeeze through. The following morning, the same procedure. By this time, my couple had arrived and taken over the pub, and I was thinking about heading home to Frinton-on-Sea, but this little cat with no home except this old boiler house preyed on my mind. As I was about to leave, she emerged from the hole in the door and came running up to me. I picked her up, and with those big eyes looking up at me, I knew I was about to take her home with me. I drove the hundred and seventy miles home with her on my lap to become one of the gang of six cats I already had, but first I took her to my local vet to make sure she was healthy and had no problems. He suddenly said she had recently had kittens, and then he squeezed her little teats and the milk flowed. That is when the realisation hit me: the kittens must have been in that old boiler house. Immediately, I put her back in the car, picked up a cat basket from home and drove the hundred and seventy miles back to the pub. Arriving in the car park of the pub, I released her from the basket and she raced to the boiler house and through the hole. I could not follow her as the door was locked, so I enquired of the barmaid who had the key. It was an elderly gentleman who used to maintain the boiler and lived just opposite the pub, and he gave me the key. When I opened the boiler house door, there she was on a pile of leftover coal and coke, feeding her two babies. I put all three safely in the basket and drove them back to Frinton to start a new life. We named the mother Willow and her two sons Smokey and Gizzy. They all lived a long life filled with much love.

CHAPTER 44

LENNIE CLUFF

Lennie Cluff was a good pal of mine from the fifties and was one of our crew at Bishopsgate Depot. Marriages finally broke up that old gang of mine and Lennie and I drifted apart. I always wondered what had happened to him and whether he was still alive. I purchased a CD that could help trace people, fed it into the computer and typed in his name, Clough. Zero information for Romford, Essex, which was the last place I remember Lennie living. About a year went by and suddenly the thought hit me that maybe his name was spelt Cluff, as opposed to Clough. I punched it in and up it came with his address. I swiftly got a letter off to him, asking whether he was my old pal and if so, to please find my phone number enclosed. Within a couple of days, he rang me, his voice full of emotion and excitement, and said, "When are you coming to see me?"

The door was opened by a short, portly guy, and I was about to ask whether Lennie was in when he threw his arms around me and said with a voice full of emotion, "Roy! Sheila, it's Roy!" he called out to his lovely wife, and she came to the door. By this time the tears were flowing for Lennie, and I was quite emotional, too. She said good-naturedly, "Come on, Len, behave yourself!" A pot of tea and sandwiches were made and Sheila said to me, "For years Lennie has spoken about you and even more so since your letter came." Lennie said to his wife, "I have never seen a guy with so many girls as this guy," pointing to me, and regaled me with an incident that I had long forgotten and still cannot remember. Apparently, quite a few of our crew had met in a certain pub in Poplar and then ordered the beer and carried it back to his house for a party. On the way back, carrying the booze, we passed a fish and chip shop and all purchased a bag of chips. A few of the guys remarked how lovely the girl was who served us. The party was in full swing when somebody remarked, "Has anyone seen Roy?" A short time later, I walked into the party with the lovely girl from the fish and chip shop on my arm. I said with a smile, "Len, you are embarrassing me!" I know this to be true because I received a phone call from one of our old pals, Terry Myring, who was at the party all those years ago and verified what Lennie had said. It would appear I was preceded by my reputation.

CHAPTER 45

KENNY NOYE

I had taken on a lovely pub in the village of West Malling in Kent and was asked to hold it until a resident manager could be appointed. I spoke to John H Stracey about putting on a boxing evening at the pub and we started to advertise it. Shortly afterwards, John and I were travelling down to the pub in my car to make final preparations for the upcoming event when John received a phone call from a friend of his who was due to meet us at the pub. I had never met this friend of John's, but by all accounts he was a solid kind of guy and had called John to ask whether it would be in order for him to bring along a friend of his. John turned to me, and I said by all means. When we arrived at the pub, they were waiting for us, and we all sat down over drinks before lunch. The guy who was with John's friend looked vaguely familiar to me, and after a while John nodded to me and we excused ourselves and headed for the toilet. John told me that the guy was Kenny Noye, who had been jailed for the Brink's-Mat bullion robbery and recently released after serving eight years of a fourteen-year sentence. During lunch, he regaled us with some of the details, which was fascinating, and on the face of it, I found him to be friendly, interesting, and entertaining. That may have belied his true character, considering the reason for his next bout of incarceration.

CHAPTER 46

MARK AARON

As I mentioned, Mark and I lost contact for a few years, but one day John Stracey called me to say he had met Mark and they had spoken about me. John passed his phone number on to me and asked me to call Mark. We met and our friendship was immediately rekindled, and we started to get about everywhere together. Mark, by this time, had become an impresario, putting on various shows incorporating singers and groups that he had under contract. I attended many of his shows and always entered free, such was his good nature. He was the most generous person I had ever encountered. He invited me to a well-known club in Essex where two of my pals were appearing in a question and answer session with the boxing public. They were former Flyweight World Champion Charlie Magri and former Welterweight World Champion John H Stracey.

The club soon became packed with men from the boxing fraternity who asked many questions of the two world champions. Mark and I circulated, stopping to say hello to various friends and people that we knew. To bring some glamour to the evening, there were quite a few hostesses who had either been invited or hired for the evening. (I never did find out which.) When Mark and I settled ourselves at the bar, we were joined by a lovely looking young girl who had the most bewitching smile that held my heart prisoner immediately. She started to chat to us and asked me where I came from. Mark suddenly took out his wallet, produced a twenty-pound note, put it in her hand and said, "Take Roy upstairs and look after him." She took my hand and we climbed the stairs to the next level where there was a line of cubicles with curtains drawn across, but I could see here and there couples involved in certain levels of enjoyment. I thought, "Oh no! This is not my modus operandi." She steered me into a vacant booth and pulled the curtain across. That's when I said, "Please sit down, sweetheart. I wish to speak with you. You are a lovely girl, but this is not for me. This is sordid, and no way could I take part. In another time and place, it would indeed be a pleasure and a privilege to romance you as you deserve. I would love having you on my arm, buying you flowers and taking you for a nice meal where I would offer you some interesting, intellectual and stimulating conversation, after which I would drive you home. At this point, and with your permission, I will continue with my rhapsody and say you are better than this! And what is going to happen now is, we are going back downstairs and Mark will say to me, 'Everything alright, Roy?' and I will say, 'Everything is fine, Mark.' You will put the money he gave you in your purse and no one will know any different." That was the moment when I thought she was about to cry. I would swear I saw the glint of silver well up in her eyes. She hugged me and said, "You are such a lovely guy, Roy." We continued downstairs and Mark asked the question I knew he would: "Everything alright, Roy?" She sat at the bar with us for one drink and squeezed my hand before she excused herself and drifted away to join some of the other girls. I did what I felt was right and what I felt comfortable with. To be involved with something like that would have been totally alien to me. God! I had daughters older than her, and at the end of that brief interlude on that memorable evening, I realised to my chagrin that I had not even learnt her name. It was just another incident that fate had set aside for me and was part of the rich tapestry of my life.

Johnny Stracey called me and said he had arranged a meet with an old friend of his who turned out to be a certain Mike Felix who was the drummer in the sixties pop group The Migil Five, who had a big hit with "Mocking Bird Hill". The meet was in a pub called The Haverstock Arms in Hampstead. In addition, we were to meet the film star Ronald Fraser, who made his name in the television production of *The Pot Carriers*, which featured prison life, and later in his career starred in *The Flight of the Phoenix*, a hugely successful film with James Stewart and Richard Attenborough. We were also looking forward to meeting Ronald's pal, none other than Peter O'Toole, famous for his role in *Lawrence of Arabia*. I had met Ronald some years earlier in a club in the West End, where he was quite well-known for his love of a good bevvy (drink), and while I was speaking with him, he became decidedly more Oliver Twist, (pissed). Ronald was already in the pub with Mike Felix and another couple of people when John and I arrived, and after touching hands all round, I remarked to Ronald that we had met before in a club in the West End and he was pissed. He countered with, "I am always pissed!" which made us all smile. He told us that Peter O'Toole would be arriving later for a drink. These two were well-known hell-raisers so we looked forward to a nice afternoon of revelry. After a while, John and I popped out to the men's toilet, which was the old-fashioned white porcelain stand-up, and in the soakaway along the bottom were a large number of copper coins. We remarked on how they could possibly have got there and that no one would dare to pick them up, considering what had been raining down on them for maybe years. Because we had arrived in my car and I never drank alcohol when I was driving, I had sparkling water in a bottle with a shot of lime. I asked the governor of the pub if he had a few copper coins I could borrow and was handed about eight old-fashioned pennies and half-pennies, poured some of my sparkling water over them in my hand and walked up to John Stracey. Before he knew what was about to happen, I said, "Here, John, I managed to pick up some of those coins in the urinal," and slapped them into his hand. He gave a shriek when he felt how wet they were and threw them up into the air. It caused much laughter after I told the company what I had done and, no doubt, much relief on John's part. After a while, there was a call for Ronald from Peter O'Toole saying that he would not be able to make the meet that day, which was a disappointment. We carried on drinking until about 6pm and then, at Ronald's suggestion, we all went back to his house in Hampstead for drinks. Against my better judgement and falling by the wayside, I had quite a few glasses of Guinness but managed to drive home safely.

Roy Wild

CHAPTER 47

RETIREMENT

I received a phone call from my pal the relief coordinator at Chef & Brewer requesting a meet at his office in Northampton. He informed me with a very solemn face that it looked as though a larger company would be making a bid to buy out Chef & Brewer and his concern was that he would be made redundant and then where would that leave me as far as work was concerned. By this time, all my work was coming from C&B.A couple of weeks later he confirmed that the takeover would be going ahead and he was, indeed, to be made redundant. I received a letter from the new company to attend a meeting at Riverside House, Northampton, where I met three of the new directors, sitting around a large table "We have been looking at your association with Chef and Brewer," one of them said, "and it would appear that you cover more work on their behalf than any other agency!"

"That would be correct," I said.

"Why do you think that is?" he asked.

"Because I am the best, and that is why the work keeps coming in!"

"You're the best?" he said with a smile on his face.

"I'm the best," said I.

"We are also looking at another agency that caters to C & B," and mentioned the name. "What is your impression of that agency?"

"I cannot see how that is relevant to why I am here at your request, and it would be unethical as well as unprofessional of me to comment on another agency."

After a further half-hour of questions and answers, he said, "Ok, thank you for your time. We will be in touch."

I then walked into my pal's office and we went to lunch together. He told me it was the intention of the incoming company to dispense with all the agencies and to form their own pool of relief managers. All they did was increase the wages of the bar cellarman who worked under the manager and let him run the pub when the manager was on holiday, but by doing that, they never had the buffer of a thousand-pound bond that we agencies held to safeguard against stock or cash deficits, which meant they would have to suffer any shortfalls.

The action by this company started to shape the way other breweries managed their pubs with alternative methods and outlay, and I could see the writing was on the wall. I received a further letter from the company telling me my services would no longer be required, which I was half expecting. At this time, I was down to two pubs for Chef & Brewer and owed them £300 for a previous stock deficit, but they owed my company £4000 for management carried out on their behalf, plus my managers' wages and my agency fee. The relief coordinator told me he had put my invoices through to the payment department some weeks ago and could not understand why they had not been paid. The payment department told him they had been instructed by the area manager not to pay me until I had paid the £300 stock deficit. I demanded to be put through to this area manager and asked him to deduct the £300 from the £4000 they owed me and send me the balance, which obviously made sense. He said their company did not operate a quid pro quo and would not hear of it. I knew they had no intention of paying me, and it would have meant my taking them to court and incurring more expense.

The two remaining pubs I had were in Northampton and the City of London. I called my manager in the Northampton pub and said I would be along in the evening to take what the brewery owed me in cash from the pub and pay him up to date with his wages as I felt sure they would replace him that very week, if not the next day. He agreed with me, and I sped up to the pub early evening. As I walked in, he started to dial a number on the phone and then handed the phone to me. He had informed the area manager of my intentions and, in turn, had called the police. So much for loyalty! While I was having an altercation with my manager, the pub door opened and in came two police officers. "We have received a complaint of someone demanding money with menaces," they said. I told them it was me and explained that it was my management that was holding the pub and the owners had refused to pay my management fee; I was there to take from the pub what I was owed and there was no menace of any kind. I showed them the invoices I intended to leave at the pub that corresponded to the money I intended to take. One of the officers said, "It is just a business dispute, then?" and I agreed. He said, "This doesn't really involve us," and he bade me goodnight, got back in their car and drove off. That is when I really tore a strip off this manager who had sold me down the river and whom I had kept in work for the past couple of years.

On the way home, I called my other manager who had only been with me a couple of months. Formerly, he had been a school caretaker and had done a couple of good jobs for me, managing with his young wife. I again explained what I wanted to do and what the brewery's intentions were and asked him how much he was holding in the pub safe. He said the previous night it had been about £4000 but by the end of business that day it would be nearer £5000. I arrived at the pub, we went into the office and he opened the safe and counted out £4000. I paid him up to the following morning and said, "The area manager will not be very happy with what I have done. If he wants you to stay on, make sure you take your wages out of the pub take every week." Before he closed the safe, I attached my invoice to the weekly statement of business, shook his hand and baled out, telling him I would send him a cheque for his £1000 bond I still held.

The following morning, sure enough, the area manager rang me at my office, rucking and ranting that he was going to call the police and what I had done was tantamount to burglary. I agreed with him that was what he should do and said maybe they would be surprised that this burglar had the agreement of the pub manager and also left behind an invoice with his company's name and address, signed "with thanks", which would probably be a first for them. He knew they were in the wrong and did not have a leg to stand on. When my manager left the pub, he called to tell me what had gone on the following morning when the area manager had arrived and was told what had taken place. My guy said he thought he would have to call an ambulance as the area manager looked as if he was about to keel over, and he never did ring the police.

I knew I had done the right thing and had taken what they owed me in cash, and that is when I baled out of the licensed trade after almost twenty years. It had been good to me; we had enjoyed some lovely houses, always brand new cars, some replaced after only eighteen months, holidays sometimes twice a year taking us back and forth all over America. The ups were many, the downs negligible by comparison and easily handled and ironed out, but I had known for some time that game shot, set and match was looming large on the horizon. I was looking forward to retirement, and to quote the epitaph on the gravestone of my old pal Frankie Shea, I am now "Free as a Bird".

REFLECTIONS

My thanks and love go to my mother and father, who helped shape my future and made me the person I am today and without whom my life story would not have been written. I have dear, indelible memories of them. Also, my thanks to my dear brother Tony for always being there for me and lending a friendly ear when it was needed, and indeed to my daughter Sandra, whose ear I occasionally bent with my progress with this book.

Also, a special mention to my daughter Gretchen, without who's help and dedication I would not have been able to record the story of my life.

After a long marriage of more than 30 years, myself and Chrissie gradually grew apart and decided the parting of the ways was our best option.

Many times I have been called a womaniser, mainly due to the substantial number of girls whom I have been seen with and who have meandered in and out of my life. Is it so wrong to be of this disposition, to appreciate a woman's shape, femininity, perfumed skin, soft hair and the beguiling smile that manifests when she feels most feminine? If it is, there are probably a couple of million guys out there just like me! Can we all be wrong? Or is it just those of us born under the sign of Scorpio? I have often heard it said, "Beware of Scorpios," and if true, I must have had the turbo version of satyriasis. And it wasn't always easy being a magnet to the iron filings of the fairer sex...Just joking!

Some people, they say, can fall in love at the drop of a hat. That never really applied to me.

When I was young, my heart just wouldn't fall.

I never knew whose lips to kiss and so I kissed them all.

I never knew whose heart to keep and whose to throw away,

And so I tried another heart every other day.

I have always treated women in a gentlemanly way, by being chivalrous and courteous. I always walked on the outside of the pavement, would open the car door for them and pull a chair out for them when we would eat out. In these days of equality, it has been my experience that most women still appreciate these shows of respect, although I occasionally think these small considerations may have worked to my detriment by forcing me to leave a few bruised hearts by the wayside, for which I wholeheartedly apologise.

In 2017, I was rushed into hospital with a perforated abdomen and required a very serious operation. My family were told it could go either way and the success rate was not favourable, but after a couple of hours under the knife, I came out of it. After three months in ICU and lying flat on my back, I was finally judged to be well enough to return home. I think somebody up there liked me and maybe said, "We are not quite ready for him yet." I now live alone with my two boys, Rudy and George. Rudy was a rescue cat from the RSPCA and George just wandered in one day about five years ago and stayed. It's us three against the world, and life is good.

Walking through the years like I have, in between the tears like I have, watching all the days go by.

Never set the sights that I should have, never reached the heights that I could have and never ever wondered why.

Roads never travelled, the world unexplored, my dreams left unravelled, suddenly I find they're not all behind me.

Suddenly the days have meaning, suddenly the leaves are greening. Just when I thought spring was good! Suddenly there's Life, suddenly there's Love.

REGRETS

Only three I can think of: the pain I caused my family, that I was not born into a vegetarian family, and finally, I never learnt to play the piano. I always had the inclination but never the time.

I hope that the many good friends I now have will not judge me as the man I once was but as the man I am now.

I went on to form two successful companies and earned more money legally than I ever did at villainy, but I always remember the buzz and the adrenaline rush. However, they were far outweighed by peace of mind; it is a mug's game.

Conclusion to my life story

I had my share of poignant moments. Throughout my lifetime I have left pieces of my heart here and there. But now I force a smile knowing my ambitions sometimes far exceeded my talents. There are now no more pretty ladies at my door.

Roy Wild

GLOSSARY OF SLANG

Bag of sand	£1000 (grand)
Benghazi (khazi)	Toilet
Bike on the nose	Glasses
Bird lime	Time
Boob	Prison
Bunsen burner	Earner
Deaf & dumb	Bum
Dolly mixtures	Pictures
Dummy	Wallet
Edmondo Ross	Boss
Face	Villain
Filth	Police
Flowery dell	Prison cell
Gene Tunney	Money
I suppose	Nose
Ice cream freezer	Geezer
Jack & Jill	Till
Jam Roll	Parole
John Bull	Pull
Khyber Pass	Arse
La-di-da	Cigar
Monkey	£500
Moriarty	Party
Mysteries	Girls
Scotch Eggs	Legs
Nelson Eddies	Readies (ready cash)
Nick	Prison
Oats and Barley	Charlie

Odd lot	Police
Oliver Twist	Pissed
Peter	Safe
Peterman	Safe blower
Pony & trap	Crap
Screw	Prison officer
Sky pilot	Vicar
Sherbet	Drink
Strides	Trousers
Sweaty socks	Jocks
Tea leaf	Thief
Thermos flask	Mask
Tomfoolery	Jewellery
Turtle doves	Gloves

Lightning Source UK Ltd.
Milton Keynes UK
UKHW020627220422
401874UK00006B/229

9 781802 273410